The Computer Industry

Recent titles in
Emerging Industries in the United States Series

The Telecommunications Industry
Susan E. McMaster

The Computer Industry

Jeffrey R. Yost

Emerging Industries in the United States

Larry L. Duetsch, Series Editor

GREENWOOD PRESS
Westport, Connecticut • London

Library of Congress Cataloging-in-Publication Data

Yost, Jeffrey R.
  The computer industry / Jeffrey R. Yost.
      p. cm.—(Emerging industries in the United States, ISSN 1539–7289)
  Includes bibliographical references and index.
  ISBN 0–313–32844–7 (alk. paper)
  1. Computer industry—United States—History. I. Title. II. Series.
HD9696.2.U62Y67 2005
338.4'7004'0973—dc22   2005004196

British Library Cataloguing in Publication Data is available.

Library of Congress Catalog Card Number: 2005004196
ISBN: 0–313–32844–7
ISSN: 1539–7289

First published in 2005

Greenwood Press, 88 Post Road West, Westport, CT 06881
An imprint of Greenwood Publishing Group, Inc.
www.greenwood.com

Printed in the United States of America

The paper used in this book complies with the
Permanent Paper Standard issued by the National
Information Standards Organization (Z39.48–1984).

10 9 8 7 6 5 4 3 2 1

For Mom and Dad

Contents

Contents

Preface

The development of the present-day computer industry has taken place in a remarkably short period of time. During the 1950s, computer technology was primarily the domain of advanced scientific research. Computer applications for business and industry were not widely adopted until the 1960s, even by large firms. During the 1970s, as the cost of computer services gradually declined, a growing number of smaller groups took advantage of the new technology for the first time. Although the market for personal computers and computer software was already healthy during the 1980s, reliance on the Internet for information exchange did not become commonplace until the 1990s. Many observers claim the development of computer technology—both hardware and software—has fostered greater prosperity and freedom for people in all parts of the world. At the same time, many others note that this new technology has heightened social divisions between the "haves" and the "have-nots."

In this volume, Jeffrey Yost examines the developmental phases of the computer industry. As the market for mainframe computers grew during the 1950s and 1960s, distinct niche markets developed for both sophisticated supercomputers and relatively inexpensive minicomputers. During the 1970s and 1980s, new software development made it possible to market less costly computers to a variety of less sophisticated users. More recently, increasingly affordable personal computers and convenient Internet access have created unprecedented interest in the computer industry throughout the world.

Yost identifies the advances that were critical to the development of the industry—and credits many individuals. Those credited with significant early contributions—people such as J.C.R. Licklider, Douglas Engelbart, Larry Roberts, Robert Taylor, Martin Goetz, Herbert Robinson, and John Cullinane (to name a few)—may not be widely known today, but Yost clearly describes their roles. Similarly, Yost credits many firms (and government agencies) with important industry advances. Firms such as IBM, Hewlett-Packard, Apple, Dell, Cisco, Microsoft, Netscape, and Google are readily identified with the industry today. Other firms—GE, RCA, NCR, Burroughs, Sperry Rand, Xerox, Control Data, Digital Equipment, Cray Research, and Computer Associates (again to name a few)—are no longer identified with the industry as strongly as they once were, but Yost examines their earlier roles as well.

Yost emphasizes that, without large-scale funding by the federal government to generate advanced scientific calculation and computer networking, the development of digital computing would have been significantly delayed. IBM, because of its prior success in selling and servicing punched-card tabulation machines, was well positioned to introduce its customers to digital computers. Wisely, the firm took up the challenge of working on large government contracts and thereby obtained technical know-how and secured the future production of commercial spin-offs. This paid off mightily. Development work undertaken for the government enabled IBM to introduce the enormously successful System/360 series, solidifying its early leadership in hardware and software. By proceeding to build its own semiconductor manufacturing capacity, the firm was able to remain at the forefront of technology and forestall opportunistic pricing by suppliers.

Gradually, more specialized computer applications were created through software programming rather than specialized hardware design. A greater scale and scope in computer applications were made possible by the increasing power and declining cost of hardware, and were then realized through greatly improved software. The development of relatively inexpensive minicomputers lent momentum to interactive computing, time-sharing, and networking. Many new software products became available during the 1970s. Yost observes that (because the marginal cost of software is minimal) the separation of hardware and software into distinct lines of business in the early 1970s was a watershed event, setting the stage for the rapid growth of the software sector by the end of the decade.

In a significant related development, during the 1980s Microsoft became the leader in both spreadsheets (with Excel) and word processing (with Word), and both were bundled with a full range of basic software as Microsoft Office. Word and Excel were not necessarily better products, but the firm benefited greatly (and continues to benefit) from its position as the supplier of the MS-DOS operating system that has been (and still is) installed on the great majority of personal computers sold in the United States. Critics argue that software innovation has been discouraged by the dominance of Microsoft in this respect. At this point, it is not clear when that dominance might erode.

By the late 1990s, browsers like Netscape and search engines like Google had transformed the Internet from a research tool and e-mail system to an increasingly broad-based communication device, making the computer industry essential to everyday life in the twenty-first century. Yost notes that many social and ethical issues connected with computing have yet to be resolved, such as those associated with social-class divisions and computer security. At this point, it is difficult—perhaps impossible—to predict how these issues will be dealt with, in large part because the industry is one that bears the uncertainties of technological change at its heart.

Larry L. Duetsch
Emeritus Professor of Economics
University of Wisconsin–Parkside

Acknowledgments

I am grateful to many individuals for their encouragement, support, and advice in the completion of this book. First and foremost I would like to thank Charles Babbage Institute (CBI) Director Arthur Norberg. Dr. Norberg read the entire manuscript and offered insightful commentary and suggestions on numerous areas, but particularly on the first decade of the computer industry. I am also greatly indebted to IBM executive and business historian, James Cortada. Dr. Cortada not only recommended me to Greenwood Press for this project, but also provided a number of significant suggestions after reading a complete draft of the manuscript.

I would like to thank CBI Assistant Archivist Carrie Seib, who helped research photographs for this book, and IBM Corporate Archivist Paul Lasewicz and Hewlett-Packard Corporate Archivist Anna Mancini, who helped provide images and obtain financial data.

I would also like to acknowledge two administrative support staff members at the Charles Babbage Institute who helped locate some resources and provided the initial proofing for several chapters: Dina Kountoupes and Kathryn Baumhover.

A number of other individuals have offered helpful commentary on parts of this book, or on other projects I have worked on that relate thematically. This, often informal, dialogue influenced my evolving ideas in a number of areas. These individuals include Janet Abbate, William Aspray, Juliet Burba, Martin Campbell-Kelly, Paul Edwards, Nathan Ensmenger, Philip Frana, Thomas Haigh, David Hochfelder, and Carroll Pursell. Martin Campbell-

Kelly and William Aspray also deserve credit for producing the first quality synthesis of the history of computing, *Computer: A History of the Information Machine* (New York: Basic Books, 1996). This insightful book provides a strong examination of the history of computing technology and extensive information and analysis on the computer trade.

I would also like to give special thanks to the founders of the Charles Babbage Institute and Charles Babbage Foundation (CBF), Erwin and Adelle Tomash, who have been extremely generous in their dedication to support the history of computing and the work of myself and many others in this field.

Finally, I would like to thank the editors of this book, Larry Deutsch, Sarah Colwell, and Carla Talmadge for their helpful suggestions and encouragement.

While suggestions from those cited above, and from other individuals too numerous to mention here, helped in many ways, I, alone, am responsible for any deficiencies or errors that remain.

Timeline

1943 In April, the ENIAC (Electronic Numerical Integrator and Computer) project begins at University of Pennsylvania Moore School of Electrical Engineering led by John Mauchly and J. Presper Eckert (funded by Army Ballistic Research Laboratory).

1945 In June, mathematician John von Neumann completes "First Draft of a Report on the EDVAC," (Electronic Discrete Variable Automatic Computer) a document defining the dominant architecture for digital computers (von Neumann architecture).

In December, the ENIAC is completed and used for calculations for the hydrogen bomb development project at Los Alamos National Laboratory.

1946 In February, ENIAC is formally dedicated and news reports on the machine begin to appear.

Moore School Lectures are held in the summer and lead to the Institute for Advanced Study (IAS) computer and other stored-program machines.

Electronic Control Company (later Eckert-Mauchly Computer Corporation) is founded by J. Presper Eckert and John Mauchly.

In September, Engineering Research Associates (ERA) is formed by Howard Engstrom, William Norris, and John Parker.

1947 ERA develops Atlas computer for Navy, a machine commercialized as ERA 1101.

In December, William Shockley, Walter Brattain, and John Bardeen complete their development of the point-contact transistor.

1949   Remington Rand completes the development of the BINAC (BI-Nary Automatic Computer) computer in March; the first BINAC installation was in August.

1950   In February, Remington Rand acquires Eckert-Mauchly Computer Corporation to enter the computer business.

Northrop engineers form Computer Research Corporation (CRC) in Hawthorne, California, initiating the West Coast computer industry.

UNIVAC (UNIVersal Automatic Computer) is completed by Remington Rand.

1951   In March, the first UNIVAC is installed (at the U.S. Census Bureau).

A British Teashop and catering firm, J. Lyons & Company, develops first business computer: LEO (Lyons Electronic Office).

MIT's (Massachusetts Institute of Technology) Whirlwind computer becomes operational, the first real-time computer.

1952   In March, John von Neumann's IAS computer is completed.

National Cash Register (NCR) acquires CRC to enter the computer business.

Grace Murray Hopper completes early compiler, A–0. A compiler is a program that translates from higher level instructions into machine-readable code.

1953   In April, IBM completes the development of its first electronic digital computer, the IBM 701.

1954   Consolidated Electrodynamics Corporation (CEC) forms Electro-Data Division to build computers.

IBM completes the development of the IBM 650—the first digital computer produced in volume.

1955   At the end of March, John Sheldon and Elmer Kubie found software service firm Computer Usage Company.

Air force launches project for major air defense and communication system (based on computer networking and radar) called SAGE, or Semi-Automatic Ground Environment.

Remington Rand and Sperry Corporation (Sperry Gyroscope) combine to form Sperry Rand Corporation.

William Shockley founds Shockley Semiconductor in Palo Alto, California.

IBM software user group, SHARE, forms and first meeting is held at the RAND Corporation in mid-August.

In December, RAND Corporation forms System Development Division to program SAGE Computers.

1956   General Electric enters computer business with ERMA (Electronic Recording Machine Accounting), an automatic check-processing system developed for Bank of America.

Burroughs Corporation acquires ElectroData to formally enter computer industry.

MIT engineers build TX-0, the first influential computer to incorporate transistors, and a model for early Digital Equipment Corporation minicomputers.

1957   In February, an IBM team led by John Backus completes the first iteration of what becomes an influential programming language, FORTRAN (FORmula TRANslator).

Former ERA engineers, including William Norris, leave Sperry Rand to form Control Data Corporation, the first company to build machines labeled as "supercomputers."

In August, former MIT engineers, Ken Olsen and Harlan Anderson, form Digital Equipment Corporation in Maynard, Massachusetts, the first company to build machines labeled as "minicomputers."

System Development Corporation is spun off by RAND Corporation as an independent corporation.

1958   First SAGE center becomes operational with programming support from System Development Corporation.

1959   Jack Kilby of Texas Instruments (in February) and Robert Noyce of Fairchild (in July) independently file for patents on the invention of integrated circuits (ICs).

In May, Department of Defense forms CODASYL (COnference on DAta SYstem Languages) to develop COBOL (COmmon Business Oriented Language), what becomes the leading programming language for business applications.

Burroughs 220 is completed.

Software service firm Applied Data Research is formed by its future leader Martin Goetz and six others.

In October, IBM announces 1401, the first digital computer to have more than 10,000 installations (sales and leases).

In November, National Cash Register completes and delivers NCR 304.

1960   In January, Control Data Corporation's first computer, the CDC 1604, is completed.

In November, Digital Equipment Corporation's DEC PDP-1 is completed (the first minicomputer).

1961 In April, IBM Stretch is completed and installed at Los Alamos National Laboratory; it is commercialized as the IBM 7030. Stretch refers to "stretching capabilities of computers."

1962 In March, Wesley Clark develops Linc-8 at MIT's Lincoln Laboratory.

H. Ross Perot founds Electronic Data Systems (EDS), a highly successful niche information technology (IT) service firm.

Department of Defense Advanced Research Projects Agency (ARPA) forms Information Processing Techniques Office (IPTO). J.C.R. Licklider is first IPTO director.

1963 In April, J.C.R. Licklider sends "Intergalactic Computer Network" memo to colleagues.

1964 IBM announces the System/360 product line of compatible computers.

Control Data finishes development of the first supercomputer, the CDC 6600, in September.

In December, Radio Corporation of America (RCA) announces IBM System/360 series-compatible RCA Spectra 70 series.

1965 In April, Digital Equipment Corporation completes the first popular minicomputer, DEC PDP-8.

1966 In June, ARPA IPTO Director Robert Taylor initiates project to develop the ARPANET.

1967 Texas Instruments develops the first handheld digital calculator.

Informatics launches Mark IV, the most commercially successful software product of its time.

1968 Digital Equipment Corporation computer engineer Edson de Castro and others from DEC defect to form minicomputer competitor Data General.

In July, Intel Corporation (initially called NM Electronics) is founded by former Fairchild Semiconductor engineers, Robert Noyce and Gordon Moore.

John Cullinane launches first major software products firm with venture capital from Wall Street: Cullinane Corporation.

1969 In June, IBM announces decision to "unbundle," or separately price, its software.

Xerox Corporation acquires Scientific Data Systems to enter the computer business.

Underlying technology of IPTO's ARPANET project completed (Stanford Research Institute and UCLA nodes are connected and become operational in October).

1970   Mansfield Amendment, included with FY 1970 Department of Defense appropriation bill, requires direct military applications for all DoD research expenditures. This formalizes trend to reduce DoD funding for basic research in computing.

1971   In February, NASDAQ (National Association of Securities Dealers Automated Quotations) market is launched using computers and networking equipment, rather than a trading floor like the New York Stock Exchange. NASDAQ becomes the market that lists (facilitates securities trading of) many IT companies in the coming decades.

In November, Intel Corporation sells the first microprocessor, Intel 4004—a "computer on a chip."

1972   Former CDC engineer Seymour Cray forms Cray Research.

In November, Charlie Thatcher, of Xerox PARC, completes design of the Alto, a machine incorporating many pioneering elements associated with subsequent personal computers.

In November, Nolan Bushnell's Atari markets Pong video game.

1973   ARPA study indicates that more than three-quarters of all ARPANET traffic is for e-mail.

1974   In April, Intel introduces the 8080 microprocessor.

1975   Micro Instrumentation Telemetry Systems (MITS) comes out with the Altair, a popular personal computer kit that is sold to early computer hobbyists for just under $400.

1976   In April, Apple Computer is formed by Steve Jobs and Stephen Wozniak.

Charles Wang founds software firm Computer Associates.

Cray Research comes out with Cray I, the most powerful computer in the world.

Gary Kildall develops CP/M operating system.

1977   In April, Apple Computer comes out with Apple II.

Larry Ellison forms database software firm System Development Laboratories in Belmont, California.

In October, Digital Equipment Corporation releases VAX (Virtual Address eXtension) 11/780 computer (first in the VAX line), launching a last wave of tremendous success for the minicomputer manufacturer.

1978   Atari comes out with popular VCS 2600 home video game system.

1979   In May, Daniel Bricklin and Robert Frankston develop VisiCalc, a personal computer spreadsheet program and the first "killer app." "Killer apps" were software application products that were so popular as to fundamentally accelerate the demand for computers.

In October, first commercial release of VisiCalc (for Apple II).

1980   Burroughs Corporation acquires System Development Corporation.

1981   In February, Microsoft licenses MS-DOS operating system to IBM for IBM PC.

In August, IBM comes out with their first personal computer: the IBM PC.

1982   System Development Laboratories is renamed after its primary product, a database called Oracle.

1983   Cullinane Corporation is the first software firm to be listed on New York Stock Exchange.

Compaq comes out with the first successful IBM PC clone.

Michael Dell begins to sell gray-market IBM compatible computers.

1984   In January, Apple Computer launches the marketing campaign for its new Macintosh personal computer with a famous two-minute television advertisement during the Super Bowl (based on themes from George Orwell's *1984*).

Michael Dell formally launches Dell Computer.

In December, Sandra Lerner and Leonard Bosack found cisco Systems (later Cisco Systems).

1985   In November, Microsoft first ships Microsoft Windows operating system.

1986   NSFNET is created by the National Science Foundation (NSF).

NSF establishes five supercomputer centers: Princeton University, University of Pittsburgh, University of California at San Diego, University of Illinois, and Cornell University.

1987   In April, IBM comes out with PS/2 personal computer.

Sequoia Capital invests in Cisco Systems, allowing for major expansion of the network equipment firm.

1988   In November, Cornell graduate student Robert Morris launches what comes to be called the Morris Internet Worm (unlike software viruses, which are transported by infected disks, worms spread over the Internet).

1989   Computer Associates acquires Cullinet Corporation.

1990   In December, Tim Berners-Lee finishes development of the underlying technology of the World Wide Web: Hypertext Markup Language (HTML), Uniform Resource Identifiers (URIs), and Hypertext Text Transfer Protocol (HTTP).

Cisco Systems diversifies beyond routers to produce LAN (Local Area Network) switches after acquiring Cressendo Communications.

1991   In October, Linus Torvalds develops a PC version of Unix called Linux, fueling the "open source" movement, and giving users access to view and modify source code. (Open source users often evangelize the open source model, and thus, it is sometimes referred to as a movement.)

1992   Introduction of Windows NT by Microsoft.

1993   ID Software develops a highly popular computer video game called Doom.

In November, the University of Illinois's NCSA (National Center for Supercomputing Applications) makes a version of the World Wide Web navigation tool, Mosaic, available for download.

1994   In March, Yahoo is formed by David Filo and Jerry Yang.

1995   In January, John Chambers becomes the Chief Executive Officer of Cisco Systems.

Internet auction firm eBay is founded in September by Pierre Omidyar and Jeff Skoll.

1996   Federal Reserve Chairman Alan Greenspan warns of an "irrational exuberance" in the stock market (due in large part to the rapid escalation of share prices of IT companies and the NASDAQ stock market).

1997   U.S. Justice Department files a complaint against Microsoft for anticompetitive practices.

So-called browser war underway between Netscape (Navigator) and Microsoft (Explorer).

1998   In June, Compaq formally acquires Digital Equipment Corporation.

In September, Google, Inc., is founded; the firm rapidly emerges as the leader in search engines.

Northern Telecom takes over Bay Networks and changes its name to Nortel.

1999   Carleton (Carly) Fiorina leaves Lucent Technologies and becomes CEO of Hewlett-Packard, the first woman to head a major IT firm.

2000   Y2K presents few problems at the start of the year, leading to reports that the potential risk was inflated by the media and firms and individuals who profited from Y2K preparations.

In March, the technology-laden NASDAQ stock market reaches its all-time peak (over 5,100).

2001   In May, Hewlett-Packard CEO Carly Fiorina orchestrates acquisition of Compaq to produce the largest PC manufacturer in the world.

In November, the U.S. Department of Justice tentatively agrees to a final settlement with Microsoft in the antitrust case.

2002   The dot.com collapse and aftermath leads the NASDAQ market to a low of just over 1,100 in October—a loss of more than 75 percent from its March 2000 high.

2003   In December, Linux 2.6.0 is released; this kernal offers greater scheduling and scalability and provides additional strength to the growing movement toward Linux and open source software programs.

2004   In August, Google goes public using an auction process—the most widely anticipated and reported initial public offering since the dot.com collapse several years earlier.

Introduction

In 1949 Edmund Berkeley published *Giant Brains, or Machines that Think*. This book, one of the first on computers, received considerable attention, but this paled in comparison to the attention received by the metaphor expressed in its title. By the early 1950s, through the reappearance of the term in many popular publications, "giant brains" became the leading metaphor for early electronic digital computers.

At the end of the twentieth century, the most common metaphor for computing technology—or more specifically, the Internet—was the "information superhighway." While it is not difficult to come up with a connection between these two metaphors—neural networks and networks of roads—they are quite distinct, particularly when understood within the context of their respective times. The popular presentation of the early metaphor was not in fact focused on neural networks, a conceptual relationship with computing primarily explored in the writings of a few gifted scientists and mathematicians, such as John von Neumann and Alan Turing. Instead, the popular presentation was on something at least partially divorced from human physiology: "giant" or "superhuman" brains. Despite nearly half a century of artificial intelligence research, computers are still far from approaching many types of human learning and thought, let alone, superhuman ones. Nevertheless, the common construction and understanding of the giant brain metaphor was fitting in several key respects. The term conjured up feelings of wonder, mystery, and fear. It fostered visions of a new machine that was rare, powerful, and like one of its early applications—the nation's nuclear program—characterized by secrecy. More generally, the giant brain metaphor reflected the fluid and creative ways that people often understand complex technologies that are still in their infancy.

The Internet was far from new when the term "information superhighway" came into common usage roughly a decade ago. Around this time, this network of networks went through a renaissance following the development and dissemination of hypertext markup language (HTML), uniform resource locators (URLs), and browser software—the foundations for the World Wide Web. The information superhighway metaphor did not signify something mysterious or frightening, but rather reflected a common image of the American landscape. Highways and roads were the backbone that supported the use of automobiles and fueled demand for a technology that Americans quickly and continuously embraced. "Superhighways" facilitated rapid movement, whether literally moving people in motor vehicles—transportation—or symbolically moving bytes of information—communication. The superhighway metaphor accurately characterized the great number of individuals who connected to the World Wide Web on a daily basis, as well as the vastness of cyberspace.

Perhaps without intention, this metaphor also symbolized a transition. While America remains a car culture, most no longer see the automobile trade as the country's defining industry. This distinction, which the motor vehicle business arguably held throughout the first three-quarters of the twentieth century, has passed to computing and related information technology industries over the past two decades. The United States' long leadership in many sectors of the computing business, our nation's continued dominance in some of the higher margin areas such as software, and the mass domestic consumption of these technologies have propelled computers and software to the forefront. Besides the impact of computing technology on our economy, our culture and business icons have changed. While Henry Ford, Alfred Sloan, Roger Smith, and Lee Iacocca were once in the media spotlight, Bill Gates, Larry Ellison, Jeff Bezos, Steve Jobs, and Carly Fiorina are now frequently center stage. The recent or current chief executives of America's Big Three (or two) automakers have become relatively inconspicuous. In homes, offices, and elsewhere, more and more Americans spend greater and greater amounts of time at work and play in front of computer screens.

To emphasize the significance of computers to our economy and contemporary culture is not to imply that Americans have universally adopted and celebrated these machines. At various times over the past half century computer technology has been attacked for, among other things, over complexity and difficulty of use, inducing unemployment, facilitating privacy invasions and computer crime, depersonalizing communications, and spawning a "productivity paradox," or an apparent decline in output despite being a "labor-saving" technology. To recent critics of computers and the Internet, the information superhighway metaphor perhaps suggests: sprawl and social and economic division (the "digital divide"), traffic congestion and crashes (overuse and software failures), and pollution (viruses and contamination of the Web with inaccurate information, annoying advertisements, or distasteful imagery). To the Web's proponents however, the metaphor tends to symbolize the road to prosperity, freedom, and the fuller realization of democracy. Whether people are computer advocates, critics, or more commonly, somewhere between the two extremes, there is no denying computer technology's influential role in our contemporary society and economy.

How did the computer evolve from a military and scientific computational tool of a small number of government, scientific, and corporate elites in the late 1940s to a ubiquitous data processing and communication technology by the mid-1990s? At the heart of this broad and challenging question is the complex story of the computer trade—an international industry that has produced annual revenues in the hundreds of billions of dollars since the turn of the millennium, and far more when embedded computer technology and the complete field of information technology products and services are taken into account.

The narrative of this industry might appear to begin with the federal government's funding of university and corporate electronics and computing research during and shortly after World War II—most notably the Army's financing of the development of the first significant electronic digital computer, the Electronic Numerical Integrator and Computer (ENIAC). The ENIAC, a wartime project at the University of Pennsylvania's Moore School of Electrical Engineering, was built to meet the Army Ballistic Research Laboratory's need to more quickly and accurately calculate complex mathematical equations for ballistic firing tables. Though the ENIAC was not completed until 1946, post–World War II defense-related computing needs remained strong as the United States almost immediately engaged in the Cold War. In the early years of this conflict with the Soviet Union, a number of new federally funded mainframe computer development projects were initiated at leading universities and national laboratories.

Beginning the story of the computer industry with these first

digital computer projects, however, would be analogous to starting a play in the second act (these projects are the topic of chapter 2). There were some fundamental technological antecedents,
most notably punched card, tabulator, and electronics technologies that formed the basis for certain essential computer functions, such as input/output systems, memory, and processing.
While technological precursors were critical, equally if not more
important were a number of organizational resources and capabilities that several leading office machine firms developed. In the
late nineteenth century the Computer-Tabulator-Recording Company (C-T-R—later renamed International Business Machines, or
IBM), National Cash Register (NCR), Burroughs Adding Machine
Company, and Remington Typewriter Company formed to create
and extend the market for labor-saving office machines. These
firms, which would all play a significant role in the post–World
War II digital computer industry, respectively led the world in the
manufacture of tabulating machines, cash registers, adding machines, and typewriters. Each firm, but particularly NCR and IBM
(behind their strong leaders John Patterson and Thomas Watson,
Sr.), developed successful sales and service operations in the late
nineteenth (NCR) or first half of the twentieth century (C-T-R/
IBM). While leaders of all four firms were cognizant of the digital
computer as a potential future business by the time the ENIAC
was completed, they showed caution in reallocating resources to
this new area that had negligible near-term demand. In just one
of many ironies that would characterize the computer trade, in the
late 1940s some business machine industry insiders and computer pioneers believed a mere handful of computers would be
able to fulfill the future computational needs of the entire nation.
The early development of sales, service, and other capabilities by
office machine firms—the prehistory of the computer industry—is
the theme of chapter 1.

When the four office machine giants turned their attention to
the computer field at varying points of the 1950s, the groundwork
for the industry to accelerate was falling into place. With the aid
of substantial federal contracts, new technologies were developed.
Soon, the market for computers extended beyond just the scientific and defense fields to include business applications at sizable
corporations. This resulted in large part from data processing
managers switching from earlier punched-card tabulation machinery to computing systems to aid with payroll, scheduling,
manufacturing, and other tasks.

Technological innovation also played a pivotal role in expanding
markets for computers during the 1950s and beyond. The first

wave of mainframe digital computers utilized thousands of vacuum tubes. This presented significant challenges, such as the requirement of very large rooms to house these machines, computer downtime from burned-out tubes, and the need for large air conditioning systems to offset the generation of tremendous heat. In the late 1950s, just over a decade after the invention of the transistor at Bell Laboratories, this technology evolved to replace vacuum tubes in many new models of digital computers, and laid the groundwork for more powerful and smaller machines.

The strategy and execution of early mainframe computer firms and the expanding range of computer applications is the primary topic of chapter 3. The chapter includes the story of IBM's System/360 series of computers. This project, to create a family of compatible machines in different price ranges, represented a watershed that solidified the company's leadership in the industry.

Prior to the late 1950s, mainframes were the sole product of the computer industry. In 1957, William Norris and other former engineers from Sperry Rand (the resulting firm from the Remington Rand and Sperry Corporation merger of 1955) formed the Control Data Corporation (CDC). Within several years this new firm would build the CDC 1604. The company's next machine, the 6600, was the most powerful computer in the world, and the first to be labeled a "supercomputer." Supercomputers were used for weather forecasting, various defense applications, and other tasks requiring extensive modeling and very rapid calculation. CDC led this segment of the industry for a number of years, until the company's top designer, Seymour Cray, left to form Cray Research and displace CDC's leadership position in the early 1970s.

Concomitant to the emergence of the supercomputer field, the Digital Equipment Corporation (DEC), under the leadership of Kenneth Olsen, pioneered the low end of the trade with its popular series of minicomputers. DEC's minicomputers, and those from competitors like Data General, greatly extended the number of organizations that could afford to buy or lease computer technology. These machines became increasingly common for use in businesses of all sizes and in smaller scientific laboratories. The rise to prominence of leading supercomputer and minicomputer firms, the techniques they employed, the demand for and use of their products, and their subsequent decline are the main subjects of chapter 4.

Chapter 5 addresses a computer industry activity that developed into a fundamental complementary business for computing: software. In the early mainframe era, programming computers was achieved by operators plugging and unplugging connections between hundreds of cords extending from the backs of the machines. This "patch cord programming" was replaced by stored memory technology, facilitating user groups and other organizations' maintenance of libraries of reusable code, and the development of high-level programming languages.

At IBM and other mainframe firms, software was an imbedded, non-priced service that was either demanded by or helped to attract customers. Recognizing that a powerful computer is only as useful as its systems and application software, a number of small software-service firms formed in the late 1950s and early 1960s. By the middle of the decade, a few companies such as Applied Data Research and Informatics began to market software products. Largely due to antitrust concerns, in 1969 IBM "unbundled" its software (discontinued it as a non-priced component of hardware).

Only a modest number of small independent companies sold software products prior to IBM's "unbundling." This move by IBM lent great momentum to the software trade. Prior to unbundling, early software firms constantly faced the threat of IBM developing new software in their area and giving it away. An announcement of future software systems or programs by IBM could cripple emerging independent firms that competed in identical or similar areas.

In addition to providing the early financial foundation for the computer trade in the mid-1940s, and remaining an important continuing market, a second critical influx of government funding for computing research began in the early 1960s. On the heels of Sputnik and the escalation of the Cold War, the recently formed Department of Defense's (DoD) Advanced Research Projects Agency (ARPA) targeted computing research by forming the Information Processing Techniques Office (IPTO) in 1962, and naming J.C.R. Licklider as the office's first director. In the coming decade, IPTO supported and managed the development of the ARPANET, the precursor to the Internet, as well as funded independent complementary research in artificial intelligence, graphics, and time-sharing. In the early 1970s, IPTO and other DoD entities significantly cut funds for basic research in computer technology, but almost simultaneously the Xerox Corporation initiated a major computer research organization, Palo Alto Research Center (PARC). Xerox PARC made major contributions to research in computer graphics, local area networks (LANs), and other areas that provided the foundation for personal computers. The government's financial support of this second fundamental wave of computer technology in the 1960s, and the legacy and continuance of similar work at Xerox PARC in the 1970s, are the main topics of chapter 6.

Chapter 7 tells the story of the emergence of personal computers and personal computer software. It begins by detailing developments at Micro Instrumentation and Telemetry Systems (MITS), Apple, IBM, and other personal computer firms, and noting how these companies benefited from previous government- and corporate-funded research. The chapter characterizes the computer hobbyist subculture and early users' roles in shaping personal computer technology. It stresses how personal computing alone, failed to constitute a revolution—contrary to common declarations during the 1980s.

The personal computer cannot be understood outside of the personal computer software industry. Much like Intel's fortuitous invention of the microchip, Microsoft was opportunistic in getting the contract to produce the operating system for the IBM PC (and of great importance, retaining the license). While Microsoft, under the leadership of its cofounder Bill Gates, soon developed a near monopoly in both operating systems and certain popular applications, many other software companies emerged to fill important niches in the personal computer software products field.

The realization of the personal computer revolution came when these machines were transformed from isolated tools used by a relatively modest number of hobbyists, students, and other individuals to play games, program, or word process, to a near ubiquitous communication device that is now used by the majority of Americans in their everyday lives. The information and communication revolution facilitated by the World Wide Web is the focus of chapter 8. The chapter explores the key roles of computer, software, and networking companies (particularly Cisco Systems); the changing nature of traditional businesses; and the emergence of a wave of new electronic commerce firms (and the subsequent industry shakeout). This chapter, and the conclusion that follows, also briefly examine some of the broader business and social implications of these developments.

Finally, it is important to comment briefly on the overall scope and the sources of this book. At its core, it is a narrative survey of the computer industry from its prehistory to the present. By necessity, it is selective. It concentrates primarily, though not exclusively, on the U.S. industry. Occasionally, developments in computing technology and the computer industries in European and Asian countries are discussed to provide context or perspective on strategy and its implementation by U.S. firms. Hardware companies are the focus, but all of the major computing and information processing sectors are addressed, from semiconductors and software to networking and electronic commerce. These different information technology industries are deeply interdependent. Software, networking, and electronic commerce were businesses characterized by very rapid technological and managerial innovation during the 1990s. By this time, the personal computer increasingly became a commodity and future advances came to rest on cost leadership, marketing, service, and process, procurement, and distribution innovations. Dell Computer excelled in all of these areas, and in turn, became the leading firm in the U.S. personal computer market.

The study draws primarily from secondary sources, many of which focus on a particular technology, individual, firm, or era. Surprisingly, the relatively vast secondary literature on the history of computing contains no book-length survey providing a narrative and analysis of the trajectory of the industry (from its prehistory to the present). The following book attempts to fill this void, but also aims to go beyond merely synthesizing and extending the temporal frame. It seeks to provide greater focus on several significant and understudied topics or themes, including marketing, sales, services, software applications, and the minicomputer and supercomputer sectors. In general, overviews and monographs on the history of computing have concentrated far more on invention and innovation, or the production of technology, than on its after-sale service, maintenance, and use. When certain developments in these and other areas are insufficiently addressed in the existing secondary literature, primary sources have been used to add value to the discussion.

—1—

The Prehistory of the Computer Industry, 1880–1939

Perhaps more than other historians, historians of technology and industry gravitate toward firsts, whether these are associated with inventors, inventions, businesses, or other topics. At times, this tendency lays a foundation for a meaningful exploration of long historical trajectories. At other times, it represents an unwarranted focus on disconnected events that, while often quite interesting, are mere anecdotes with little relationship to the larger scope of historical change, especially broad economic, social, and cultural transformations. Histories of the computer industry and computer technology are not immune to this latter phenomenon.

Charles Babbage, a British economist and inventor, has rightly been celebrated in recent years for his partial construction of the Difference Engine and his design of the Analytical Engine during the 1820s and 1830s. The latter machine, a remarkable precursor to the modern computer, not only included specifications for mechanisms capable of advanced mathematical calculation, but also included the concept of stored memory. In retrospect, the design of the Analytical Engine appears to be a major first step in the history of computing. Further reflection, however, indicates that it was a step that did not lead anywhere. Babbage's Analytical Engine suffered not only from his failure to concentrate on a single design, but also from inadequate financial resources, limited potential commercial applications, lack of government support, and challenges of precision manufacturing. A Babbage machine was not built for well over a century (and then, only as an antiquarian, though operational, artifact by the Science Museum of London). Babbage's designs neither influenced the work of engineers in the middle of the twentieth century, who built the first electronic digital computers, nor individuals who worked on intermediate technologies that proved useful to these engineers. Babbage's work on calculating-machine design is full of intrigue and is a potentially useful episode to see how an idea for an invention can arise before its time, but it is of little value in comprehending the continuities and connections within computing technology and the computer industry.

Similarly lacking any direct connection to digital computer technology, but reflective of a nation searching for machine solutions to mathematical problems, were several projects of the interwar period and early World War II era: the Differential Analyzer and the Harvard Mark I projects. In the late 1920s, Vannevar Bush, an instructor at MIT, invented the Differential Analyzer—a path-breaking analog computer. Analog computational devices consisted of mechanical models or analogs of physical phenomena. Such machines were far from new. In fact, their history dates back nearly 2,000 years. The earliest analog tools, however, showed little resemblance to the more sophisticated devices of the nine-teenth century, such as a tide-predicting machine invented by Lord Kelvin in 1876.[1] Like Lord Kelvin's tide predictor, most ana-log calculators of the first quarter of the twentieth century were highly specialized. Bush's Differential Analyzer changed this. Although it could only calculate ordinary differential equations (calculating the area under curves), such mathematical problems had a wide number of applications in the physical sciences, and to a lesser extent, the social sciences. In the 1930s, copies of Bush's Differential Analyzer were built at the University of Pennsylvania and General Electric's Schenectady plant. The Differential Ana-lyzer had a margin of error of about 2 percent, a deviation that was not prohibitive for some scientific and mathematical work. On the other hand, directly using numbers rather than models, and achieving complete accuracy, was optimal for certain applications, such as calculating ballistic firing tables during World War II. Before digital computers, human computers, often with the aid of mechanical calculators, analog computers, and logarithmic tables, were used.[2] This, however, proved to be only partially successful.

Like the Differential Analyzer, the Harvard Mark I grew from the needs of scientific calculation. Harvard doctoral student Howard Aiken was working on his dissertation on vacuum tube design in 1936 when he came up with the idea for a machine to calculate nonlinear differential equations (a type of differential equation that could not be solved with a Differential Analyzer). He proposed the idea to George Chase, the chief engineer of the Monroe Calculating Machine Company. While Chase supported the project, he could not get Monroe's financial backing. Conversely, IBM's chief engineer, James Bryce, was able to secure the support of IBM president Thomas Watson, Sr., to fund the work. Unlike any of the digital computing pioneers, Aiken drew inspiration (though no technical ideas) from the writings and work of Charles Babbage as he formalized his proposal. After receiving some training in engineering from IBM in the late 1930s, Aiken began work on the project with $100,000 from the company (more than six times his original estimate). Operational by January 1943, this large electromechanical machine was the first fully automated calculating device. It utilized a fifty-foot drive shaft that ran off a five horsepower electric motor. This unprecedented calculator was capable of doing three additions or subtractions per second, and multiplication problems in six seconds.[3]

The Mark I was a useful computational machine during the late–World War II period. It was used for producing mathematical tables for the U.S. Navy and other tasks. It could run without continual human intervention, following a long set of instructions coded or programmed on paper tape. Long laborious instructions, however, were always necessary because it lacked conditional capabilities ("if this, then that"). This liability, coupled with its slow operations, resulted in it being quickly overshadowed in the age of digital computers. The Mark I's moving parts simply could not compete with the speed of fully electronic digital processing. While technologically isolated from digital computers, from an organizational standpoint, the Mark I project was meaningful to subsequent computing technology in two respects.

First, it introduced a small number of individuals at Aiken's laboratory and IBM to computer technology. For some, this exposure left a deep impression, and these individuals continued in the computer or programming fields. Most notably, Grace Murray Hopper, a future rear admiral in the navy, followed her work on the Mark I with becoming a pioneer in developing, refining, and promoting influential compilers and programming languages in the 1950s and 1960s.

Second, it indicated the early willingness of IBM and Thomas Watson, Sr., to invest in research in computer technology.[4] At the official dedication ceremony for the Mark I in 1944, Aiken ignored IBM's engineering and financial role and took full credit for the machine. This infuriated Watson, but did not detract from his interest in computing technology. In fact, it led him to hire Columbia University Professor Wallace Eckert to establish the Watson Computer Laboratory (at Columbia), and to build a similar but more powerful automatic electromechanical machine, the Selective Sequence Electronic Calculator. In the 1950s, as a legitimate computer industry was beginning to displace the development of one-of-a-kind machines, IBM and other office machine firms led the way in bringing a substantial number of computers to market. The remainder of this chapter examines such office machine specialists, and the business relationships, capabilities, and skills that they developed between the late nineteenth century and the start of World War II. These relationships, capabilities, and skills would prove critical shortly after the advent of electronic digital computers.

THE BEGINNINGS OF A BUSINESS MACHINE INDUSTRY IN THE UNITED STATES

The lack of connection between much of the technology and business context of computers (both analog machines and electromechanical calculators) of the interwar period and later electronic digital computing might suggest that the latter emerged out of nowhere at the end of World War II. Though concentrated efforts and funding in electronics and computing during the war were fundamental to the development of electronic digital computers, these machines had a significant and long technical, organizational, and business prehistory that dated back to the late nineteenth century.

With regard to the computer trade that emerged in the second half of the twentieth century, there is a meaningful distinction between the business machine industry, and a subset of that industry, the tabulating machine and punched-card field. Both were important to the future computer industry, but with many office and business machines (such as typewriters) the connection to the future industry was primarily one of brand recognition, developing sales and service know-how, and marketing.[5] This was true of the tabulating machine and punched-card sector as well, but in this area there was also the far closer technological connection of data processing automation. In the nineteenth century, clerks achieved most data processing needs in Europe and the United States through painstakingly slow manual tabulation. By the start of the following century, this changed dramatically in the United States.

Europe, with a more firmly entrenched infrastructure resulting from its earlier industrialization, lagged behind the United States by a decade or two in widely embracing tabulating machine and punched-card technology, and more generally, adopting the mechanized office. Even after World War I however, American businesses continued to be captivated by office machinery to a greater degree than their European counterparts, and U.S. firms led in many areas of the international office machine industry. A number of factors were likely responsible for this leadership: American's fascination with efficiency; the fact that a smaller office labor force and higher wages in the United States made automation more attractive; America's far greater domestic market relative to any single European country; and a host of talented U.S. business machine entrepreneurs, including William Burroughs, John Patterson, Thomas Watson, Sr., and James Rand. Another inventor-entrepreneur, Herman Hollerith, however, played the greatest role in establishing the technology. He did this through his design skills and leadership in developing tabulating machines, and by forming the company that would, by the mid-1950s, begin to evolve into the world's largest and most successful computer firm.

HERMAN HOLLERITH AND THE ORIGINS OF INTERNATIONAL BUSINESS MACHINES

For decades following the first U.S. Census of 1790, census-taking represented by far the greatest tabulation problem facing either the public or private sectors of the nation. By 1880, the census-taking chore had become even more arduous as a result of both population growth and the expanded data that was gathered and processed on individuals and families. Nearly 1,500 clerks were employed for this census, and the tedious manual tabulation work took seven years to complete. A young engineer, Herman Hollerith, cognizant of this huge and expensive burden, would build a machine to greatly ease the effort of the following census. In doing so, he set the stage for rapid growth in the information-processing machine industry.

Upon Hollerith's graduation from Columbia University with an engineering degree, one of his professors, who happened to serve as an advisor to the U.S. Bureau of the Census, helped him get a job as an assistant with the bureau. Shortly after starting his new position, Hollerith heard the director of vital statistics, John Shaw Billings, remark on how there "ought to be a machine" to do the tedious work of tabulation, "something on the principle of the Jacquard Loom."[6] After a couple years, Hollerith left the bureau to teach at MIT, and subsequently worked at the U.S. Patent Office in Washington, D.C. He did not forget the words of Billings, however, or the problems he saw at the Bureau of the Census.

While traveling by train and observing the conductor using a punch device to record physical characteristics of passengers on their tickets, Hollerith had the idea for a punched-card tabulating machine.[7] He built a prototype that he patented in 1884. By the latter part of the decade, he had set up shop in downtown Washington, D.C., and had refined his machine so that it could tabulate using punched cards and electric sensors. In 1888 the new superintendent of the Bureau of the Census, Robert Porter, initiated a contest for devices and methods to ease the work of taking and tabulating a census. The following year, Hollerith's tabulating machine was tested against two different manual methods. In this small-scale test, Hollerith's machine was the clear winner of the contest due to the time it saved in the mechanized tabulation phase of the operation. Hollerith subcontracted and supervised the manufacturing of his tabulating machines at Western Electric and at Pratt and Whitney.[8] Though he had sold his services and tabulating machines to a few local or national government agencies before this, these deals were small compared to the 1890 Census. The census project changed Hollerith's life and was a momentous event in the history of data processing.

The Bureau of the Census contracted to use fifty-six Hollerith machines for the 1890 Census for an annual rental fee of $1,000 per machine. Soon after the initial contract, it added forty-four more Hollerith machines. As a result of the high cost, the bureau ran the machines both day and night and stipulated a penalty schedule for any prolonged breakdowns. Through Hollerith's diligence, no machines were ever down for long and he never had to pay a penalty. Each machine operator could tabulate results with productivity equivalent to twenty manual tabulating clerks. The machines used contact pins that completed electrical circuits when a hole was punched. If a circuit was completed, a mechanical counter tabulated the result. Thanks to Hollerith machines, the 1890 U.S. Census was processed in only two and a half years, faster by nearly a factor of three than the 1880 Census. The overall 1890 Census included 26,408 pages of reports, roughly a quarter more than the 1880 Census, and the $11.5 million cost was estimated to be $5 million less than it would have been without using Hollerith's tabulating machines.[9]

In the early 1890s, Hollerith moved his shop to a two-story brick building in the Georgetown area. The building would undergo a number of expansions in subsequent years to serve as a development laboratory, card-manufacturing plant, final assembly installation, and repair shop. He continued to outsource subassemblies to a number of different suppliers. In December 1896, Hollerith established a new company, the Tabulating Machine Company, to commercialize his technology. He managed to get a contract for the 1897 Russian Census, but soon shifted his primary attention to supplying machines for the 1900 U.S. Census. For the latter, he received an annual rent of $1,000 for each of fifty machines plus an option to rent one hundred more, the same compensation per machine as for the prior U.S. Census.[10] Even before the 1900 Census was complete, however, Hollerith knew he could not count upon the next U.S. Census for another large financial boost. With the assassination of President William McKinley, Robert Porter was replaced as the superintendent of the Bureau of the Census. His successor felt Hollerith's rates for the 1900 Census were exorbitant and that the 1910 Census contract should be given to a different punched-card machine producer, James Powers.

Not long after the turn of the century, Robert Porter went back to his native Great Britain and formed Tabulating Limited to produce tabulating machines similar to those of Hollerith for the British market. This firm, which changed names to the British Tabulating Machine Company (BTM) in 1907, would become Britain's leading computer manufacturer.[11]

After losing the Bureau of the Census contract, Hollerith concentrated on commercial business and produced a number of new automatic tabulating machines. He particularly targeted railway companies and secured business with New York Central, among others. By 1908 he had thirty customers, and by 1911 he had about a hundred. He worked tenaciously on the engineering, financial, and marketing sides of the business. His heavy work schedule contributed to his suffering from a series of health problems and a desire to spend more time with his family. Already possessing great wealth, in 1911 Hollerith retired and sold the Tabulator Recording Company to financier Charles Flint. Hollerith, however, remained a technical consultant and worked on a more modest schedule for the firm for more than a decade. Flint, immediately after purchasing the company, merged it with two other firms: the Computing Scale Company and the International Time Recording Company. The resulting enterprise was named the Computing-Tabulating-Recording Company (C-T-R). In 1924, C-T-R changed its name to International Business Machines (IBM).

In reflecting on Hollerith's achievements, the importance of his first government contract for the 1890 Census cannot be overemphasized. Even with his success on this project, however, he still had difficulty bringing his machines to a wider market. The 1900 Census gave him more time and resources, and by late in the first decade of the twentieth century, he had built a successful business, independent of U.S. Census work. This pattern of development, major government funding over a span of years as a new technology is refined and markets are cultivated, would play itself out again and again in the early electronic digital computer industry of the post–World War II period.[12] It is difficult to speculate on when and if the tabulating machine and its market would have developed without Hollerith's early government contracts. Likewise, it is uncertain when and if digital computing would have developed and been brought to market had it not been for the substantial government funding in computing and electronics in the name of national defense during and after World War II. In these counterfactuals, the technologies and businesses may have developed, but they would have been far later and likely of different form.

The information processing of the tabulating machine and punched-card business was particularly conducive to future success with developing digital computing technology. This, however, was but one factor in placing IBM in a strong position for the digital computer industry. A key component in its future success in the new trade was the strong leadership and organizational capabilities that IBM developed during the interwar period. The story of this leadership actually begins with another of the office machine giants.

NATIONAL CASH REGISTER, JOHN PATTERSON, AND THOMAS WATSON, SR.

In 1878, Dayton, Ohio, restaurateur James Ritty was traveling through Europe. After observing a ship-propeller-counting device, Ritty had an idea for a machine that could calculate cash at his restaurant. The following year he and his brother completed the construction and patenting of such a machine. In doing so, the basis for one of America's great companies, National Cash Register (NCR), was born. The brothers only sold one machine, but, of great importance, John Patterson, the owner of a retail coal business, purchased it. This transaction appeared an insignificant event at the time, and the Ritty brothers soon sold the rights to their machine and company to Jacob Eckert for $1,000. Patterson, however, was quite impressed with the machine he had purchased, and in 1884 bought the controlling interest of the firm for $6,500. He immediately renamed it the National Cash Register Company. Patterson would become a legend for the unparalleled marketing and sales skills that he practiced and taught at NCR. In fact, he has been dubbed "the father of modern salesmanship."

During Patterson's first year at the helm, his firm sold 359 cash registers.[13]

NCR's early success placed it in a position to integrate into both upstream acquisitions of materials and subassembly manufacturing, as well as downstream retail sales. In the late nineteenth century, office equipment companies tended to use wholesalers and nonspecialized sales agents to sell products.[14] With technologically complex machinery, such as cash registers, this had the disadvantage of using sellers who often were uneducated in the finer technical points of their products. By integrating into both upstream and downstream operations, and maintaining a centralized managerial structure, employees involved in manufacturing could communicate technical details to the sales force. Equally important, the sales personnel could convey the wants and needs of customers back to engineers. These engineers then would refine products and incorporate the most desirable features into subsequent models. Maintaining a high degree of integration also led to economies of scale and reduced the inherent cost of transactions.[15]

NCR's vertical integration and Patterson's management proved a winning combination. In 1894, NCR engineer Charles Kettering, who would later invent the electric starter for automobiles, designed and built the first electrical cash register. That same year, Patterson ran the first sales school in U.S. industry.[16] By the turn of the century, NCR's annual sales volume grew to 200,000 cash registers, and by 1922 the company was selling more than 2 million of the machines annually.[17] The importance of Patterson's sales skills and his abilities to teach his knowledge and practices to others cannot be overemphasized. Patterson would force his sales representatives to memorize and recite sales pitches, have highly charged motivational meetings, and set ambitious goals. These goals were recorded as official quotas to be met and were based on past sales data for particular territories. First and foremost, a salesperson was an educator who rationally convinced customers of the merits of a product. Patterson saw selling as a science, something that required knowledge and skill, but also something that could be taught. In doing so, Patterson, more than anyone else in the late nineteenth century, elevated sales to become an esteemed occupation. He molded a number of individuals into top sellers of NCR machines, and he did this through discipline and maintaining complete control. If he ever felt he had lost control of one of his sales representatives or sales managers, he would fire them without hesitation. Both his ability to teach sales and sales management skills, and his propensity to dismiss successful employees who had gained enough confidence to challenge his strong opinions, led NCR to become a training ground for those who would go on to become talented sale managers and executives at other companies. Of these individuals, none would be more influential than Thomas Watson, Sr.

Thomas Watson, Sr., was born in East Campbell, New York, in 1874. His father encouraged him to study business for a year at Miller School of Commerce in Elmira, New York. The elder Watson subsequently pushed his son to leave nearby Painted Post, New York, and his job selling pianos and organs. Showing strong sales ability from the start, Watson left to seek work in Buffalo in 1895. Following his dismissal from one job for celebrating a sale by drinking in a saloon while his horse, buggy, and merchandise were stolen, he had difficulty finding steady work. Within a year, however, he succeeded in getting a sales job at NCR's Buffalo office. After just four years, Watson was named the sales manager of the firm's faltering Rochester, New York, office. A mere three months later, he turned the office into one of the company's most successful and was called to the home office in Dayton, Ohio, to meet with the famed John Patterson.

By the early twentieth century, the high quality of NCR cash registers, ironically, began to hurt the company to a certain extent by creating a widespread secondhand market and reducing opportunities for new machine sales. Recognizing this, Patterson developed a plan to covertly finance a business specializing in selling used NCR equipment and to keep its relationship to the parent company secret. He placed Watson in charge of the operation. Watson would locate near major competitors that sold used office machinery and would undersell them, or use other techniques to put them out of business. While he was very successful at this, he did not enjoy it, and was pleased when NCR's deceitful practice ended and the secondhand business was absorbed into the larger sales operation. Shortly thereafter, in 1908, Watson was named the assistant sales manager of NCR. Two years later, he became the sales manager.

NCR's near monopoly—nearly 90 percent of the cash register market in the United States—and the tactics it used to maintain and extend its power, did not go unnoticed at the U.S. Justice Department. In 1912, Patterson, Watson, and some other top employees were found guilty of violating the Sherman Antitrust Act (engaging in illegal anticompetitive business practices). Patterson and Watson both were given the maximum sentence of one year in jail. While the case was being appealed, there were major tensions between the two individuals. Patterson was suspicious of the power and respect Watson had achieved with all the salesmen and engineers at the firm and made Watson's life at the company unpleasant. This came to a head in 1913, when Patterson forced Watson to resign. Despite having his first child on the way, Watson was selective in his job search. In 1914 he accepted the position of general manager at C-T-R.

THOMAS WATSON, SR.: EARLY YEARS AT C-T-R

In 1915, after an appeals court cleared Watson of any criminal offense in the Justice Department's antitrust case, the C-T-R Board of Directors named him the new president of the company. Watson, however, had difficulties with Herman Hollerith, the founder of C-T-R. Hollerith believed that Watson's focus on sales was wrong in principle, thinking that a concentration on engineering and on targeting a small number of customers who could benefit most from the machines, was preferable. The tension diffused when Hollerith resigned from the Board of Directors soon after Watson's arrival.

Watson is often remembered for his unwritten, but very real, dress code (the legendary IBM dark-blue suit and dark tie) and many paternalistic prohibitions (including one on alcohol—he opposed drinking ever since his horse and buggy were stolen while he was in a saloon). While Watson never wavered in emphasizing sales, he did not ignore the technical side of the firm. More than anything, Watson was deeply influenced by Patterson and the successful integrated operation he observed at NCR. He later reminisced, "Nearly everything I know about building a business comes from Mr. Patterson."[18] This included strong central management and placing great importance on both sales and engineering, and perhaps most significantly, communication and interaction between the two operations. Other key elements of Patterson's that were immediately reproduced at C-T-R included sales quotas and rewarding successful sales staff with substantial commissions.

Within his first year as president, Watson started a new engineering department for tabulation-machine development in New York City. Two years later he moved this division and the engineering department of the firm's Time Recording Division to Endicott, New York. Watson brought in James Bryce to supervise Time Recording's research and development. In 1922, Bryce would become the chief engineer of C-T-R. By this time, Watson became increasingly involved in strategic planning for his firm's technological leadership. The company's only real competition in tabulating machines and punched cards over the past decade had been

Thomas Watson, Sr., at his desk at the Computer-Tabulating-Recording Company, or C-T-R, 1914. (Courtesy of IBM Archives)

the Powers Accounting Machine Company—the firm begun by James Powers, the individual who won the 1910 U.S. Census contract over Hollerith. Powers Accounting Machine would later merge with a larger office machine company, resulting in a more formidable competitor for IBM.

REMINGTON TYPEWRITER

In the early 1870s, an increasingly diversified manufacturing firm, the Remington Company, would enter a new business by teaming up with retired newspaper editor Christopher Latham Sholes of Milwaukee, the inventor of the first practical modern typewriter in 1868. Unlike tabulating machines, competition from numerous small firms was evident soon after Remington started marketing its Remington 1 typewriter. Nevertheless, Remington rapidly achieved and maintained its position as the industry leader. By 1890 the firm was making more than 20,000 typewriters a year. Typewriters were the first volume business to demonstrate that a major office machine industry in the United States was coming into being in the 1880s. Setting a precedent for the computer, and to a lesser extent some other office machines previous to computing, the typewriter was a technology that could be effectively marketed only if trained users existed. The shortage of male office clerks quickly opened the door for women in this new profession. Many typing schools emerged in the 1890s, and soon thereafter typing classes were offered at other types of schools. The 1900 U.S. Census identified approximately 112,000 individuals as typists or stenographers, and 77 percent of these individuals were women.[19]

The 1890s also represented the decade of the first vertical filing systems. James Rand, Sr., became one of the pioneers in this area when he patented a visible index system of dividers, color strips, and tabs to be held in vertical files. In 1898 he formed the Rand Ledger Company and quickly became the leading provider of record-keeping systems for corporations. His son, James Rand, Jr., who worked at the company, invented a continually expandable card record-keeping system that he named Kardex. The younger Rand soon left his father's firm and started the Kardex Company, an enterprise that quickly surpassed the successful Rand Ledger Company in sales revenue. In 1925, father and son merged their two firms to create Rand Kardex Company. This enterprise had 4,500 field representatives in 219 offices. In 1927, the Rands wanted to diversify into other areas of office equipment and merged with Powers Accounting Machine and Remington to establish a tabulator machine and punched-card division. The combined firm, Remington Rand, had assets of $73 million and was by far the world's largest business machine company.[20]

BURROUGHS ADDING MACHINE COMPANY

A final major player in the late-nineteenth- and early-twentieth-century office machine industry was the Burroughs Adding Machine Company. William S. Burroughs, a former bank clerk, established the American Arithmometer Company in 1886 in St. Louis after patenting an adding and listing (printing) machine. The firm had moderate initial success, but would not grow rapidly until the early years of the following century—something William S. Burroughs never saw as he died in his mid-forties in 1898. By 1904 the company's annual sales of adding machines were in the thousands. That year, the company moved from St. Louis to Detroit and was renamed the Burroughs Adding Machine Company. In 1905 the firm had a sales force of 148 and was selling about 8,000 adding machines a year. Three years later machine sales grew to 13,000. The firm became the leading adding machine enterprise in the world, but it had a number of U.S. competitors such as Felt and Tarrant.[21]

Burroughs, however, differed in a number of ways from its many adding machine competitors. First, it was focused not just on selling adding machines, but also on the service of integrating them into the businesses of its customers. The firm also was not a one-technology enterprise. In addition to adding machines, it diversified into more sophisticated full-scale accounting machines. Advanced knowledge and capabilities in accounting systems became instilled in its sales force. Finally, the success of the company placed it in a better financial position, with far greater assets than most of its competitors. All of these were influential factors helping to explain why Burroughs was the only adding machine company that made a meaningful transition into the computer industry in the second half of the twentieth century.

THE GREAT DEPRESSION AND THE OFFICE MACHINE INDUSTRY

The stock market crash in October 1929, and the unprecedented depression that followed, presented extreme challenges to American corporations. Some of the major New York Stock Exchange indexes would not reach their 1929 highs again until the 1950s. Many firms did not survive, while others forever changed or were scarred by the prolonged economic collapse. The four American office machine giants—NCR, IBM, Remington Rand, and Burroughs—all made it through these difficult years, but their relative positions changed significantly. While they each led in producing a different primary product (cash registers, tabulating machines, typewriters, and adding/accounting machines), they competed against one another to varying degrees. For instance, Burroughs and IBM competed on some accounting machines, and IBM competed directly against the tabulating-machine division of Remington Rand. By far, the most striking change during the Depression years of the 1930s was the massive growth of IBM—in a decade in which the other firms declined in revenue and profitability (see Table 1.1).

In 1928 Burroughs' revenue was 63 percent higher, and NCR's revenue was 149 percent higher, than IBM's. Nevertheless, both Burroughs and NCR had lower revenue than IBM in 1939. Relative changes in earnings were even more striking during this period. Of the four office machine leaders in 1928, IBM had the lowest net earnings at $5.3 million. In 1939, IBM's bottom line had grown to $9.1 million, and the next highest of the four firms

Table 1.1
Differential Impact of Depression on U.S. Office Machine Industry Leaders (all figures in millions of dollars)

	1928		1939	
Company	Revenue	Profit	Revenue	Profit
Burroughs	$32.1	$8.3	$32.5	$2.9
IBM	$19.7	$5.3	$39.5	$9.1
NCR	$49.0	$7.8	$37.1	$3.1
Remington Rand	$59.6	$6.0	$43.4	$1.6

Source: Annual issues of Moody's Industrial Manual. Taken from James W. Cortada, Before the Computer: IBM, NCR, Burroughs, and Remington Rand, and the Industry They Created (Princeton, NJ: Princeton University Press, 1993), 153.

was NCR with just $3.1 million. In the latter year, when more than 23 percent of IBM's revenue remained as net earnings, the profit margin for all three of the other firms was well below 10 percent. IBM was able to achieve these phenomenal results (in both absolute and relative terms) in large part because it relied on leasing far more than selling its machines. It also had steady revenue streams coming in from its sale of punched cards. This allowed it to have far more predictable and sustained earnings during the years when few firms could invest in purchasing new business machines. Furthermore, Thomas Watson, Sr., did not cut his manufacturing or sales workforce during the Depression. He continued to push forward and encouraged his sales personnel to be all the more aggressive. Watson became legendary in these years for the courage he displayed and instilled in others through his commitment to his workers.[22]

At the outbreak of World War II, IBM was in an unrivaled position among America's office machine giants. Furthermore, it was the clear leader in tabulator and punched-card systems, the technologies that would translate most directly to the early era of electronic digital computers. Such computers were developed during and shortly after the war primarily in university and government (rather than corporate) settings. Without the exigencies of a massive war and a shift in U.S. foreign policy from relative isolationism to deep involvement in the global political arena, electronic digital computing would not have developed for a number of years. The first digital computer firms were relatively small enterprises that extended from wartime government-funded computing research and development projects. All of the large office machine companies let these smaller enterprises test the new waters, but at varying points in the 1950s the large firms each took differing approaches to investing in this emerging industry. Their strategies for entering this business, however, began long before they instituted a direct plan to manufacture digital computing machines— and advancing their capabilities in electronics and other related research proved critical. The following chapter outlines the early university and military digital-computing research, the emergence of small commercial firms attempting to capitalize on this new technology, the subsequent entry (by internal expansion or acquisition) of the office machine leaders into this business, and the early strategy and trajectory of the new industry.

NOTES

1. Martin Campbell-Kelly and William Aspray, *Computer: A History of the Information Machine* (New York: Basic Books, 1996), 61.

2. Prior to World War II, the term "computer" referred solely to people who engaged in calculating work, not machines. Government agencies and certain businesses often employed a large number of individuals to do calculations. In the late 1940s and early 1950s, electronic digital calculating and information processing machines increasingly displaced these workers. As this occurred, the term "computer" became common to refer to machines, not people.

3. Campbell-Kelly and Aspray, *Computer*, 69–74.

4. As will be discussed in the next chapter, Watson and others at IBM were reluctant to use the term "computer" for such research.

5. Typewriters, of course, were precursors to computer keyboards, but such input systems were not developed for a couple decades.

6. James W. Cortada, *Before the Computer: IBM, NCR, Burroughs, and Remington Rand and the Industry They Created, 1865–1956* (Princeton, NJ: Princeton University Press, 1993), 47.

7. Campbell-Kelly and Aspray, *Computer*, 22.

8. Ibid., 22–23.

9. Ibid., 26.

10. Cortada, *Before*, 53.

11. Emerson Pugh, *Building IBM* (Cambridge, MA: MIT Press, 1995), 14–18.

12. With the ENIAC and other early digital computer projects, the government paid for the initial research and development. This differed from Hollerith's initial census contract in that the government merely paid for

completed machines. Proceeds from Hollerith's first contract, however, provided him with capital to refine his technology.

13. Cortada, *Before*, 70–72.

14. Pugh, *Building*, 30–31.

15. Vertical integration was a successful strategy for NCR at this time and often has been for producers of complex technological products with many different components. This, however, differs depending on the degree of engineering talent of supply firms, and the structure, competitive environment, and maturity of an industry. For instance, automobile producers benefited from outsourcing and the development of close communicative relationships with their suppliers which enabled them to cut product development time and enhance responsiveness to changing demand in the early U.S. (1896–1915) and more recent Japanese (the mid-1960s to the present) auto industries.

16. Cortada, *Before*, 68–71.

17. Ibid.

18. Thomas J. Watson, Jr., and Peter Petre, *Father, Son, & Co.: My Life at IBM and Beyond* (New York: Bantam Books, 1990), 11–13.

19. Campbell-Kelly and Aspray, *Computer*, 34–35.

20. Ibid., 36.

21. Ibid., 37–39.

22. Cortada, *Before*, 153.

— 2 —

The Advent of the Mainframe Digital Computer, 1940–1957

Like the automobile a half-century earlier, the digital computer at its origin was a complex technology composed primarily of existing components. Vacuum tubes, which gave computers their power to process information, and punched cards and tabulation systems—the means for the input and output of data—had been around for decades. In many respects these fundamental computer components were analogous to the motive power of cars—internal combustion engines—and motor vehicles' ancestral transportation technologies: wagons, carriages, and bicycles. While there is no individual or team that *invented* the automobile or digital computer, both technologies took great ingenuity and insight to successfully design and assemble. The first Americans to build automobiles, Charles and Frank Duryea, like the first ones to build a digital computer, John Vincent Antanasoff and Clifford Berry, have their place in history. Both sets of individuals, however, will never be as celebrated as those associated with producing the first wave of *useful* cars and computers, or the people (and firms) that later marketed such complex machines in substantial volume. With regard to automobiles, these individuals were William Durant (Buick and General Motors), Ransom Olds (Olds Motor Works and REO), and Henry Ford (Ford Motor Company); in the digital computer field, they were John Mauchly and J. Presper Eckert (Eckert-Mauchly Computer Corporation and Remington Rand), and Thomas Watson, Jr., (IBM). Despite some commonalities between the origins of these technologies, the differences are equally striking. Entrepreneurs, who only needed modest start-up capital (and often relied on generous credit from established component suppliers from the carriage and bicycle trades), typically built the first automobiles. On the other hand, it was the scientists' and engineers' quest for knowledge, not riches, coupled with a wartime demand for unprecedented calculating power, that led to the first digital computers. By the beginning of the twentieth century, the road to commercial success for automobiles was clear enough to attract private capital.[1] With digital computer development in the 1940s, however, the path was so cluttered and uncertain that without the real and perceived computational needs of the Department of Defense (DoD) during World War II and the beginning of the Cold War, the large-scale, economically blind investment in digital computers by the federal government would not have occurred and the advent and growth of computing technology and the computer industry, at the very least, would have been significantly delayed.

JOHN MAUCHLY, J. PRESPER ECKERT, AND THE DEVELOPMENT OF THE ENIAC

John Vincent Antanasoff and his graduate student, Clifford Berry, built a primitive digital computer at Iowa State University between the late 1930s and early 1940s. It was not a powerful machine, and debates continue on the degree to which it was even operational. In 1944 Antanasoff entered military service and would never return to his Antanasoff-Berry Computer (ABC). There is also a cloud of uncertainty about the nature and extent of the influence that a 1941 meeting between John Mauchly and Antanasoff had on Mauchly's ideas and subsequent accomplishments in digital computing. Most likely, Antanasoff inspired Mauchly to make his and J. Presper Eckert's subsequent ENIAC project all the more ambitious. Beyond that, it is difficult to say, and existing resources conflict and offer few clues. The issue did become critical to a subsequent court case, *Honeywell v. Sperry Rand*, in which Antanasoff's work proved important to the invalidation of Sperry Rand's ENIAC patent—a patent that claimed Eckert and Mauchly's invention of the electronic digital computer.[2] Court interpretations aside, from both a technological and industrial standpoint, Eckert and Mauchly's work is the proper place to begin the formal story of digital computing.

The Ballistic Research Laboratory's (BRL) need for calculating complex firing tables brought about a collaboration between the BRL and the University of Pennsylvania's Moore School of Electrical Engineering in the late 1930s. From the BRL's perspective, the Moore School's Differential Analyzer and skilled engineers were the primary attraction. Though the Differential Analyzer was slow and limited, it was the best tool at the time to help calculate ballistic trajectory equations. A typical firing table, however, took the machine hundreds of hours, under the guidance of many dozens of operators, to make the thousands of necessary calculations. A new and more powerful computational machine clearly was needed.

Shortly after America's entrance into World War II, John Mauchly, a physics instructor at Ursinus College, and Arthur Burks, a philosopher at the University of Michigan, took part in the Moore School's Engineering, Science, and Management War Training Program. As the name suggests, the program was designed to prepare scientists and engineers to contribute to America's war effort. Impressed by the faculty and having won over the department, in early 1942 Mauchly and Burks accepted posts as Moore School instructors. By summer of that year, Mauchly proposed building an electronic digital computer to better address the problem of ballistic firing-table calculation. J. Presper Eckert, a talented Moore School electrical engineering research associate, was captivated by Mauchly's idea. In August 1942, Mauchly completed a formal proposal that he submitted to both the director of the Moore School and Lieutenant Herman Goldstine, the BRL liaison officer to the Moore School. Goldstine became a strong advocate of Mauchly's proposed project, and the following year he helped gain approval of what would become a $400,000 BRL contract for the development of a digital computer. The machine, which would consist of 18,000 vacuum tubes and have dimensions of thirty by sixty feet, was named the Electronic Numerical Integrator and Computer (ENIAC). Mauchly contributed the grand idea and broader conceptualization for the project and Eckert provided the electrical engineering expertise.

Work on the ENIAC proceeded steadily, but as a result of various challenges, the machine was not completed until months after the war. During the project, a chance meeting between Herman Goldstine and John von Neumann led to the latter's direct involvement with the ENIAC project. Von Neumann, a leading mathematician and Manhattan Project consultant, convinced the group to submit a proposal to the BRL for the design and development of a subsequent digital computer, the Electronic Discrete Variable Automatic Computer (EDVAC), that would address some of the limitations of the ENIAC. Though Eckert, Mauchly, and others had a direct hand in the planning, von Neumann wrote up the now famous report in June 1945, entitled, "A First Draft of a Report on the EDVAC."[3] This report contained the critical stored-program concept that an internal memory device could hold both the instructions of a program and the data to be processed. The stored-program concept set the stage for the development of programming languages in the early 1950s and, later in the decade, the beginnings of artificial intelligence research. The EDVAC report established the dominant architecture, or logical structure, for digital computers—what became known as the von Neumann architecture.

Von Neumann's involvement with the ENIAC and EDVAC projects, along with his nuclear weapons research at Los Alamos National Laboratory, also provided the connection for the first practical test of the ENIAC in late 1945. The machine was used to calculate equations related to the feasibility and power of the "Super," the classified U.S. project to develop a hydrogen bomb. While the underlying issues were classified, the equations themselves were not. The mathematical problems were successfully run on the ENIAC at its new home at Aberdeen Proving Ground in Maryland, and results were sent to Los Alamos in December 1945.[4]

Though the ENIAC was the first useful large-scale digital computer project in the United States, others soon followed. Of particular note, was von Neumann's computer development project at Princeton's Institute for Advanced Study (resulting in the IAS Computer) during the late 1940s, and Jay Forrester's Whirlwind Project at MIT's Servomechanisms Laboratory that was completed in the early 1950s.[5] Though the latter started as a relatively modest flight simulator project, Forrester, through skillful research and rhetoric, transformed it and received government funding to build an advanced digital computer. Whirlwind led to advances in real-time computing (near-simultaneous networked computer communication) and time-sharing (a system facilitating multiple networked computers' concomitant use of the resources of a large mainframe), and also lent momentum toward establishing MIT as a fundamental center for future computing, software, and networking research at the school's newly formed Lincoln Laboratory.

THE PIONEERING COMPANIES: ELECTRONIC CONTROL COMPANY/ECKERT-MAUCHLY COMPUTER CORPORATION AND ENGINEERING RESEARCH ASSOCIATES

Around the time the ENIAC was completed, Eckert and Mauchly became excited about the future commercial possibilities for digital computing. The two formed the Electronic Control Company in 1946 with the aim of not only building computers for scientific calculation, but also for data processing applications in business. The company began operations in a downtown Philadelphia facility. Eckert and Mauchly, much like Herman Hollerith, first targeted the U.S. Census Bureau as a potential customer. Despite projections that building a machine based on the EDVAC's specifications would cost about as much the ENIAC, they accepted a contract for $100,000 less. They hoped they would make up for the loss with future sales.

By fall 1947, the firm had twelve engineers and was working on a new machine designated as the Universal Automatic Computer, or UNIVAC. The term "Universal" was chosen to signify that the machine was appropriate for both scientific and business applications. In 1947, Eckert and Mauchly changed the firm from a partnership to a corporation to accommodate the wishes of the U.S. Census Bureau, and renamed the enterprise the Eckert-Mauchly Computer Corporation (EMCC). The American Totalisator Company, a firm that had built sophisticated mechanical calculating machines, agreed to purchase a 40 percent interest of EMCC for $500,000 and also to make some loans to the struggling computer firm. A tragedy, however, soon eclipsed this source of funding. American Totalisator's primary backer of the deal, vice president Henry Strauss, died in a plane crash, and the firm pulled out of the partnership.[6] Initial difficulties in selling contracts for UNIVAC computers led to further financial struggles for the firm and to its reluctant consent to build a smaller scientific machine for Northrop Aircraft Corporation; the machine was a computer named BINAC (BINary Automatic Computer). The BINAC contract, however, was not enough to put Electronic Control on stable footing, and the firm was quickly drifting toward insolvency.

In spring 1948, the media company A. C. Neilson contracted for a UNIVAC, and a deal to build one for Prudential Insurance quickly followed. Again, however, Eckert-Mauchly was forced to settle for prices that failed to cover its manufacturing and delivery costs. EMCC was in such poor financial shape that Eckert and Mauchly reluctantly met with International Business Machines (IBM), National Cash Register (NCR), and Remington Rand to potentially sell a controlling interest of the company. Though IBM may not have had any serious interest, its lawyers killed any possibility of a deal by warning Thomas Watson, Sr., that antitrust action would likely follow such an acquisition. In 1950, Remington Rand, a firm with far less market share in the information processing field than IBM, bought EMCC for $538,000. For a mere 7.6 percent more than

Remington Rand's Universal Automatic Computer, or UNIVAC; the acronym became synonymous with mainframe digital computers during the 1950s. (Courtesy of Charles Babbage Institute, University of Minnesota, Minneapolis)

American Totalisator's planned offer two years earlier (for a 40 percent stake), Remington Rand received complete ownership of the firm. This left Eckert and Mauchly as salaried employees (at an annual compensation of $18,000 each) of the firm they had founded.[7]

The early history of Eckert-Mauchly was an engineering triumph and business failure. With the uncertainties of the development costs of this new technology, cost-plus contracts clearly would have been preferable and might have placed the two in a position to retain control of their firm. Whether it could have successfully secured business on such a basis is difficult to say, but by forging ahead as it did, Eckert-Mauchly helped press the office machine giants to continually evaluate whether they were allocating adequate resources toward research and development in this new field. Despite the fact that the office machine leaders were initially only concentrating on computing research, and not the development of products, Eckert-Mauchly was not alone in the digital computer business in the mid-1940s.[8]

In 1946, almost simultaneous to the formation of EMCC, Howard Engstrom, William Norris, and John Parker, engineers who had worked together in the U.S. Navy during World War II, founded a company called Engineering Research Associates (ERA) in St. Paul, Minnesota. They wanted to keep together the engineering talent of their wartime code-breaking group and successfully secured modest investment capital. Though a private company, ERA began by strictly doing naval projects in the code-breaking area and related electronics research and development. In the summer of 1947, the navy approved a contract for ERA to build an electronic digital computer named Atlas. The contract was similar in scale to the army's funding for the ENIAC project. ERA petitioned and received permission to build a nonclassified version (with certain Atlas machine-instructions removed), which it could sell commercially, the ERA 1101. Unlike the UNIVAC, the ERA 1101 was specifically targeted for scientific work. It had relatively strong internal processing capabilities for the time, but lacked sophisticated input/output technology. This liability, coupled with the firm's lack of marketing experience, made it difficult for the firm to secure contracts to produce ERA 1101 computers.[9]

During development of the 1101, ERA continued to receive some naval contracts for noncomputing equipment, but the firm failed to thrive financially. In 1952, Remington Rand decided to further boost its computer development and manufacturing resources by purchasing ERA. Given the firm's financial uncertainty, John Parker was eager to sell the company. Before the acquisition, ERA had received a naval contract to build a more powerful computer, the Atlas II. With this machine, the company's engineers had a clearer sense of developing features that might make it more marketable to a range of scientific users, and sought to incorporate such specifications in the product development stage (although they remained attentive to the navy's needs). The UNIVAC 1103 (Remington Rand took the name UNIVAC for its entire computer division) was a technically sophisticated machine, and it sold better than the 1101. The 1103 model that Remington Rand delivered to the National Committee of Aeronautics (NACA) in 1954 used magnetic core memory, a major advance over the tube memory being used by most other digital computer producers at that time.

Engineering Research Associates (ERA) research laboratory, circa late 1940s. (Courtesy of Charles Babbage Institute, University of Minnesota, Minneapolis)

BUYING INTO THE COMPUTER INDUSTRY: OFFICE MACHINE GIANTS AND THE START-UPS THEY ACQUIRED

Economist Kenneth Flamm and a number of historians have highlighted the head start that Remington Rand had in the computing field by acquiring the first two U.S. digital computer firms. Remington Rand also had existing internal resources in punched-card tabulation and computer research and development.[10] These resources, while significant, somewhat distort an assessment of Remington Rand's "lead" over IBM in computing. IBM was conducting extensive research in electronics and computing by the time of Remington Rand's acquisitions of EMCC and ERA. Similar to Remington Rand, many dozens of engineers were involved in computer-related research at the punched-card and tabulation machine giant. IBM's base of business customers in data processing also mitigated advantages that otherwise might have accrued from Remington Rand bringing digital computers to market several years ahead of the New York–based firm. Furthermore, to fully benefit from its first-mover status in product development and delivery, Remington Rand needed to quickly integrate its computer business resources from its facilities in Norwalk, Connecticut (Remington Rand), Philadelphia (EMCC), and St. Paul (ERA). Existing evidence indicates that the firm failed in this effort.[11]

Much like Eckert and Mauchly, most of the engineers at ERA were disappointed by Remington Rand's takeover of the firm. From the start, there were cultural clashes and conflicts between the facilities. Eckert had an arrogant demeanor and always wanted to be in control. By some accounts he saw the former ERA firm and Norwalk as merely job shops to support his Philadelphia operation. While few if any questioned Eckert's electrical engineering skills, many found communicating with him quite difficult. Technical talent existed at all three of the firm's computer research facilities, and the former ERA engineers resented Eckert's air of superiority.[12]

Furthermore, there was a problem of resources. While Remington Rand demonstrated a commitment to the computing field through engaging in some pre-1950 internal work and acquiring the first two American firms in digital computing, it did not shower the Philadelphia or St. Paul divisions with funds. Both of these operations believed that resources were spread too thinly to appropriately conduct their various projects. Allocations indicate that while the company expected computers would be important for its punched-card tabulation or data processing division, the firm was not willing to transform its overall nature or focus.

Remington Rand, more than any of the other office machine leaders, was a conglomerate, and James Rand and other top executives had no interest in making the firm primarily a digital computer company. In addition to its large typewriter and filing-system products, the company was heavily involved in the consumer electronics area, selling electric razors and other devices. The diversity of its businesses contributed to the overall decentralized management of the firm. This, in turn, helped perpetuate both independence and distant relations between facilities, even—and perhaps particularly—among those facilities that overlapped in certain product areas.

Remington Rand's punched-card tabulation division had always been less than one-fifth the size of IBM's, and as data processing (DP) evolved into the era of digital computers, this same proportion remained intact between the two firms' DP divisions. In retrospect, it is easy to point out some of Remington Rand's strategic shortcomings in the several years between its acquisition of EMCC and IBM's launch of its first digital computer in 1953, the IBM

701. In reality, it is not likely that a different approach by Remington Rand would have altered the relative position of the two firms' computing businesses to any significant degree. From its sales capabilities, customer base, lease structure, and technical resources, IBM simply had too much of the right infrastructure in place to be anything but an early leader in the digital computer field. Remington Rand was certainly not alone in its struggles to compete. The companies that perhaps could have mounted the most formidable challenge in the early years, RCA and General Electric, chose to explore the business on a tentative basis. NCR, Burroughs, and others also took a cautious approach, similar to, and several years behind, Remington Rand.

Adding- and accounting-machine specialist Burroughs developed its first digital computer in 1951 for its Philadelphia research facility. Two years later it sold an enhanced version of the machine, called the Unitized Digital Electronic Computer (or UDEC), to Wayne State University. The firm recognized the potential future importance of computing, but was facing challenges from IBM and others in its accounting-machine business and was reluctant to risk large amounts of capital on a market that was uncertain and could take years to develop.

The Detroit-based company decided to explore entry into the computer business in a modest way through a joint venture with the British Tabulating Machine Company (BTM), a firm in a similar position that had some complementary technologies for computer development. BTM had been the British licensee of IBM punched-card and tabulating machine products for more than four decades. In 1949, however, IBM severed the partnership. IBM had received an amazingly high 25 percent royalty from BTM for years, but was disappointed with the level of the British firm's punched-card and tabulating machine sales and thought it could do better by marketing in the United Kingdom on its own.[13] Thomas Watson, Sr., also may have been reluctant to license products in the future, given IBM's increasing research-and-development expenditures and its potential move into computing technology. This left BTM with existing tabulating machine designs, but a severe deficiency of new product development capabilities. Though Burroughs and BTM engineers worked for several years on the HOBO (Hollerith-Burroughs) project to jointly develop digital computers, they abandoned the partnership, and in the end, both followed a strategy similar to Remington Rand's in competing against IBM: engaging in acquisitions. BTM merged with another British firm, Power-Samas, while Burroughs acquired the ElectroData Corporation.[14]

In the early 1950s, ElectroData had been launched as a division of an electronics firm, Consolidated Electrodynamics Corporation (CEC) of Pasadena, California. In 1954, CEC spun off ElectroData as an independent business, and two years later Burroughs acquired the company. ElectroData already had a small-scale digital computer on the market, the ElectroData 205, and was completing a more powerful machine, the ElectroData 220. This gave Burroughs an immediate presence in the computer business. While less significant than acquiring two producers of large mainframes as Remington Rand had done, the Burroughs' acquisition was similar in making a modest entrance into the computing field without significantly diverting resources and risking lost opportunities in its profitable existing lines (especially electromechanical accounting machines). Burroughs continued to allocate 75 percent of its research and development expenditures for innovating electromechanical accounting machines and only 25 percent for basic research. Of this basic research, only a fraction went toward electronics. Despite significant sales of ElectroData 205s and 220s, the firm's level of spending on electronics research was insufficient to significantly expand its computing business in the second half of the 1950s.[15] Even though Burroughs' annual revenues from digital computers reached $14 million during 1957, the revenue from this division did not even approach 20 percent of the company's total sales until 1960. This, however, was a significantly higher percentage than at NCR and many of the other competitors in the computer industry at this time.[16]

National Cash Register moved into the computing business in 1952, several years earlier than Burroughs and only a couple years after Remington Rand. It positioned itself in this new field by purchasing the Computer Research Corporation (CRC), a firm founded by Northrop Aircraft engineers in 1950. CRC, located in Hawthorne, California, was similar to ERA in that it was sponsored by Department of Defense contracts, and its formation was an attempt to keep together engineers who had engaged in electronics and computer-related military research during and shortly after the war—in this case for the air force rather than the navy. Chief among the projects many of these engineers had worked on was the Magnetic Drum Differential Analyzer, which was built for airborne guidance applications in the late 1940s. CRC, like CEC a few years later, largely grew out of engineers migrating from Northrop, Raytheon, and other established defense contractors, as well as freshly minted engineers from California Institute of Technology. Aircraft firms were critical to spawning the engineers that gave the West Coast a major presence in the early computer industry.

From the start, NCR president Stanley Allyn wanted to integrate CRC within its existing operation and centralize manufacturing at NCR's Dayton facilities.[17] The firm believed that its cash register and accounting-machine technology could provide the necessary input/output mechanism for integrated data processing technology.[18] CRC's first computer, the 102, and the revised and more successful 102A, were midpriced smaller machines geared for the scientific market. Soon after the acquisition, Allyn decided that replicating computer-manufacturing facilities in Dayton, when the infrastructure already existed at the Hawthorne plant, was impractical. Thus, NCR changed course and decided to produce its computers at its California facility.[19]

The tasks that lay ahead for NCR involved continuing to serve its core customers with cash registers, meeting the needs of a small number of government and corporate entities for scientific computers, and integrating its technology for data processing computer systems in a way that would appeal broadly to the business community. NCR's management expected immediate results in regard to this latter goal, which did not materialize. The CRC division was losing money in the first years after the acquisition, and Allyn had difficulty maintaining enthusiasm for the firm's plans in computer technology when the traditional cash register business continued to be highly profitable. In the middle of 1954, the firm discontinued CRC manufacturing operations, and reorganized CRC as NCR's Electronics Division, led by general manager Donald Eckdahl. The Electronics Division consisted of a talented group of engineers that developed a small general-purpose digital computer, the 303, which was a revised and improved version of the firm's 102 series. Allyn, however, had growing reservations about this new field, and NCR did not provide significant resources for computer research and development.[20] Instead, the firm began to take a more conservative approach to the new technology by the mid-1950s. Exemplifying this strategy was the nature of the partnership the firm entered into with another American industrial leader, General Electric.

Through the firm's banking work, NCR became involved with the Bank of America's bank automation programming project, Electronic Recording Machine Accounting (ERMA). Bank of America had contracted with General Electric (GE) to build the computers based on ERMA (a computing system developed for Bank of America by the Stanford Research Institute, or SRI), and Allyn subsequently approached GE about National Cash Register collaborating on this endeavor. This resulted in an alliance in 1956 between General Electric and NCR. The agreement stipulated that GE would build central processors and memory for both of the firms' computers, and NCR would provide card readers, printers, and other peripherals. Engineers at Hawthorne were stunned and angered by this retreat from full-fledged computer development work. Some contemplated leaving NCR, and many believed it set the firm back at least two to three years in digital computing development capabilities. The impact was long-term for a firm in the fast-moving computing field. Even by 1962, a decade after entering the industry, 80 percent of NCR's research and development expenditures remained in traditional mechanical engineering, spending that was primarily geared to facilitate innovation of its cash registers.[21]

UNREALIZED OPPORTUNITIES AT THE MAJOR ELECTRONICS COMPANIES: GENERAL ELECTRIC AND RADIO CORPORATION OF AMERICA

The business machine giants of the first half of the twentieth century had certain advantages in marketing and technology that aided their entry into the digital computer business, not least of which were established customers and design know-how in certain areas related to computer systems. These firms still faced a major task, however: to internally develop, or acquire and integrate, advanced understanding and ability in electronics. In many respects, leading electronics firms' technical advantage for computer development was far greater than the office machine specialists. General Electric and the Radio Corporation of America (RCA) explored this potential advantage in the 1950s.

In the early 1950s the general manager of the GE Specialty Electronics Division, George Metcalf, attempted to market a version of a computational machine his group had built several years earlier for the Wright Field Aerodynamics Group. Metcalf began by contacting a couple of insurance companies as potential customers for this product. Though the machine in question was not of the scale and power of the UNIVAC or computers IBM would soon market, it caught the attention of IBM President Thomas Watson, Sr. Watson contacted GE President Ralph Cordiner to ask that Metcalf stop calling on IBM customers or the office machine giant would withdraw all its business from GE. Watson realized that GE's considerable talent and infrastructure in electronics, coupled with its massive revenue (more than six times that of IBM's in 1955), could make it one of his firm's fiercest competitors if it entered the computer field. Though current GE sales to IBM were modest, Cordiner took Watson's threat seriously and established a formal policy to stay out of the general computer business.[22] GE manufactured some one-of-a-kind computers for individual customers (for scientific and defense applications), but no computers that were broadly marketed in the early- to mid-1950s.

GE's entrance in the commercial computer business in 1956 was not a formal change in strategy, but instead a product of circumstance. This began in its response to the Bank of America's request for proposals to build a machine similar to a SRI's prototype, ERMA. ERMA was created to automate check processing, an increasingly challenging endeavor for Bank of America and other large financial institutions. Cordiner agreed to bid for the contract. He saw it, like other GE projects, as an arrangement to produce a specialty machine, not a general-purpose computer. GE received the contract and placed Barney Oldfield in charge of the ERMA project that called for thirty-six computers. Having no experience in some areas of computing systems, GE needed a partner for the peripheral devices and chose NCR. GE built the NCR 304 computer and the Dayton firm marketed it. Thus, GE indirectly broke its policy of staying out of the general-purpose computing/data processing business.

The ERMA-style computer, renamed the GE 100, was a success and soon the Bank of America was using these machines at its processing center to handle more than a million transactions per day. General Electric quickly built another computer focused on financial applications, but more general in nature, the GE 210. With this machine, GE had formally entered into the general-purpose computer business. The GE 225 soon followed, and the subsequent GE 265 offered time-sharing capabilities. The 200 series was GE's most profitable line of computers.[23]

General Electric's entrance into computing, however, failed to attract a broad base of customers (within computing, it focused on the financial industry) and the firm's top management never made the computer division an integral part of the firm's corporate strategy. One potential reason why it never mounted a serious threat to IBM was its bias toward sales rather than leases. GE also never diverted sizable internal resources, or raised substantial venture capital, to develop its computing business.[24] After a decade and a half, GE sold its computer division to another electronics firm, Honeywell. While RCA and Honeywell's experiences were different in a number of respects, they shared General Electric's great talent in electronics design and development, as well as a reluctance to stray in any significant way from their long-term successful core businesses. Honeywell and GE both developed some impressive computing technology, but neither succeeded in consistently generating net income from their computer businesses.

In the early 1950s, RCA developed sophisticated computing devices, including the analog RCA Typhoon, but it was the firm's announcement of a new large-scale business digital computer in 1955 that symbolized its most serious commitment to the commercial computer business up to that time. Though creative and ambitious, the Bizmac, which carried a price tag of $4 million, was unsuccessful in the marketplace. In fact, only one Bizmac system was installed, and it was at a military (an army facility in Detroit) rather than corporate setting. A primary problem with Bizmac was its divergence from the dominant von Neumann architecture, an attempt to advance computing specifically for business applications. It sought to enhance efficiency by substantially increasing the number of drives for mass storage, thereby obviating the need for an operator to frequently mount and demount drives. Recent advances in tape-drive performance, core memory, and processing speeds, however, mitigated the benefits of this and it was more efficient to use computers with fewer drives and have a human operator shift them as necessary. More generally, the failure of the relatively specialized Bizmac demonstrated the ascendancy of general-purpose computers over those designed for specific markets (increasingly, software, not computer hardware, was understood as the proper place to specialize for particular types of applications).[25]

In the early 1960s, RCA shifted from a differentiation to an imitation strategy to compete in the industry. Specifically, RCA tried to mimic and undersell IBM by making IBM-compatible machines. For a time this proved far more successful than its efforts with the Bizmac, but as the next chapter will discuss, this strategy was not sustainable for the long term in the rapidly changing industry. While Remington Rand, Burroughs, NCR, General Electric, and RCA each had certain resources and capabilities that could contribute to successfully competing in the early industry, only one company seemed to possess them all: IBM.

THE PRE-DIGITAL COMPUTER AND POST-DIGITAL COMPUTER DATA PROCESSING INDUSTRY LEADER: INTERNATIONAL BUSINESS MACHINES

Given the early achievements of EMCC, ERA, CRC, and CEC, the story of IBM appears to be one of early negligence—in "falling behind" in the computer industry, and subsequent triumph—in overcoming the substantial lead of other firms. This interpretation could not be more inaccurate. The history of the early computer industry is one where all the large established companies showed great caution (IBM, Remington Rand, NCR, Burroughs, General Electric, and RCA), while small start-ups (Electronic Control, ERA, CRC, CEC, and others) took risks to build products when demand for these expensive machines was relatively low. Remington Rand did acquire the Eckert-Mauchly Computer Corporation fairly early (1950), but it certainly did not focus the firm's overall strategy around this acquisition or new product area. In fact, its investments in computer research, development, manufacturing, and marketing were quite modest.

IBM triumphed in the computer industry because of what the firm had been before the advent of digital computing—the leader in punched-card tabulation machines with excellent technical, sales, and service operations, and because of what the firm did from the mid-1940s onward—put increased resources into electronics research and development. Specifically, in the mid-1940s the firm established a special laboratory in Poughkeepsie, New York (under the leadership of Robert Palmer), that was devoted to electronics research (IBM's primary research and development laboratory was at its Endicott facility). At the time the ENIAC was completed, IBM was not dismissive of computing, nor was it a proponent of this technology. IBM was achieving high profit margins and had strong cash flow from its dominance in the data processing field, a field that at the time was based on punched-card tabulation systems. The firm was interested in maintaining and extending its dominance in data processing, and perceived electronics as a fundamental means of achieving this over the long term.

The ENIAC was a machine that was practically obsolete from the moment it was completed, and posed no particular challenge to IBM. The UNIVAC, however, was a different matter. The threat of this machine was not simply that IBM was going to miss out on this *new* industry. The UNIVAC could read information off magnetic tape and efficiently rearrange data in memory and thus posed a competitive challenge to IBM's traditional line of electromechanical punched-card tabulation machines. IBM's commitment to electronics research had been to best prepare the firm for future technical leadership, given an unforeseeable future. The UNIVAC represented a likely preview of where technology was headed, and IBM was ready to act.

IBM had come out with the IBM 604 Electronic Calculating Punch in 1948, a machine with 1,400 vacuum tubes that could perform addition, subtraction, multiplication, and division electronically. Though it lacked the full range of capabilities that the UNIVAC would possess, it was a technical and commercial success. The machine rented for less than $600 a month, and over its ten-year life 5,600 IBM 604s were installed and serviced.[26] The substantial revenue streams that IBM began to receive as it ramped up its electronics research proved critical to the firm as it developed and marketed successive waves of computers to protect and extend its leadership.

In September 1949, Thomas Watson, Jr., the son of Thomas Watson, Sr., was named the executive vice president of IBM. With this promotion, he became the clear future successor to his father. Tom Watson, Jr., was a strong proponent of extending electronics research at IBM, a position that was strengthened when he saw the commercial success of the IBM 604. In 1949 he secured authorization from his father to hire twenty-five additional electrical engineers, half of whom would work under Ralph Palmer at the Poughkeepsie electronics lab. Palmer, a gifted electrical engineer who had been with the firm since 1932, was able to hire twelve more electrical specialists the following year.[27] Even before this, however, Palmer had begun to focus on enhancing IBM's capabilities for the development of a large-scale electronic digital computer. With the start of the Korean War in June 1950, an opportunity to test these capabilities came into play.

Following up on the firm's Tape Processing Machine, which was completed in the spring of 1950, Palmer soon began to examine the possibility of a computer for military applications. After cost estimates were made, the firm approached select customers to secure contracts before development. IBM received more than twenty favorable responses, and commitments for more than a dozen machines remained after the monthly rental price estimates nearly doubled to as much as $17,600.[28] The pre-orders combined with the elder Watson's patriotism led to his agreement to move ahead with what became known as the Defense Calculator project (after its completion, it was called the IBM 701). Though a true digital computer based largely on von Neumann's IAS machine, the name "computer" was consciously avoided as a result of the senior Watson's opposition to the term at that time. At its peak, more than 150 individuals were working on the Defense Calculator, and IBM completed the project by the end of 1952. The first model went to IBM's headquarters in the New York City office and the second to Los Alamos National Laboratory. Refinements were made and new models were constructed: the IBM 700 series (including the 702, 704, 705, 709). Each carried the prefix EDPM, or Electronic Data Processing Machines—once again, avoiding the use of the word

Thomas Watson, Sr., congratulating his son Thomas Watson, Jr., as the elder Watson passed control of IBM to his son, 1956. (Courtesy of IBM Archives)

computer. Beginning in 1955, and continuing thereafter, the number of installed IBM computers exceeded that of Remington Rand.[29]

Concomitant to the 700 series, IBM also developed an advanced successor to its IBM 604, the IBM 650 Magnetic Drum Calculator. This machine, which was actually a small-scale computer comparable to those being marketed at the time by CEC's ElectroData division and others, was a tremendous commercial success. It had a shorter life, but became the Model T of computing—the first mass produced machine of its kind. It had one thousand ten-digit words of memory and rented for a mere $3,250 a month. Between the mid-1950s and early 1960s more than 2,000 IBM 650s were installed—more than a hundred times that of the powerful IBM 702s that rented monthly for about $15,000. With the IBM 650, the firm established commercial superiority in computing and used its excellent sales staff and customer base to bring its electromechanical calculating machine customers into the computer age. Further highlighting this ongoing transition to computers, in 1956 Thomas Watson, Jr., an increasingly strong advocate of the firm's computer research and computer business, succeeded his father as chief executive officer. IBM's development of computers with unprecedented power would not come until the early- to mid-1960s, and even then, would be short-lived. The firm's leadership of the computer industry, however, would continue.

THE DIGITAL COMPUTER AND DIGITAL COMPUTER INDUSTRY IN THE MIDDLE TO LATE 1950S

By the mid-1950s the computer industry had begun to meet more than just the scientific computing needs of the U.S. military, national laboratories, major universities, and select companies (many in aviation). While the UNIVAC had paved the way by bringing digital mainframes to a small number of major corporations, other firms came out with less expensive computers that were beginning to make headway by slowly replacing traditional electromechanical data processing machines for financial, manufacturing, engineering, and other applications. IBM's successful practice of leasing machines, coupled with its reputation and data processing customer base, led to the firm's rapid ascent to the top of the computer industry when it shifted its focus from more basic electronics research to product development in the early- to mid-1950s.

Despite the growing number of computer installations, for most Americans computers were something they saw only through media representations. The UNIVAC made a high-profile television appearance when CBS used it to predict results during its presidential election coverage in 1952. Playing to and reinforcing the stereotype of computers as giant brains, CBS and Remington Rand representatives added flashing lights covered by numbered half ping-pong balls to a nonoperational UNIVAC on stage. Meanwhile, in a back room, a working UNIVAC was predicting a landslide for Eisenhower over Stevenson—a result far different than the polls, which indicated that the candidates were running neck and neck. Not trusting the UNIVAC, CBS continued to present it as a close race until it was obvious that the UNIVAC had been right all along. The public needed to see a computer as an expert, but those in charge, whether at broadcasting companies or other corporations, were still somewhat skeptical. Media representations of the UNIVAC as a giant brain, and the fact that it was the first large mainframe that saw nonmilitary use, resulted in the machine's name becoming synonymous with all mainframe computers for many Americans during the 1950s. Given the hundreds of thousands of dollars needed to purchase a UNIVAC, the brand recognition of Remington Rand (after the 1955 Remington Rand and Sperry Corporation merger, the firm became Sperry Rand) did not necessarily translate into many additional sales.

Nearly all of the large digital computer projects of the first half the 1950s were funded by the Department of Defense for advanced scientific and engineering calculation and computer networking. It was all behind the scenes, but computing technology was becoming a critical factor in the early years of the Cold War. From the ENIAC's initial raison d'être, ballistic firing-table calculation, to the Semi-Automatic Ground Environment (SAGE), real and perceived defense needs were the driving force behind the rapid developments in computer technology in the decade and a half following World War II.

Behind the strength of Jay Forrester's Whirlwind project and MIT's commitment to develop a laboratory (Lincoln Laboratory) dedicated to air defense research, MIT received extensive Defense Department funding.[30] SAGE was designed to be a large-scale command-and-control networked radar and computing system, a system believed to be critical to meet the growing Soviet nuclear threat. Many participants in the early computing industry received contracts for SAGE during the second half of the 1950s, but the largest share of the business went to IBM to work in collaboration with MIT engineers. According to Forrester, the MIT research team favored IBM over other top contenders (Remington Rand and Raytheon) as a result of IBM's "closer ties between research, factory, and field maintenance."[31] The agreement called for fifty-six large-scale IBM digital computers. In the end, SAGE brought a half-billion dollars of revenue to IBM. Both the technical experience developed working on SAGE computers and the massive influx of funds were fundamental factors facilitating the expansion of IBM's design capabilities and its continuing leadership in the computer business.[32]

Besides the role of the digital computer as a tool in the Cold War, it also influenced peoples' lives in other indirect ways. In 1952 John Diebold's book *Automation* came out, popularizing a term originally coined a half-decade earlier at Ford Motor Company.[33] Diebold's focus was on the industrial uses for feedback mechanisms, with the digital computer as the primary tool for such systems. Much of the early metrics for evaluating the desirability of corporate investment in expensive digital computing

Air force officer at Semi-Automatic Ground Environment (SAGE) display console. (Courtesy of Charles Babbage Institute, University of Minnesota, Minneapolis)

technology rested on the number of jobs that computers could replace. Journalists and others emphasized the technological utopia that computers could potentially create, an environment where tedious jobs of the past could be done entirely by computers. Other writers, such as Kurt Vonnegut in his dystopian novel *Player Piano* (1952), emphasized the dehumanizing affects on both blue-collar and white-collar workers of being replaced by automated systems.[34] Demonstrating that the potential downside to computerized factories was not limited to fiction, historian David F. Noble's *Forces of Production: A Social History of Industrial Automation* (1984) elegantly analyzed some of the deleterious impacts of computer automation on industrial laborers, and showed how such systems did not always boost efficiency.[35]

For better or worse, large corporations increasingly were using computers for payroll, engineering, manufacturing, logistics, and financial analysis by the second half of the 1950s. Leading consultants, such as the firm Canning, Sisson, and Associates

(CS&A), were holding informational workshops and developing client lists to educate corporate data processing departments in the range, nature, and techniques of using digital computing equipment. CS&A's Richard Canning went on to become the editor and publisher of the influential *EDP Analzer* in the early 1960s, a newsletter that provided computer and software technology advice to thousands of data processing managers nationally and internationally.[36] In the late 1950s, while Canning and Roger Sisson were conducting research for large department stores (on computer purchasing applications) and other clients, American Airlines was finalizing arrangements with IBM to build its massive airline reservation system, Sabre, which would operate in real time. The firms' initial research had begun five years before, and the computer network system was completed a half-decade after accepting IBM's 1959 proposal. As IBM did with many early corporate and government projects, the firm leveraged its new expertise—in this case IBM developed a Programmed Airline Reservation System (PARS) for other customers during the second half of the 1960s.[37]

At the end of the 1950s, there were more than 6,000 computers operating in the United States. U.S. firms also produced many of the machines installed in Europe, and though there were some competing computer firms in foreign markets (such as the British Tabulating Machine Company and Powers-Samas in the United Kingdom), American companies, and particularly IBM, dominated the early post–World War II international computer trade. Solid-state or transistor technology came to replace vacuum tubes on new models of digital computers (discussed in chapter 3) and represented the first step in an ongoing trend toward miniaturization. As computers became smaller, they also became cheaper and more powerful. This, coupled with advances in software (the focus of chapter 5), led to an unprecedented number of computer installations (both leased and sold) and scientific and business applications. IBM's decision to focus on electronics research in the late 1940s, but to wait for the more receptive markets of the mid-1950s to launch commercial digital computer products had proven successful. Nevertheless, the office machine giant had only established its leadership, the firm still had the challenge of solidifying its dominance in this new field—and in any high technology industry, the future is always uncertain. At the end of the decade new market niches would emerge, such as minicomputing and supercomputing (which are both outlined in chapter 4). With this changing environment in the industry, IBM would face a number of ongoing strategic decisions, particularly regarding which technologies it would invest in and which market segments it would seek to serve.

NOTES

1. Government investment in succeeding decades for the infrastructure of roads and highways was fundamental to the accelerating demand for automobiles.

2. Judge Earl R. Larson, *Findings of Fact, Conclusions of Law, and Order for Judgment* (U.S. District Court, 4th Div.), 1973; Honeywell, Inc., "*Honeywell v. Sperry Rand" Records, 1846–1973* (Minneapolis: Charles Babbage Institute, University of Minnesota).

3. A reprint of von Neumann's EDVAC report is in the appendix of Nancy B. Stern's *From ENIAC to UNIVAC: An Appraisal of the Eckert-Mauchly Computers* (Bedford, MA: Digital Press, 1981).

4. Herman H. Goldstine, *The Computer from Pascal to von Neumann* (Princeton, NJ: Princeton University Press, 1972), 215. Honeywell filed suit against Sperry Rand and its subsidiary, Illinois Scientific Instruments, Inc., in U.S. District Court (No. 4-67-Civ. 138, Minnesota District, 4th Div.) in 1967. John W. Mauchly and J. Presper Eckert filed the ENIAC patents in 1947.

5. The full significance of the IAS project lay in the fact that copies of the IAS computer were built at the laboratories that received contracts on the project. This included ILLIAC I (ILLInois Automatic Computer) constructed for the army by the University of Illinois, ORDVAC (ORDnance Variable Automatic Computer) at Aberdeen Proving Ground, MANIAC I (Mathematical ANalyzer Numerical Integrator And Computer) at Los Alamos National Laboratory, AVIDAC (Argonne's Version of Institute's Automatic Computer) at Argonne National Laboratory, ORACLE (Oakridge Automatic Computer Logical Engine) at Oakridge National Laboratory, and the JOHNNIAC (named after von Neumann) at the RAND Corporation.

6. Martin Campbell-Kelly and William Aspray, *Computer: A History of the Information Machine* (New York: Basic Books, 1996), 110–112.

7. Campbell-Kelly and Aspray, *Computer*, 119.

8. The most in-depth history of Eckert-Mauchly Computer Corporation, is Arthur L. Norberg's *Computers and Commerce: A Study of Technology and Management at Eckert-Mauchly Computer Company, Engineering Research Associates, and Remington Rand, 1946–1957* (Cambridge, MA: MIT Press, 2005). This important work also provides the most thorough examination of the history of Remington Rand and Engineering Research Associates.

9. Frank C. Mullaney, interview by Arthur L. Norberg, June 2 and 11, 1986, Minneapolis, MN (Charles Babbage Institute, University of Minnesota).

10. Kenneth Flamm, *Creating the Computer: Government, Industry, and High Technology* (Washington, DC: Brookings Institution, 1988), 107.

11. Ibid.; William Butler, interview by Arthur L. Norberg, November 8, 1984, and December 11, 1984; Frank Mullaney, 1986 (Charles Babbage Institute, University of Minnesota).

12. Ibid.

13. Thomas J. Watson, Jr., and James W. Birkenstock, interview by Arthur L. C. Humphreys, April 25, 1985, Armonk, NY (Charles Babbage Institute, University of Minnesota); Martin Campbell-Kelly, *ICL: A Business and Technical History* (Oxford: Oxford University Press, 1989), 140–143.

14. "HOBO Reports," meetings held in Detroit, Michigan, September 24, 1951, and November 23, 1951 (Charles Babbage Institute, University of Minnesota).

15. James W. Cortada, *The Computer in the United States: From Laboratory to Market, 1930 to 1960* (Armonk, NY: M. E. Sharpe, 1993).

16. James W. Cortada, *Before the Computer: IBM, NCR, Burroughs, and Remington Rand and the Industry They Created, 1865–1956* (Princeton, NJ: Princeton University Press, 1993).

17. Stanley C. Allyn, *My Half Century with NCR* (New York: McGraw-Hill, 1967), 166.

18. Richard S. Rosenbloom, "Leadership, Capabilities, and Technological Change: The Transformation of NCR in the Electronic Era," *Strategic Management Journal* 21 (2000): 1087.

19. Ibid., 1089–1090.

20. Allyn, *My Half Century.*

21. Ibid., 1090–1091.

22. J.A.N. Lee, "The Rise and Fall of the General Electric Corporation Computer Department," *IEEE Annals of the History of Computing* 17, no. 4 (1995): 24.

23. Ibid., 31.

24. Ibid., 42.

25. Paul Ceruzzi, *A History of Modern Computing* (Cambridge, MA: MIT Press, 1998), 55–56.

26. Emerson Pugh, *Building IBM* (Cambridge, MA: MIT Press, 1995), 152.

27. Ibid., 163–169.

28. Ibid.

29. Ibid., 170–179.

30. The most extensive and impressive analysis of Whirlwind and SAGE is Kent C. Redmond and Thomas M. Smith's *From Whirlwind to MITRE: The R&D Story of the SAGE Air Defense Computer* (Cambridge, MA: MIT Press, 2000).

31. J. F. Jacobs, *The SAGE Air Defense System: A Personal History* (Bedford, MA: MITRE Corporation, 1986), 43–44.

32. Flamm, *Creating,* 88.

33. John Diebold, *Automation* (New York: Van Nostrand, 1952).

34. Kurt Vonnegut, *Player Piano* (New York: Dell Publishing Company, 1952).

35. David F. Noble, *Forces of Production: A Social History of Industrial Automation* (New York: Oxford University Press, 1984).

36. Richard Canning, interview by Jeffrey R. Yost, August 23, 2002, Vista, CA (Charles Babbage Institute, University of Minnesota).

37. Duncan G. Copeland, Richard O. Mason, and James L. McKenney, "Sabre: The Development of Information-Based Competence and Execution of Information-Based Competition," *IEEE Annals of the History of Computing* 17, no. 3 (1995): 30–36.

─── 3 ───

The Broadening Scale and Scope of the Mainframe Computer Industry, 1957–1964

IBM's success as it achieved industry leadership in computing during the mid- to late-1950s resulted from its effective development of new technological know-how while working on large government contracts, particularly on the Semi-Automatic Ground Environment (SAGE), along with its great sensitivity to the needs of users when developing computers for market. The commercially successful IBM 650 and IBM 1401 computers demonstrated the latter. Unparalleled marketing and service operations, punched-card sales, and the firm's leasing structure also provided important opportunities and substantial and predictable revenue.[1] Punched-card and tabulation machines had not only been the key to IBM's past growth, they remained fundamentally important to the company's top and bottom lines. At the end of the 1950s, IBM was still receiving 65 percent of its domestic revenue from this class of products, and in international sales, the figure was 90 percent.[2] IBM's punched-card input-output systems were also a major factor in its customers remaining loyal to the office machine giant as they upgraded from electromechanical tabulators to digital computers. Between the end of World War II and 1956, IBM went from approximately 20,000 employees to more than 70,000.

IBM, however, faced a number of challenges in the early 1960s, and had to decide how to address a future defined by rapid technological change. Concomitantly, the firm's much smaller computer industry competitors had to develop innovative strategies to protect their own position in the industry and their revenue from predigital computing products, all while attempting to take market share from IBM. By the first half of the 1960s, the use of computers had broadened in the sciences, and computer-based data processing applications had grown substantially within mid-to-large-size corporations. The stakes grew alongside rising demand, and competition amongst the major computer manufacturers became increasingly fierce.

TRANSISTORS, INTEGRATED CIRCUITS, AND THE GROWING FOCUS ON TECHNOLOGICAL INNOVATION

The IBM 1401, which was announced in 1959, was the transistor-equipped and advanced version of the firm's highly successful IBM 650 vacuum-tube computer. The company installed over 10,000 IBM 1401 computers during the 1960s. It was not the first transistor-equipped computer, but IBM did not miss much business by being a year or two later than a few firms (such as National Cash Register with its NCR 304) in incorporating the new technology for computer memory and processing. As with IBM's slightly delayed entrance into digital computer products, which occurred several years after Remington Rand's UNIVAC hit the market, the New York–based firm demonstrated great insight as to when a technology could be produced and installed at a cost that would yield considerable profits.

As with many inventions, the development and diffusion of advanced know-how, coupled with several rounds of technological innovations, had to occur before transistors could be logistically and economically feasible for computers. Physicists William Shockley, John Bardeen, and Walter Brattain had invented the transistor at AT&T's Bell Laboratories back in 1947. Research in this area had grown out of advances in quantum mechanics and wartime research to develop amplifiers out of semiconductor materials. Largely to appease antitrust regulators after a 1956 consent decree, Bell Laboratories disseminated information about its work in solid-state electronics, or transistor technology, at a minimal cost to other firms and organizations.[3] By the early- to mid-1950s, transistors, which were already in use in some areas of electronics outside of computing, began to be used in computers on an experimental basis, including on the U.S. National Bureau of Standards' Eastern Automatic Computer (SEAC) in 1950 (which used a mixture of vacuum tubes and transistors) and the TX-0 at MIT in 1954. By the end of the 1950s and early 1960s, transistors became standard equipment for new models from most computer manufacturers.

The transistor was a revolutionary technology for computing.

While vacuum tubes characterized the first generation of digital computing technology, transistors became the defining element of second-generation computers. Transistors were small, worked quickly and efficiently, and did not create the enormous heat of vacuum tubes. While there were a number of new computer hardware inventions and innovations (primarily memory devices) developed and used during the 1950s and early 1960s (such as mercury delay lines, Williams tubes, and magnetic cores), the transistor, unlike the others, soon was recognized as a technology that could fundamentally transform computing machinery, an invention that through subsequent innovation could bring continual advances in miniaturization and performance-to-cost ratios.

Some established electronics and communications companies became involved in manufacturing transistors by the mid-1950s, including AT&T's manufacturing operation, Western Electric; Raytheon; General Electric; RCA; and Texas Instruments. In the mid-1950s transistors were expensive for the performance they delivered and were used primarily for areas of electronics where miniaturization was critical and cost was secondary, such as for hearing aids and various military applications. Nevertheless, nearly one million transistors were sold annually by mid-decade.[4] By the late 1950s, manufacturing costs had come down, and demand escalated for transistors in computing and other fields. U.S. production of transistors had grown to 30 million a year by 1957, with nearly one-sixth being manufactured by Western Electric. Unit costs had fallen dramatically to only a dollar or two per transistor, and annual sales reached $100 million.[5] By 1963 the annual value of transistors used in computers had reached $41.6 million, far more than in any other industry, but roughly a third of the value of the devices used in military equipment and systems (aircraft, missiles, communication systems, etc.).[6]

The most critical innovation came right on the heels of the early commercial adoption of transistors in computing. In 1958, Texas Instruments engineer Jack Kilby and Fairchild Semiconductor founder Robert Noyce, independently developed methods of combining circuits on a single chip.[7] The following year they both filed patents, Kilby in February and Noyce in July, for what were soon referred to as integrated circuits (ICs). While Kilby was first with his patent, Noyce's application described techniques that more closely matched what would become the standard practice for producing ICs: developing photographic images on silicon wafers using chemical processes to create conducting lines. This process of photolithography made it possible for Noyce and his colleagues to produce hundreds of transistors on a single piece of silicon.

Other firms quickly began using similar processes, and in the early 1960s RCA pioneered the application of metal oxide semiconductor (MOS) transistors to integrated circuits based on Fairchild Semiconductor's planar process (placing a layer of silicon oxide on top of transistors, sealing out dirt and other contaminants). With the rapid growth in manufacturing efficiency and the wildly accelerating demand for integrated circuits in computing and other areas of electronics, the total annual revenue in the U.S. semiconductor industry exceeded $1 billion by the early 1960s.[8]

STRETCHING IBM

Given this fast-paced technological change and IBM's past benefit from working on large government projects, it is not surprising the firm was interested in building a state-of-the-art computer on contract for the Atomic Energy Commission's (AEC) Lawrence Livermore National Laboratory in 1954. Such a project could be critical in building new computing technical capabilities. The AEC contract, however, went to Remington Rand's UNIVAC division to build the Livermore Advanced Research Computer (LARC). This made IBM all the more determined to get the next government contract to develop and build a cutting-edge computer. In 1955, IBM submitted a proposal to develop a high-speed computer for Los Alamos National Laboratory, and in late 1956 it received the contract. The project and the computer it produced became known as Stretch, a moniker emphasizing how the machine was stretching the capabilities of computing technology. Steve Dunwell, a cryptographer during World War II who later became one of IBM's leading engineers, was placed in charge of Project Stretch. Stretch was to be one hundred times faster than IBM's most powerful existing commercial computer.

This project represented a change for IBM in computing. For the first time the firm made a large bet that the benefits of advancing its technical know-how and the future production of commercial spin-offs would outweigh the inadequacy of a contract to even approach development and delivery costs.[9] The contract was for $3.5 million, while design, development, and installation expenses were estimated to be around $20 million.[10] This figure turned out to be at least $5 million less than the actual cost when Stretch was set up in Los Alamos National Laboratory in 1961. Project Stretch approached but did not meet most of its technological goals. Overall, only eight Stretch-based machines, sold as IBM 7030s, were ever installed. Thomas Watson, Jr., publicly criticized Project

John Mauchly (left) and Arthur Draper (right) in front of Sperry Rand's LARC, circa early 1960s. (Courtesy of Charles Babbage Institute, University of Minnesota, Minneapolis)

Stretch for cost overruns and failure to deliver original perfor-mance specifications. Stretch, however, was a more advanced computer than Remington Rand/Sperry Rand's LARC, and early judgments by Watson and other members of IBM's top manage-ment proved shortsighted. The project had many intangible bene-fits with regard to both organizational (running a massive computer development project) and technical know-how. Stretch-based technology was incorporated into subsequent IBM second-generation computers, including standard modular systems (SMS) and printed circuit cards. More importantly, Stretch possessed ar-chitectural elements that were precursors to IBM's famed Sys-tem/360 series: fixed and variable word length operations, an emphasis on alphabetical characters, and advances in magnetic tape recording.[11]

SPREAD AND THE IBM SYSTEM/360

In addition to the many technological benefits that the IBM Sys-tem/360 received from Stretch, it also shared a descriptive name with the earlier machine. The number "360" referred to 360 de-grees, or the full circle of applications possible on System/360 se-ries computers. The System/360 series contained a number of different machines that varied significantly in price and process-ing power. If the IBM 650 and IBM 1401 were analogous to the Model T and the mass production that defined "Fordism," the IBM System/360 series could accurately be described as "Sloanism," for General Motors President Alfred P. Sloan's strategy of price dif-ferentiation and production of models for "every purse and pur-pose."[12] Purchase prices within the series varied from $133,000 to $5.5 million, but most customers were leasing the machines from IBM for between $2,700 and $115,000 per month.[13] While com-puters at the low end of the scale were becoming more affordable, they were still far too expensive and complex to formally meet the "every purse and purpose" criteria—something General Motors (GM) did not fully achieve either. Nevertheless, by the mid-1960s, with the advent of the IBM System/360 series and successful com-puters at other firms, a substantial number of businesses were installing digital computers for the first time in order to help with payroll, human resources, factory automation, and a number of other tasks.

Despite the evolutionary elements of the System/360 project, it also represented a major break with the past. In late 1961, IBM had initiated a task force, the SPREAD (Systems, Programming, Review, Engineering, And Development) Committee, to develop a new plan for computing and programming. This group, which consisted of senior engineers and software and marketing managers, concluded that IBM's products had to change significantly for IBM to maintain its competitive advantage over other firms. Though IBM was the industry leader, its future looked uncertain. Manufacturing its seven completely different business and scientific computers led to high production costs. Even the talented and knowledgeable IBM sales force was not capable of effectively marketing all of these different computing systems.[14] By far the most costly aspect, however, was that the various IBM computers could not use the same software. This lack of compatibility among IBM computing systems was in stark contrast to the firm's highly unified Punched Card Division. While IBM had some computers at different price points, customers could not shift between them without incurring major switching costs from system incompatibility. To address this problem the SPREAD Committee came up with a strategy called Solid Logic Technology (SLT) to implement a compatible system for a range of new computers at different prices. Most importantly, the system would be backward compatible with IBM's successful 1401 computers (could run software of the 1401). Given the thousands of 1401 computer installations, this was a critical step to capitalize on the firm's past success and ensure the loyalty of its customers. The plan also called for designing these machines to use common peripheral equipment. The five planned computers would all use solid-state, or transistor, technology. By early 1962 the SPREAD Committee's ideas solidified into System/360. If the Stretch Project was a business risk, it was just the tip of the iceberg compared to this new series of computers.

The SPREAD Report, which was presented by the committee to IBM's senior management at the start of 1962, contained a recommendation for spending $125 million on software development alone. This was more than twelve times the firm's entire current budget for programming. IBM, in many respects, was competing against itself with its ambitious new operating system, OS/360. This operating-system project was by far the largest programming effort that had ever been undertaken by the firm. The project faced a number of challenges, the system was late in delivery, and it had major cost overruns. OS/360 Project Manager Frederick Brooks, in an insightful and engaging book, *The Mythical Man Month*, detailed the small-scale, craft nature of programming and the substantial difficulties he and his team had in trying to scale up, or produce software code on a much larger scale. In developing the OS/360, Brooks discovered that adding programmers late in the project could actually slow down rather than speed up the process.[15]

Despite the challenges, delays, and tremendous costs, OS/360 was successful. In the near term the compatible operating system was a critical element that facilitated System/360's success in a range of different price/performance categories. Customers could move between different systems with relative ease and use the same applications software on different IBM models. The applications software of the time was highly specialized and the result of large programming costs that had been incurred either directly or indirectly by customers (developed internally or outsourced to service firms). In the longer term, the OS/360 greatly expanded the managerial and technical knowledge that would benefit the firm on future large-scale programming projects.

It is difficult to overstate the significance of the IBM System/360 hardware and software to the firm's leadership in computing. Not having a compatible line of quality machines would have gradually eroded IBM's computer business. At the same time, the enormous investment was a tremendous risk. A *Fortune* magazine journalist, Tom Wise, described the System/360 project as "IBM's $5 billion gamble."[16] In addition to the massive investment in software development, the plans included initiating major internal semiconductor production capacity—a critical move to integrate backward into component manufacturing on a large scale, and a decision that Thomas Watson, Jr., made in part because of tensions with IBM's primary semiconductor supplier, Texas Instruments. Watson also was uneasy with the level of electronic component integration at RCA (funded in part by the U.S. Army's Micromodule Program), a firm that was in many respects IBM's greatest challenger in the mid- to late-1960s.[17] By building semiconductor manufacturing capacity, IBM simultaneously addressed the threat of being outdone technologically and of potential opportunistic pricing from semiconductor suppliers.

Despite the System/360's success in addressing IBM's incompatibility issues and the learning that took place within the corporation, the system also had its downside. Most importantly, it did not allow for time-sharing. Time-sharing was a programming tool to conserve valuable computer time through networking smaller, cheaper machines to a mainframe system that allocated resources in rotation so swiftly as to be invisible to users. Nevertheless, when IBM announced the System/360 product line in March 1964 the response was tremendous. In some respects, there was too much interest. In the first two years IBM was able to fill only about half of its 9,000 orders for System/360 machines.

IBM System/360 installation, 1964. (Courtesy of Charles Babbage Institute, University of Minnesota, Minneapolis)

The firm's revenue grew to over $5 billion and employment increased by 50 percent in the three years following the launch of System/360.[18]

THE SEVEN DWARFS AND THEIR COMPUTING STRATEGIES

The major competitors of IBM each had less than 5 percent of the domestic computer market. IBM controlled roughly two-thirds of the trade by the early 1960s and three-quarters by the end of the decade.[19] While there were some commonalities between IBM's seven primary computing competitors—the "seven dwarfs" as they were commonly referred to in the press—they were a diverse group of companies. Burroughs, Sperry Rand, and NCR were three of the long-time suppliers of office machines, and shared a similar, though much smaller, customer base relative to IBM. Sperry Rand continued to be a conglomerate and NCR had a successful near monopoly in the expanding cash register field. General Electric and RCA were large electronics firms with immense capital, but computing was at best a modest focus for these firms (see Table 3.1). Control Data and Digital Equipment Corporation were new

Table 3.1
Data Processing Revenue of IBM and Competitors, 1963
(in millions of dollars)

Company	Revenues
International Business Machines	$1,244
Sperry Rand	$146
Control Data	$85
Burroughs	$42
General Electric	$39
National Cash Register	$31

Source: Franklin M. Fisher, James W. McKie, and Richard B. Mancke, *IBM and the U.S. Data Processing Industry: An Economic History* (New York: Praeger, 1983), 65.

companies leading the way in two emerging niches of the industry, supercomputing and minicomputing, respectively.

BURROUGHS AND THE BENEFITS AND BURDENS OF THE PAST

By 1956, Burroughs had achieved a small but meaningful commercial presence in the computer industry with the Burroughs 205 (formerly the ElectroData 205). The successor to this machine, the Burroughs 220, was already in the works at the time of its acquisition of ElectroData in 1956. Like IBM, Burroughs had benefited from significant government contracts. This included work on SAGE equipment, as well as the design and construction of computers for the air force's Atlas ballistic missile guidance system. These two projects brought more than $70 million to the firm, and though this was a small fraction of what IBM received from the Department of Defense (DoD) on SAGE alone, it helped Burroughs advance its technical capabilities in computing.

The Burroughs 220, a vacuum tube machine, hit the market at the beginning of 1959 in an environment full of announcements of second-generation transistor-equipped computers. It had only modest commercial success, as Burroughs sold around fifty 220s for between $600,000 and $1.2 million (depending on memory specifications and peripherals).[20] Though Burroughs had recently boosted its investment in computer research and development, it did not have the resources to design and manufacture new computer systems at the pace of IBM. Burroughs' B5000, which came out several years later, was a technically advanced machine, but was not market-driven in its design, and only had limited success in the marketplace. The B5000 operating system, the Master Control Program, was impressive at multiprocessing, but both the hardware and software were designed around the programming language ALGOL (ALGOrythmic Language). COBOL (COmmon Business Oriented Language), however, was backed by the DoD, and was becoming the standard programming language for business computing. This further hurt B5000 sales and leases. The early customers for B5000 systems included government agencies, insurance companies, universities, and banks. The machine generally received a better reception in scientific and academic settings than in the corporate sector.[21]

Despite some differences, Burroughs, in many respects, offers the purest comparison with IBM—and highlights the importance of some of the latter's advantages. Both firms saw a critical need to transition into computers and recognized that, in time, their previously successful electromechanical products would become obsolete. Most of the other dwarfs had a greater range of products or specialties outside of data processing and accounting machines (especially General Electric, RCA, and Sperry Rand), some in areas where continued demand and solid revenue growth were more predictable.

The relative success of IBM compared to Burroughs is indicative of the benefits the industry giant received from its long history in the punched-card and tabulation field, its excellent base of data processing customers, and its internally built capabilities in computing. By the time Burroughs had quality computers on the market, IBM had already established itself as the most trusted brand in data processing. In many respects, this had begun long before the first electronic digital computers emerged in the mid-1940s, and there was undoubtedly some basis for the often-quoted statement that no purchasing or corporate data processing manager "ever got fired for choosing IBM." The fact that Burroughs succeeded in getting substantial business in the banking area is indicative of how past customer relationships proved critical; unfortunately for Burroughs, IBM had a far greater number of customers in a vast array of industries where computers would be the fundamental future technology for data processing. As Burroughs made modest moves forward with its computer business, it continued to harvest revenue from its traditional accounting machine lines. Demand for these earlier machines, however, began to diminish as computers became less expensive and programming services and software products made computers all the more versatile for business users in the 1960s.

REMINGTON RAND/SPERRY RAND'S CONTINUING COORDINATION PROBLEMS

Remington Rand (and later Sperry Rand) had some of the same difficulties as Burroughs. Though Remington Rand appeared to possess an important first-mover advantage after its acquisition of Eckert-Mauchly Computer Corporation and Engineering Research Associates in the early 1950s, its products were not attractive or cost-effective for most corporations and organizations of the time, and division and conflict plagued its computer organization. In addition to clashes between the two formerly independent computer companies, there was also a lack of focus on computing and inadequate resources from corporate headquarters. Such lack of coordination was evident when the computer for Lawrence Livermore Laboratory (LARC) was delivered more than two years late because engineers on the project were transferred to help address ongoing problems with the design of the UNIVAC II.[22] The overall dissension among managers and engineers led to a loss of talent and delayed the completion of projects. William Norris and others left to form the Control Data Corporation, and talented Sperry Rand engineer Seymour Cray soon joined them. There also was far less focus on marketing computers at Sperry Rand than at IBM, and poorer cooperation and communication between the design engineers and the sales-and-marketing side of the corporation.

The IBM System/360 announcement sent ripples throughout the industry, and Sperry Rand's top management almost immediately convened a task force to work on a responsive UNIVAC product strategy. The firm expanded its line to include the 1050 and 1004, and developed the 1108 and 1109 to be compatible with the existing 1107. The following year the task force also announced the 9200 and 9300, computers that would be compatible with the IBM System/360 series. This goal, however, was only partially realized, and none of Sperry Rand's machines even approach the success of those of the IBM System/360 series.

RCA AND THE IMITATION GAME

If imitation is the sincerest form of flattery, then Radio Corporation of America's (RCA) imitation of the IBM System/360 series was laying it on thick. RCA was a large highly integrated electronics firm with advanced research-and-development infrastructure, and thus had the ability to adopt a strategy of building computers compatible with the IBM systems on a large scale—by replicating the architecture and instruction codes used by the computer industry leader on RCA's Spectra 70 series. Most of the other dwarfs could not have even considered pouring $50 million into developing IBM-compatible computers. RCA was large enough, however, that this represented only a modest investment and business risk.

Commercial success using an imitation strategy depended fundamentally on substantially underselling the first-mover. This was particularly important to compete with firms such as IBM that had strong brand loyalty and production economies. RCA first publicized its Spectra 70 series in December 1964, only months after IBM's System/360 announcement. RCA had actually considered such a strategy before IBM's announcement, and the System/360 seemed to be the appropriate time to test its implementation. The Spectra 70 series, which consisted of four computer models, was designed to be entirely compatible with and mimic the machines of IBM's System/360 series.

RCA sought to achieve a cost advantage from its internal electronics manufacturing capabilities, a resource that could produce integrated circuits for less than the Solid Logic Technology (SLT) used by IBM.[23] The Spectra 70 series did achieve some cost and performance advantages and was a financial success for roughly half a decade. During the 1960s, in large part as a result of the Spectra 70 series, RCA's computer revenues increased fifteen times to $211 million.[24] This, however, was less than 5 percent of IBM's revenues and a small portion of the radar and consumer electronics specialist's overall revenue.

Imitation, however, meant quickly shifting direction whenever IBM made a change, something that could be both costly and difficult for the imitator. The RCA computers that were created in response to IBM's subsequent System 370 series destroyed the market for the Spectra 70 series rather than taking market share from IBM. This misstep, and other challenges associated with always being in a reactive position, highlighted the long-term difficulties with imitation, and RCA sold its computer division to

Sperry Rand in 1971. In contrast to imitation, product differentiation was a less expensive and more attractive alternative for most of IBM's competitors.

DIFFERENTIATION AND STRATEGIC CROSS-DIVISIONAL INTEGRATION AT NCR

National Cash Register (NCR) was a methodical producer of successful computing systems that only sold modestly, but typically exceeded the firm's conservative market projections. NCR spent $10 million developing its 304, one of the earlier solid-state computers. The 304, announced in 1957 and delivered first in 1959, was priced around $1 million. Overall, NCR sold thirty-three of this model, eight more than the firm's initial target. NCR also moved into the services area, doing inventory and accounting for a number of midsized firms that lacked sufficient data processing departments. In 1960, NCR developed a smaller computing system, the NCR 315 that rented for about $12,000 a month. It successfully integrated sales of this computer with its cash register products, allowing for register data to be input into the 315 for processing. To facilitate communication of data between the NCR 315 and the company's traditional cash registers, hardware modifications and extensive programming were required.[25] By selling or leasing more than 7,000 315s, the machine became an important product for NCR, increasing its Data Processing Division revenues from $308,000 to nearly $31 million in the five years following 1958.[26] Like Burroughs, NCR was able to take advantage of its successful base of banking customers from its precomputing days.[27]

GENERAL ELECTRIC: TOO LITTLE, TOO LATE

General Electric, like RCA, took advantage of its substantial electronic component manufacturing divisions to achieve production economies in computing. Following the ERMA installations at Bank of America branches, the firm sought to broaden its computing efforts. In 1959, it began to develop a line of 24-bit computers named MOSAIC. Prior to IBM, GE announced a compatible group of computers, the 400 series. This was followed rapidly by the 600 series to compete with the IBM System/360. Overall, the 600 series was less efficient and only achieved a small number of installations. During the second half of the 1960s, General Electric's computer division faced an increasing turnover of managers and key engineers. The firm also discontinued several product lines, such as the WXYZ series in the early 1960s, and the 600 series in the late 1960s.[28]

The IBM System/360 series had created a new hurdle in the industry for computer firms to focus on the compatibility and sustainability of systems. Completely discontinuing relatively new systems undermined customer confidence and hurt General Electric's reputation in computing. By the late 1960s, a task force was established that soon recommended merging with another computer firm. At decade's end, General Electric's computer division merged with Honeywell Information Systems into a new Honeywell division.[29] As with RCA, General Electric's massive amount of capital and capabilities in electronics might have enabled it to seriously threaten IBM in the first decade of the industry. After IBM's stronghold was established with the System/360, however, it likely would have been prohibitively expensive to consider expanding to the scale necessary to pose a major challenge to IBM's industry leadership. With the exodus of both General Electric and RCA by the early 1970s, the moniker "IBM and the seven dwarfs" had evolved to "IBM and the BUNCH" (Burroughs, UNIVAC, NCR, Control Data, and Honeywell). This acronym, however, left out one of the industry's important firms of the 1960s and 1970s, Digital Equipment Corporation, or DEC (Control Data and Digital Equipment Corporation are the focus of chapter 4).

DEMAND-SIDE PERSPECTIVES: UNDERSTANDING EVOLVING COMPUTER APPLICATIONS, 1956–1964

The first decade of the history of the digital computer and the digital computer industry are correctly associated with scientific and defense applications of computers and computing systems. With the emergence of a substantial and growing business market by the mid-1950s, historical analyses have tended to focus on the supply side of the computer companies and the machines produced. These studies have emphasized the growth of the trade as computers became common for certain applications at corporations during the late 1950s and early 1960s. While this focus on *production* is critical for understanding the history of the computer industry and is addressed substantially in this book, computing and data processing *consumption*, or the demand side, is equally important. While business installations began to outpace scientific applications at some point in the early- to mid-1950s, both categories continued to expand in number and form. The importance of government funding for computing continues to the present. Examples include the development of a range of special computing technologies for the DoD, Department of Energy (DoE), the National Science Foundation's CISE (Computer and Information Science and Engineering) and ITR (Information Technology Research) Directorates, and Internet2 (a government, higher education, and corporate collaboration to provide broadband for scientific research). The demand side is periodically addressed in certain areas of my supply-side discussion, such as General Electric and NCR's ERMA computer system for the Bank of America in chapter 2. The following sections, however, provide brief, concentrated syntheses of some of the areas in which computers began to be used by individuals, companies, and other organizations from the mid-1950s to the mid-1960s, each of which contributed to the growth of new systems and the revenue and profits of computer manufacturers.

REVISITING GOVERNMENT FUNDING FOR COMPUTING RESEARCH AND DEVELOPMENT

Although computer projects funded by the DoD (such as the ENIAC, ERA 1101, and Whirlwind) in the late 1940s to early 1950s, and the work of the DoD Advance Research Projects Agency's (ARPA) Information Processing Techniques Office (IPTO) starting in the early 1960s have received the most attention, government funding for computer technology was continuous in the intervening decade. The Cold War was a critical factor in the continuing high level of funding for computer research. The National Research Council has estimated that by 1950, government investment in computing amounted to $15 million to $20 million a year.[30] This figure grew rapidly as the cost of IBM's work on SAGE reached a half-billion dollars by the end of the 1950s. While IBM was the largest computing contractor on SAGE, there were other sizable contractors, including the System Development Corporation, which received approximately $150 million between the mid-1950s and mid-1960s for software and systems work.[31] The impact on computer companies, and particularly IBM, was immense. During the 1950s, federal contracts supported half of the research and development at IBM and, as of 1963, continued to provide more than one-third of the funds for the firm's annual research-and-development expenditures.[32]

In addition to substantial government contracts to corporations, there were also government organizations that spent heavily on internal computing research, such as the National Applied Mathematics Laboratory of the National Bureau of Standards. This laboratory was responsible for building the Standards Eastern

Automatic Computer (SEAC) for the air force and the Standards Western Automatic Computer (SWAC) for the navy (both in 1950). Other government laboratories, including Lawrence, Los Alamos, and Argonne, were fundamental sources of capital for computer development projects. The RAND Corporation was another important source of research talent in computing. RAND, initially formed by the U.S. Air Force and Douglas Aircraft in a joint venture, became an independent nonprofit corporation in 1956. In addition to training hundreds of computer engineers and programmers, this organization has completed extensive research on social policy and defense issues involving computers, such as computer security and privacy.

The influence of the Cold War on computing technology was not limited to increased government funds and new systems, it also helped shape our cultural understanding of computers. Even when computers were not directly involved in military applications, their rhetoric was critical to establishing and reinforcing military ideological constructs. Information scholar Paul Edwards, in an insightful monograph, *The Closed World* (1996), illustrates how, politically, technologically, and ideologically, computers were part of a "closed world" where all events were perceived within the context of the Cold War between the United States and the Soviet Union.[33]

THE LEGACY OF PUNCHED-CARD TABULATION SYSTEMS IN SCIENTIFIC COMPUTING AND GOVERNMENT FUNDING

The legacy of IBM's many tabulating-machine business customers is frequently and appropriately emphasized as an important factor in its preeminence in the business computing market by the end of the 1950s and early 1960s. Less frequently made is the association between pre–World War II scientific computation (particularly in astronomy and physics) that used IBM punched-card tabulation-machine technology and the firm's success in obtaining the most prestigious and largest government digital computer development projects of the 1950s (especially the primary SAGE computer contract). Columbia University Astronomer Wallace Eckert was critical to developing, refining, and publicizing IBM's work in using punched cards for scientific computation at the Thomas J. Watson Astronomical Computing Laboratory in the late 1930s.[34] Far more than the other office machine firms during the pre–digital computing era, IBM established itself as a significant force in scientific computation.[35] While the extent of the connection between IBM's leadership in punched-card scientific computation and its subsequent success in winning DoD digital computer development contracts is not entirely clear, it was undoubtedly a factor. Cuthbert Hurd, along with the Applied Science Department that IBM established in 1949, built upon and expanded a tradition in scientific computing begun by Eckert.

CONTINUING AND EVOLVING NATIONAL DEFENSE AND OTHER SCIENTIFIC APPLICATIONS

Despite the fact that Remington Rand's UNIVAC was so-named to emphasize its universal applicability for science and business, and Remington Rand succeeded in securing installations in both areas, most computer models from other firms during the 1950s were designed, marketed, or at least perceived by potential customers, as either scientific *or* business machines. Though the growing concept of the general-purpose computer was beginning to take hold in the latter portion of the decade and in the early 1960s, it was the introduction of IBM's System/360 that really began to shift the balance toward computer models being seen as appropriate for both realms. This was largely based on the notion that specialized programming or software, and increasingly software products, were the best tools to prepare computers for particular tasks.[36]

COMPUTING IN THE PHYSICAL SCIENCES

Physics and chemistry were the first two scientific disciplines to extensively use digital computers. In fact, it was a particular type of physics problem, the BRL's need to quickly calculate ballistic firing tables that led to the first meaningful electronic digital computer, the ENIAC. Digital computers continued to be fundamental tools in physics and chemistry calculations, such as the DoD's development and evaluation of the Super (hydrogen bomb project). Most work at national laboratories was defense-related, and computers played a fundamental role in many areas of physics and engineering research in radar, missile guidance (Atlas), early detection systems (SAGE), and aeronautics and flight simulation (Whirlwind). By the early- to mid-1960s, computers were also becoming increasingly prevalent in physics education. For instance, the U.S. Air Force Academy utilized a Burroughs B5500 in its curriculum. While military academies were often leaders in bringing computers into undergraduate classrooms in the physical sciences, other higher education institutions soon followed.[37]

THE EMERGENCE OF COMPUTER-BASED COGNITIVE SCIENCE AND ARTIFICIAL INTELLIGENCE

Increasingly in the 1950s, scientific computing included areas outside of those directly related to national defense. Many of the larger research universities in the nation had computer laboratories or centers by late in the decade. These laboratories and centers were used for both computation (in fields such as physics, chemistry, and mathematics) and data processing (in areas such as taxonomy). Academic computing applications also made their way into the disciplines of psychology and cognitive science beginning in the mid-1950s.

At this time, Herbert Simon and Allen Newell of Carnegie Institute of Technology pioneered efforts to shift the focus of cybernetics from biological mechanisms to symbolic systems (they also engaged in research for the RAND Corporation in this area). MIT's John McCarthy, who was soon working on similar research, organized a famed 1956 conference at Dartmouth University, and coined the term "artificial intelligence" for this new area of research. Edward Feigenbaum, who had completed his doctorate at Carnegie Institute of Technology under Simon and Newell, began to collaborate with scientists in other disciplines to lead the way in applying artificial intelligence to chemistry and medicine, using "expert systems" such as DENDRAL and MYCIN during the late 1960s and 1970s. These systems combined a database with an "inference engine" (a heuristic or set of rules) for drawing meaning or conclusions from the scientific data. The broader application of expert systems evolved into what has become known as knowledge engineering.

MEDICAL COMPUTING

Concomitant to the emergence of the field of artificial intelligence, digital computers were used for the first time in medicine. Robert Ledley, Lee Lusted, J. Octo Barnett, and several other physicians worked with computer specialists to pioneer computer applications in medicine in the late 1950s.[38] These physicians used computers to compare individual patient records with growing databases of medical histories. Often computing laboratories at universities were used to process information, as few hospitals had invested in mainframe computers prior to the mid-1960s. The advent and commercial growth of networking and time-sharing, coupled with the emergence of relatively powerful low-cost mini-computers, however, brought down costs and soon led to the acceleration of computer installations in medical laboratories and hospitals. Exchange of medical information over computer networks became increasingly common in the late 1960s and computers began to grow beyond merely serving as discrete diagnostic tools into networked systems fundamental to evaluating information on public health and epidemiology. Hospitals also increasingly used computers for administrative work by the late 1960s. Collaborations between physicians and computer technicians are indicative of the growing need for computer/programming service providers by this time.

COMPUTER ELECTRONIC DATA PROCESSING DEPARTMENTS, SERVICE PROVIDERS, AND FACILITATING BUSINESS APPLICATIONS, 1956–1964

Corporations purchased computers for a number of different purposes between the mid-1950s and the mid-1960s. Firms installed computers to automate aspects of manufacturing, to take care of administrative chores such as payroll, and to a lesser extent, explore the role that these machines could play in operations management (coordinating activities on the shop floor). Administrative work was by far the primary area for business applications and typically firms that already had punched-card tabulating machines were those that graduated to digital computers. The previous tabulating-machine work often came under the control of a formal data processing department. These departments were composed of individuals engaged in new occupations, such as programmers and computer operators. Sales personnel commonly marketed computers as "revolutionary," but generally most computer applications of the period were evolutionary and fairly mundane in nature.[39] Computers tended to yield efficiencies, but only after substantial initial investments were made in setting up and programming the machines to conduct routine tasks. Typically the focus was less on the computers themselves than on automating office work through electronics. Until well into the 1950s, it was anything but certain that the computer—an expensive machine that was still often perceived as a "giant brain" for scientific and government use—would become the primary piece of electronic equipment to usher in the electronic office.[40]

Ironically, a British teashop and caterer named J. Lyons & Company was the first firm in the world to broadly apply computing systems to create an electronic office—one that handled its finances and the major task of coordinating inventory and delivery of baked goods to its nearly 200 teashops.[41] J. Lyons & Company's leadership in business office applications was unlikely for three primary reasons. First, it was a tea-and-food company that had no background in the office machine or electronic industries—the ancestry of most computer firms of the time. Second, the company created its own computer, which it named LEO (Lyons Electronic Office). Though components were outsourced, most design activity, assembly, and programming were done internally. Finally, the British computer industry was slow to develop despite some impressive early digital computing design work at a few leading universities (Cambridge and Manchester) and the National Physical Laboratory immediately following the end of World War II. This last point, however, probably indicates why J. Lyons & Company felt compelled to build its own computer.

Once the investment had been made in designing and building LEO, the firm decided to take advantage of the machine by spinning off a computer manufacturing division, Leo Computers, Ltd., in late 1954. This company had marginal success and was eventually taken over by English Electric. During the 1950s and 1960s English Electric and the other major players in the British computer industry (including the British Tabulating Machine and Powers-Samas) combined and became part of the government-endorsed "national champion" computer firm, International Computers Limited (ICL). By this time, the British government believed that a single company with concentrated resources was the best way to compete with IBM, and other U.S. firms. Overall, the British computer industry provided only modest competition to IBM in the United Kingdom and had no significant presence in the U.S. market. Other U.S. computer manufacturers also had manufacturing and/or sales operations in Great Britain and other European countries. IBM, however, dominated the international computer industry by the 1960s.

In the United States, full office automation came right on the heels of the J. Lyon's & Company's activities, but did not appear to be influenced by it. The million-dollar price tag of Remington Rand's UNIVAC was a fundamental factor preventing its wider adoption by corporations in the early 1950s. IBM, by building some smaller computers such as the IBM 650, demonstrated that it was more receptive to the needs and constraints of corporations of the time. Burroughs's acquisition of ElectroData yielded the 205, which it saw as appropriate for both scientific and business users. The same was also true of the Burroughs 220. When Burroughs management started new projects however, such as the B5000, it tended to be less receptive to the needs of business users during the design process. Burroughs executives of the 1950s later reflected on this as a missed opportunity.[42]

Understandably, the role of the customer in defining certain specifications and performance characteristics was often evident in the first few years of digital computing, when manufacturers frequently designed a machine under contract for a single scientific laboratory or government agency. Firms often had the idea that the same or a very similar model could be marketed to a limited number of other scientific users. Gradually, computer manufacturers learned the benefits of understanding its customer's needs and applying such knowledge to future design-and-programming work. IBM, which had the broadest scale and scope of data processing customers from its pre–digital computing punched-card tabulation days, had a clear advantage over its competitors. There were also differences between industries. Management scholar JoAnne Yates found there was considerable feedback between corporate users and computer manufacturing suppliers in the insurance industry.[43]

Increasingly during the 1950s and beyond, more and more specialization was achieved through programming rather than specialized hardware design. Some service work was done by computer manufacturers and buried within the cost of the computers they were selling or leasing. Service companies, however, did a substantial amount of programming. The service sector is perhaps the least studied component of the computer industry, yet it was of fundamental importance in making computers useful for businesses. This sector will be examined in discussing the software industry (chapter 5).

While many types of computer applications in business were similar across industries, there were also considerable differences. Computing work within aerospace firms differed significantly from that in the petroleum, life insurance, or banking industries. Analyzing computer applications and their impacts on various trades is still in its infancy. A few industries, such as life insurance, have been studied in depth.[44] Historian James W. Cortada has recently engaged in a multivolume project to survey digital computer applications in dozens of industries.[45] While computer applications can in some respects be considered a topic outside of the computer industry (more related to the scientific or industrial field being addressed), it is critical to understanding the evolution of the demand side of the computer trade.

A greater scale and scope of computer applications was made possible by the increasing power and declining cost of computer hardware and the increasing knowledge and tools available (particularly software) to use these systems. Two new emerging sectors of the digital computer industry during the late 1950s and early 1960s, minicomputing and supercomputing, were also fundamental contributors to the proliferation of computing technology. In 1956, a mere 600 digital computers were installed in the United States. The cumulative total that were in use that year was only 800. During 1964, there were 7,500 new digital computer installations, contributing to the 24,000 in use in the United States that year.[46]

NOTES

1. A 1956 consent decree, in resolution to a Justice Department antitrust suit brought against IBM in 1952, required the computer firm to allow customers to purchase, rather than just lease, IBM machines.

2. Martin Campbell-Kelly and William Aspray, *Computer: A History of the Information Machine* (New York: Basic Books, 1996), 130.

3. A 1956 consent decree to settle the Justice Department suit against AT&T prevented the telephone giant from selling transistors to non-government entities and kept the firm from competing in the computer market.

4. Michael Riordan and Lillian Hoddeson, *Crystal Fire: The Invention of the Transistor and the Birth of the Information Age* (New York: W. W. Norton, 1998), 226–227.

5. Ibid., 254; Ernest Braun and Stuart MacDonald, *Revolution in Miniature: The History and Impact of Semiconductor Electronics* (Cambridge, London; Cambridge University Press, 1978), 91, 153. While a 1956 consent decree limited AT&T transistor sales to only the U.S. government, this was the primary market for the devices in the 1950s and first half of the 1960s. During much of this period more than half of the value of overall transistor sales were to the government. By 1972, however, three-quarters of the semiconductor market was for private industry.

6. Braun and MacDonald, *Revolution*, 91.

7. Fairchild Semiconductor was founded by Robert Noyce and other defecting engineers from the first semiconductor firm in Silicon Valley, William Shockley's company: Shockley Semiconductor Laboratory. While a gifted scientist, Shockley proved unable to lead this business venture and alienated Noyce and other talented scientists and engineers he had hired.

8. Riordan and Hoddeson, *Crystal*, 274.

9. IBM, however, had invested in basic research (outside of specific computer projects) in electronics for years.

10. Franklin M. Fisher, James W. McKie, and Richard B. Mancke, *IBM and the U.S. Data Processing Industry: An Economic History* (New York: Praeger, 1983), 47–50.

11. Ibid.

12. As with nearly all analogies, this one is imperfect in that IBM had

more computers than the 1401 (Ford Motor Company, for many years, produced only one mass-produced "pleasure car," the Model T).

13. Emerson Pugh, *Building IBM* (Cambridge, MA: MIT Press, 1995), 276.

14. Campbell-Kelly and Aspray, *Computer*, 137–139.

15. Frederick P. Brooks, Jr., *The Mythical Man-Month: Essays on Software Engineering* (Reading, MA: Addison-Wesley, 1975).

16. Thomas A. Wise, "IBM's $5,000,000,000 Gamble," *Fortune*, September 1966, 118. The design work on the System/360 project cost approximately $5 million, and IBM soon had $4.5 billion in capital invested in equipment, facilities, and leased machines; Nancy S. Dorfman, *Innovation and Market Structure: Lessons from the Computer and Semiconductor Industries* (Cambridge, MA: Ballinger Publishing Company, 1987), 66.

17. Pugh, *Building*, 280–282.

18. Campbell-Kelly and Aspray, *Computer*, 144.

19. Ibid., 147.

20. George T. Gray and Ronald Q. Smith, "Before the B5000: Burroughs Computers, 1951–1963," *IEEE Annals of the History of Computing* 25, no. 2 (April–June 2003): 56.

21. "Discussion: The Burroughs B5000 in Retrospect," *Annals of the History of Computing* 9, no. 1 (1987): 45.

22. Fisher, McKie, and Mancke, *IBM*, 56–57.

23. Campbell-Kelly and Aspray, *Computer*, 145–146.

24. Pugh, *Building*, 297.

25. Stanley C. Allyn, *My Half Century with NCR* (New York: McGraw-Hill, 1967), 168–169.

26. Fisher, McKie, and Mancke, *IBM*, 86–88.

27. Ibid., 147.

28. John A. N. Lee, "The Rise and Fall of the General Electric Computer Department," *IEEE Annals of the History of Computing* 17, no. 4 (1995): 24–45; John A. N. Lee, "The Rise and Sale of the General Electric Computer Department: A Further Look," *IEEE Annals of the History of Computing* 22, no. 2 (2000): 53–60; H. R. Oldfield, "General Electric Enters the Computer Business—Revisited," *IEEE Annals of the History of Computing* 17, no. 4 (1995): 46–55.

29. Ibid.

30. National Research Council, *Funding a Revolution: Government Funding for Computer Research* (Washington, DC: National Academy Press, 1998), 87.

31. Claude Baum, *The Systems Builders: The Story of SDC* (Santa Monica, CA: System Development Corporation, 1981), 13.

32. National Research Council, *Funding*, 87–88. The total estimated cost of the "Digital Information Handling Program" that resulted in SAGE was estimated at $2.04 billion in 1948 dollars by MIT's Servomechanisms Laboratory; Henry S. Tropp, moderator, "A Perspective on SAGE: Discussion," *Annals of the History of Computing* 5, no. 4 (October 1983): 382–383.

33. Edwards, Paul, *The Closed World: Computers and the Politics of Discourse in Cold War America* (Cambridge, MA: MIT Press, 1996).

34. Wallace J. Eckert, *Punched Card Methods in Scientific Computation* (New York: Thomas J. Watson Astronomical Computing Bureau, Columbia University, 1940). [Reprinted as part of Charles Babbage Institute Reprint: Series (Cambridge, MA: MIT Press and Los Angeles: Tomash Publishers, 1983)].

35. Peggy Aldrich Kidwell, "American Scientists and Calculating Machines—Novelty to Commonplace," *Annals of the History of Computing* 12, no. 1 (1990): 31–40.

36. For analysis of the IBM System/360 series' applicability to both the business and scientific fields, see Emerson W. Pugh, Lyle R. Johnson, and John H. Palmer, *IBM's 360 and Early 370 Systems* (Cambridge, MA: MIT Press, 1991).

37. John F. Ahearne, "Introductory Physics Experiments Using a Digital Computer," *American Journal of Physics* 34 (1966): 309–333; Roger D. Hartman, "Use of Computers in an Undergraduate Light and Optics Laboratory," *American Journal of Physics* 34 (1966): 793–798.

38. Jeffrey R. Yost, *A Bibliographic Guide to Resources in Scientific Computing, 1945–1975* (Westport, CT: Greenwood Press, 2002).

39. Thomas Haigh, "The Chromium-Plated Tabulator: Institutionalizing an Electronic Revolution, 1954–1958," *IEEE Annals of the History of Computing* 23, no. 4 (2001): 75–76.

40. Ibid.

41. Georgina Ferry, *A Computer Called LEO: Lyons Teashops and the World's First Office Computer* (London: Fourth Estate, 2003).

42. "Discussion: The Burroughs B 5000 in Retrospect," *Annals.*

43. JoAnne Yates, "Coevolution of Information-Processing Technology and Use: Interaction Between the Life Insurance and Tabulating Industries," *Business History Review* 67, no. 1 (Spring 1993): 1–51; JoAnne Yates, "Early Interactions Between the Life Insurance and Computer Industries: The Prudential's Edmund C. Berkeley," *IEEE Annals of the History of Computing* 19, no. 3 (1977): 60–73.

44. Ibid.

45. The first volume of Cortada's important new series is *The Digital Hand: How Computers Changed the Work of American Manufacturing, Transportation, and Retail Industries* (New York: Oxford University Press, 2003).

46. Braun and MacDonald, *Revolution,* 114.

—4—

The Industry's Supercomputing and Minicomputing Sectors, 1957–1975

Cost leadership was a strategy employed by a number of IBM's competitors from the late 1950s through the 1960s. While this sometimes took the form of building computers of similar power and trying to sell or lease them for less than IBM, increasingly, as IBM came to be seen as the standard in computing, the strategy involved firms attempting to create IBM-compatible computers. This practice proved either hard to accomplish, or at very least, difficult to profit from over the long-term.[1]

The other fundamental strategy of IBM's competitors was differentiation. All computing systems that were not built as clones had distinct features and performance characteristics. Nevertheless, these differences were typically modest within a particular class of computing system. With the exception of specially designed computers, built under contract as one-of-a-kind products or in small quantities, there was usually a relatively comparable IBM machine. This, coupled with IBM's strong brand and the firm's quality service network to back up its products, made competing against the computer giant a great challenge. There was, however, one potential opportunity, extreme differentiation, or developing completely novel types of computers (in terms of components, price, performance, etc.). In 1957, just as IBM was solidifying its hegemonic position in the computing field, two new companies formed to create classes of computing systems outside the spectrum of those produced by IBM or any other computer manufacturers of the time. These firms were Control Data Corporation (CDC) and the Digital Equipment Corporation (DEC), and the classes of computers they created became known as super-computers and minicomputers respectively.

CDC sought to build machines of unprecedented power to serve a relatively small and specialized group of government agencies and major research universities that had advanced scientific and engineering computational requirements. Conversely, DEC attempted to build desktop systems that had modest processing capabilities, but were priced low enough to bring many new business and scientific users into the market for computers. While neither threatened to displace IBM's overall leadership in computing, and in many respects they posed less of a business challenge to IBM than some of the firm's other competitors, they nevertheless redefined the computer trade to include two fundamental new segments, and in doing so, made the computer giant take notice. With regard to CDC, IBM had to decide the real and perceived technological and business benefits that accrued from building the world's fastest computers. DEC, on the other hand, forced IBM to consider whether it wanted to compete at the ultra low end of the computer market. The remainder of this chapter focuses on these two new segments, primarily through an examination of CDC and DEC, and their visionary leaders William Norris and Kenneth Olsen.

WILLIAM NORRIS, SEYMOUR CRAY, AND THE CONTROL DATA CORPORATION

William Norris, born in 1911 and raised on a Nebraska farm, graduated with an engineering degree from the University of Nebraska in 1932. With the tight job market in the early years of the Great Depression, he was unable to find an engineering job in the private sector and joined the U.S. Marine Corps. At various times during the 1930s and first half of the 1940s, Norris served as a Marine, helped run his family's farm, worked as a salesperson for Westinghouse, and as a naval cryptographer. After the end of World War II, Norris and some his fellow naval engineers founded Engineering Research Associates (ERA) to manufacture mainframe digital computers and other electronic devices in St. Paul, Minnesota.

Norris was a strong individualist with deep convictions and was dissatisfied with the management of Remington Rand after the conglomerate took over ERA in 1952. He had opposed the merger from the beginning. While ERA President John Parker believed the additional capital that Remington Rand could provide would be critical to allowing ERA to compete effectively in the computer industry, Norris doubted the corporation would adequately fund the St. Paul operation and believed the real value of ERA lay in the creativity and talent of energetic former navy engineers (himself among them) who had been the nucleus of the St. Paul enterprise from the beginning. Seeing IBM's emerging leadership in computing by the mid-1950s fueled Norris's frustration. He was general manager of the St. Paul facility and felt his group's potential had been limited by managers at other divisions (particularly the UNIVAC division in Philadelphia) and Sperry Rand's senior executives (the firm's new name after the Remington Rand and Sperry Corporation merger in 1955). The latter, in Norris's opinion, lacked "vision and commitment" in computing.[2] Chief among the problems was the poor coordination between the facilities and the absence of adequate funds.

Norris and eleven managers and engineers (some from the old ERA firm and other, young engineers who had joined since Remington Rand's acquisition of ERA) decided to leave Sperry Rand to form their own computer company, the Control Data Corporation (CDC). Norris was the oldest at forty-six, with the average age of the "defectors" being thirty-four. Other key executives at the start included Vice President and Treasurer Arnold Ryden, Director of Engineering Frank Mullaney, and Marketing Director Willis Drake. Frustrated by their loss of engineering talent, Sperry Rand quickly filed suit and alleged CDC's illegal use of trade secrets. The case did not have much merit, and CDC won the legal battle.[3]

Control Data set up operations in a vacant warehouse in St. Paul in 1957. The company was financed through a stock issue of 600,000 $1 shares. From the start, the firm did not want to compete directly against IBM. In fact, Norris sought business as a supplier to IBM in 1957.[4] Generally speaking, CDC planned to supply various computer components to original equipment manufacturers (OEMs) as well as build a powerful new computer for end-market customers. While Norris wanted to avoid overt competition with IBM, he knew that the New York–based firm would see CDC's powerful scientific computers as a competitive challenge, even though the computer giant was not currently building anything in CDC's class, and its focus was increasingly on the data processing business market for computing technology.[5]

One of the engineers who left Sperry Rand to join the new firm was Seymour Cray, a University of Minnesota–educated electrical engineer. Cray's desire to resign from Sperry Rand, however, caused some uneasiness with Norris, Mullaney, and other CDC executives. They all knew of Cray's great engineering talent and wanted him at the company, but he was the key designer on a

Sperry Rand project for the navy. The last thing CDC wanted was to alienate the navy, given the important role future naval contracts might play for Control Data. Norris worked to smooth things with Navy Commander Hank Forest, and CDC executives allowed Cray to join the firm in late 1957. Forest and other naval personnel knew Cray's fierce individualism and idiosyncrasies nearly as well as the CDC executives, and everyone thought it best to let Cray follow through on his plans rather than to perpetuate a difficult situation.[6] Further evidence that there was no lasting ill will came in 1959 when CDC signed a contract to supply the navy with a special-purpose computer system for firing control applications on the submarine-based Polaris missile.

Many who came to know Seymour Cray considered him a genius. Cray developed the highest-speed computer circuitry in existence, which was used on a project Control Data soon engaged, the CDC 1604. Norris and others believed IBM was increasingly focused on the business market and that the smaller high-end scientific field would be a niche CDC could effectively target. At the beginning of 1960, the CDC 1604 computer was completed and delivered to the first customer, the U.S. Navy Bureau of Ships. The machine sold for $600,000, a lower price tag than for some computers with far less processing power. CDC was able to sell for less as a result of Cray's unparalleled circuitry and because the firm did everything on a shoestring compared to the giants in the computer field. The company had a small engineering staff and only two salesmen when the CDC 1604 was completed.

Another area where CDC saved on the 1604 was software; unlike business customers, users of powerful scientific computers often did all of their own programming. Other early customers of the CDC 1604 included the British government (for its intelligence agency), and Atomic Energy Commission (AEC) laboratories. While CDC's success with building an efficient world-class computer is undisputed, the company did struggle in the early years with providing adequate service to keep all installations up and running, and improving upon this was a fundamental focus for Norris and other CDC executives in the early 1960s.[7]

Concomitant to the 1604, under Cray's technical leadership, the firm also developed the CDC 160, a small computer that could be used as an input/output data processor for the larger mainframe machine, as well as for other scientific and engineering applications. The CDC 160, and its successor, the CDC 160A, were small, but with Cray's circuitry, these machines had significant power relative to their size. The CDC 160A sold as a stand-alone device for $60,000 and could arguably be considered the first minicomputer.[8] In 1963, the company also came out with the CDC 3600 as a successor to the 1604, a machine that achieved a modest presence in the commercial data processing field.[9] The substantial technical, and lesser though significant financial success of the CDC 1604, CDC 160, CDC 160A, and CDC 3600 led Control Data to embark upon an even grander project, the CDC 6600.

Seymour Cray worked long and irregular hours. He often liked to work alone, or at very least, with only a small number of familiar individuals. He found the St. Paul facility distracting and asked Norris if he could set up a laboratory in his hometown, Chippewa Falls, Wisconsin, and take a number of the firm's best engineers to work with him to design and build the CDC 6600. Knowing Cray's unique personality and work habits, as well as his ability to achieve great results, Norris agreed to this unusual request. All told, the Chippewa group included thirty-four individuals, mostly engineers. Announced in 1962 and on the market two years later, the CDC 6600 was the world's first supercomputer. The first 6600 system was delivered to Lawrence Livermore National Laboratory in September 1964.

The CDC 6600 created more public attention than any computer since the ENIAC and UNIVAC.[10] The machine rekindled a public notion of computers as giant brains that could revolutionize the future of science. *Businessweek* called the 6600 a "triumph" and emphasized how it would open up "a whole universe" of opportunities in scientific calculation "that have been impossible to contemplate."[11] Shortly after the 6600 came out, the firm became the third leading computer company in the world, behind only IBM and Sperry Rand's UNIVAC division.

Directly, the CDC 6600 did not provide a major challenge to IBM's revenue streams and profitability. Even though it did substantially cut into the computer giant's sales and leases for IBM 7090 and 7094 computers, the company was rapidly growing its data processing installations with other machines. The 6600 sold in low volumes to select customers, slightly more than 100 units over a decade, but at an average price of $8 million per system, it contributed nearly a billion dollars in revenue to the Twin Cities–based firm. Customers consisted of government entities (national laboratories, the National Security Agency, etc.), larger university computing centers, and a small number of major corporations. The computers bought by these government and non-government organizations, however, were widely reported in the popular and trade presses, and a sign of great prestige.

With the Soviet Union's successful launch of the Sputnik I satellite in 1957 still a recent memory, and the Cold War at its height,

Control Data Corporation's CDC 6600, the most powerful computer in the world, and the first to be termed a "supercomputer," circa mid-1960s. (Courtesy of Charles Babbage Institute, University of Minnesota, Minneapolis)

the concept of scientific and technological leadership was on the minds of many individuals in industry and government. For competing high technology companies, it was seen of paramount importance. IBM's Thomas Watson, Jr., was dismayed that a laboratory in a small town in Wisconsin with less than three-dozen employees could create a machine that was by far the most powerful computer in the world.[12] With Stretch, IBM had wanted to build and extend various organizational capabilities, but there was also a race to be seen as the industry's technological leader after Sperry Rand won the contract for LARC. Watson pushed his System/360 team hard to outdo the CDC 6600 (with the IBM System/360/90). The challenges of maintaining compatibility within the System/360 family, as well as the design skill of Cray on the CDC 6600, however, proved too great to overcome. IBM had lost technical leadership at the high end of computing to a small start-up in St. Paul doing its most advanced work out of a relatively tiny Chippewa Falls laboratory.

The anger of Thomas Watson, Jr., over CDC's technical leadership in computing mirrored that of his negative reaction to the

Stretch Project after it failed to meet specifications when it was completed a couple of years earlier. By 1966, Watson had come to grips with Stretch. He revised his opinion, focusing more on the project's many successes in positioning IBM to succeed commercially with the highly profitable IBM System/360 series. That year, Steve Dunwell, Stretch's project leader, was named an IBM Fellow, the company's greatest honor for technical achievement. At the IBM Annual Awards Dinner, Watson made a point of paying special tribute to Dunwell's achievement in leading Project Stretch and "publicly corrected the record" with regard to his and other IBM executives past critiques of the project.[13]

Even though the IBM System/360/90 was inferior to the CDC 6600 in terms of processing speed, it offered compatibility within the firm's system, and IBM aggressively and successfully marketed the machine, along with others in the System/360 series. CDC claimed IBM used illegal predatory practices in trying to sell and lease the System/360/90 and filed a lawsuit in 1968. This was a daring move on Norris's part, as many outside the company thought it foolish to take on the computer giant. IBM, feeling the weight of a number of simultaneous suits, settled out of court and agreed to sell its Service Bureau Corporation to CDC for $16 million, a fraction of its market value, and provide the Minneapolis-based firm $101 million in cash and contracts. The Service Bureau Corporation had 1,700 experienced employees and more than 20,000 customers. The CDC suit was in all likelihood a significant contributing factor in IBM's decision to "unbundle" its software (to price it separately from hardware) the following year. This had a positive impact on many hardware firms, including CDC, and lent great momentum to an independent software industry (see chapter 5).

The IBM settlement proved critical to CDC. Losing the suit might have threatened the firm's existence. Much of the early negotiations of the settlement were held secretly in 1971 and 1972 between Norris and IBM's new chief executive officer, Thomas Learson. Learson had succeeded Thomas Watson, Jr., following Watson's heart attack and subsequent resignation from the position in 1970.[14]

In the wake of the 360/90, IBM quietly explored the possibility of pushing harder and moving into the supercomputing field, but soon abandoned these plans. Watson had recognized that overcoming CDC's leadership in supercomputing was probably ill advised from a business and legal standpoint. The IBM System/360 series had been a tremendous financial boost to IBM even though it contained no machines as technically advanced as CDC supercomputers. This reinforced for Watson the valuable lesson that his firm did not have to build the most powerful computers to be the most successful computer company. Meanwhile, CDC enjoyed great success on a smaller scale. Its machines represented around 5 percent of the value of installed computers around the world by the late 1960s, and it continued to hold this share during the first half of the 1970s. Most CDC computers were sold to government agencies and universities for science and engineering applications. Many of the scientists and engineers involved with purchasing decisions appreciated the personalized service they received from a firm that was far smaller and less bureaucratic than IBM.[15]

While CDC successfully designed, built, and sold supercomputers, it was also very successful at marketing services to a range of customers. Norris became increasingly interested in this side of the business throughout the 1960s and 1970s. Back in 1961, Norris had appointed a young and talented recruit, Robert Price, to head the Application Services Division. Norris not only wanted to target the large scientific and engineering organizations that did their own programming, but also the smaller scientific laboratories that needed assistance with software and analysis. The settlement CDC received from IBM (especially obtaining the IBM Service Bureau) lent great momentum to this business within CDC.

Both Cray and Frank Mullaney wanted the firm's primary concentration to be computer hardware, but Norris saw the expansion of the services business as an important opportunity. Norris also recognized that each new supercomputer project was a substantial risk, especially for a firm such as CDC that had far fewer resources than a number of firms in the computer industry, especially IBM and Sperry Rand. Cray ran into some difficulties in designing a new supercomputer, the 8600; and along with his frustration at the growing focus on services within CDC, he resigned from the company in 1972. Control Data continued with the development of this system, and more broadly, in the supercomputer field. The firm, however, began to scale back research-and-development in supercomputing and its commitment to attaining unprecedented technical advances. With this reduced concentration, CDC would soon be outdone in this market segment.

Unlike the exodus of Sperry Rand engineers to form CDC, Cray's departure was friendly on both sides. Norris appreciated what Cray had done for CDC over the years, and Cray was grateful for the autonomy that Norris and CDC had given him to establish the Chippewa Falls laboratory. After about a year of rest and reflection, Seymour Cray formed a new company, Cray Research, Inc., to be devoted exclusively to designing and building supercomputers. CDC even invested $500,000 in stock of the new firm, a wise move that yielded Norris's company a 200 percent profit when the firm sold the shares several years later. Cray Research allowed its leader to focus on processing speed, and after four years of development, it came out with the successful Cray-1, the first supercomputer to use chips rather than magnetic core memory. This proved more flexible in allowing Cray to successfully use vector processing and yielded the fastest computer in the world.[16] Los Alamos National Laboratory immediately purchased a Cray-1 for its rapid processing speed, despite the fact that it meant reprogramming system and applications software. Other potential customers, such as the U.S. National Center for Atmospheric Research, however, would only buy the $8 million Cray-1 if the supercomputer manufacturer would provide system software. Among corporate customers, there was even greater pressure to concentrate on programming and ease-of-use rather than merely a blind focus on achieving greater heights in computer processing speed.[17] In short, during the mid- to late-1970s, given a new and increasingly diverse base, there was a growing need for CDC to concentrate on customers. Norris and others at CDC had anticipated this and tried to achieve it both within and outside of the supercomputing field.[18]

Shifting from a focus on supercomputing to become more of a diverse and service-oriented business was simultaneously a bold repositioning of Control Data and a conservative move with regard to reducing up-front capital expenditures on research-and-development. In one new area, however, educational services, it was extremely ambitious and full of financial risk. Norris also became heavily focused on refining and instituting computer-based educational instruction, a project named PLATO, or Programmed Logic for Automated Teaching Operations, that had originated at the University of Illinois.

Back in the mid-1960s, CDC had begun Control Data Institute to educate and train the firm's employees. In the early 1970s, Norris decided to convert this in-house resource to sell educational and vocational services, and several years later, to incorporate PLATO as the primary tool. Norris also was interested in getting PLATO into K–12 education. Despite his early recognition of the importance of information technology access and education to opportunity (especially for the economically disadvantaged—in essence what came to be termed "the digital divide" in the subsequent personal computer and World Wide Web era), lack of course-

Control Data Corporation founder and longtime president William C. Norris in front of CDC 1604 console at a museum exhibit, circa 1970s. (Courtesy of Charles Babbage Institute, University of Minnesota, Minneapolis)

ware and financial challenges led to problems with implementation. At the press conference to announce his retirement in 1986, Norris spoke of future opportunities for PLATO and despite the system's many past challenges, he cited it without hesitation as the proudest accomplishment of his career.[19]

Over time, the once-smaller branches of peripherals (plug-compatible products such as disk drives), data services, engineering services, professional services, financial services, and education would collectively become the foci of CDC's evolving enterprises. These areas brought a mixture of financial success and failure, and the firm would never again lead a design-and-manufacturing sector of the computer industry, as it had for a number of years after initiating the field of supercomputing. The company, behind Norris's creative leadership, also focused on restoring the economic health of impoverished neighborhoods, and many other philanthropic endeavors. Norris would transform CDC into one the nation's most innovative and involved corporations on a range of social issues. Much of the firm's economic troubles can be attributed to changes in an information technology services environment resulting from the increasingly widespread proliferation of personal computers during the early 1980s. The Digital Equipment Corporation would also be victimized by this fundamental change in the computer industry.

KENNETH OLSEN AND THE DIGITAL EQUIPMENT CORPORATION

There were a couple of fundamental early differences between CDC and the Digital Equipment Corporation, aside from the fact the two firms competed at opposite ends of the price spectrum in the computer trade. While Norris and CDC knew where they wanted to focus from the start—advanced scientific computers, or supercomputers—DEC experimented for several years before finding its identity. A further difference was that supercomputing and the advanced circuitry that made it possible were internally developed by Cray and others at CDC. With regard to minicomputing, the fundamental technologies came from a university setting—MIT—and the general advancement in integrated circuit technology during the 1960s.

Kenneth Olsen and Harlan Anderson formed DEC in 1957. Olsen, who was born and grew up in Bridgeport, Connecticut, was thirty-one years old at the time. He had graduated from MIT with an electrical engineering degree seven years earlier and had gone on to work as a research associate at MIT's Lincoln Laboratory on Project Whirlwind (where he engineered the system's core memory). In the early 1950s, Olsen had spent a year in residence at IBM as a MIT representative involved with oversight of the first Semi-Automatic Ground Environment (SAGE) computer.

Harlan Anderson, immediately following completion of his B.S. in Engineering Physics and M.S. in Physics from the University of Illinois, joined MIT's Digital Computer Laboratory, and soon shifted to become an engineer at Lincoln Laboratory. Like Olsen, he worked on computer circuitry design and implementation of magnetic core memory, as well as administrative and technical oversight on IBM's SAGE computer project. Olsen and Anderson's work at Lincoln Laboratory gave them excellent experience on the most advanced digital computer transistor implementation work in the early 1950s, while their time at IBM provided exposure to the strong organization and management of the emerging industry leader in mainframe digital computers.

By the middle 1950s Olsen and Anderson became interested in establishing a firm to compete in the computer business. Starting a new computer company, however, posed great challenges by this time. Barriers to entry, substantial at the start of the industry,

DEC Founder and President Kenneth Olsen. (Courtesy of Charles Babbage Institute, University of Minnesota, Minneapolis)

had grown considerably with IBM's emerging dominance. While CDC overcame the barriers, it had a core group of engineers from one of the established mainframe firms, and was able to raise enough start-up capital to begin on a skeletal basis. Additionally, the firm was anything but secure in its first few years. To compete effectively in the mainframe industry by this time firms not only needed advanced processing technology, programming capabilities, and peripheral products, they also needed effective sales personnel. To buy their way into these capabilities, Olsen and Anderson would need far more than the initial $70,000 they received from American Research and Development (AR&D), a firm formed by pioneering venture capitalist and famed Harvard Business School professor George Doriot.[20]

DEC began in a sizable facility (formerly a textile factory) in Maynard, Massachusetts, as a component manufacturer supplying circuit boards for the expanding electronics industry.[21] For $70,000, and a $30,000 line of credit from AR&D, DEC had to pay dearly in stock—70 percent went to the venture capital firm. This stock would be worth billions of dollars several decades down the road. DEC not only would initiate a new sector of an industry, but like Shockley Semiconductor's and Fairchild Semiconductor's role in bringing Silicon Valley to prominence, the Maynard, Massachusetts, firm, in time, would be a major contributor to establishing Route 128 as a critical corridor for electronics and computing enterprises. Many of DEC's engineers came from MIT in the early years, just as many engineers and programmers for Silicon Valley firms came from Stanford University and the University of California, Berkeley. Shockley Semiconductor, Fairchild Semiconductor, and DEC would be training ground for many engineers that would lead operations or companies in semiconductors and minicomputing for years to come.

Among the engineers who came to DEC from MIT, none would play a greater role in the firm's success than Gordon Bell. Bell, who joined the company in 1960, became the technical guru behind DEC's innovative new class of computers. He had received his B.S. and M.S. from MIT in engineering before using a Fulbright award to study in Australia, where he set up the British computer-maker English Electric's Deuce computer. He returned to MIT in the late 1950s to work on his doctorate, but left the program after meeting Olsen. He found the engineering atmosphere of this atypically engineering-friendly company preferable to the research world of academe. Despite this, Bell always held the opinion that deep corporate associations with top universities such as MIT were critical to competing effectively in high technology businesses. This was reflected in his own career choices, leaving DEC in 1966 to join the faculty of Carnegie Institute of Technology, but returning to Digital Equipment as the vice president of engineering between 1972 and 1983.[22]

After several years of manufacturing and selling circuit boards for memory testing to customers such as Cal Tech and Bell Laboratories, Olsen and DEC had the capital needed to initiate their first computer project: the Programmed Data Processor, or PDP-I. DEC took advantage of changes in transistor technology that yielded smaller, faster, and cheaper electronic components. The computer, which was modeled on the circuitry of MIT Lincoln Laboratory's TX-0 and TX-2 (two of the first transistorized machines, and decedents of Whirlwind), was to sell for a mere $125,000. Olsen chose its name to avoid having to overcome the commonly held belief that "real" computers cost in the range of $500,000 to several million dollars or more, as well as AR&D's concerns about articles in the financial press that predicted limited potential for the computer business.

George Doriot was particularly negative about computers as a result of the successful American electronics giants RCA and General Electric losing money in the field. In fact, Doriot's negativity toward the computer business was the basis for the firm's name of Digital Equipment Corporation, instead of the originally proposed name of Digital Computer Corporation. The resulting decision was emblematic of the influence Doriot would have on Olsen and DEC for many years.

Despite its name, the PDP-1 was very much a real computer, and though less powerful than its expensive counterparts in the mainframe area, it was nevertheless a highly advanced machine and an amazing achievement given its price. The computer achieved its performance capabilities at a low cost based on several factors. First, the price of computers varied considerably based on their peripheral equipment, something early DEC machines lacked. Burrough's 220, for instance, sold for $1.2 million with peripherals, or roughly twice as much as the price of the machine without them. DEC's PDP-I also was geared to a scientific market (smaller scientific laboratories) and did not include extensive software, leaving the specialized and expensive programming services to its customers, individuals and groups that had fairly unique needs.[23] Furthermore, unlike other computer manufacturers, given the market DEC was targeting, it spent very little on promotion and sales.

The PDP-1 and a wave of subsequent DEC computers were technical achievements and saw modest commercial success. Users did not have to wait hours or overnight for their job to queue up, as was the case with the mainframe/batch processing model.[24] Early customers included Lawrence Livermore National Laboratory, and ITEK (a typesetting firm). Bolt Beranek and Newman (BBN) also purchased the machine, and this was one of the factors that led to BBN's work on computer time-sharing.

From a financial standpoint, the most important order came from International Telephone & Telegraph (ITT), which purchased about half of the fifty-three PDP-1's that were ever manufactured. Notwithstanding DEC's success with the ITT contract, Olsen thought that the low price would create its own buzz, reduce the need for heavy marketing expenditures, and lead to many orders (unlike IBM, DEC only sold machines, it did not lease them). In theory, he was right, but it would take a few additional years, experimentation with a series of new models, and far greater advances in performance-to-cost ratios in semiconductors to achieve this.

DEC's fortunes changed with the introduction of the PDP-8 in 1965, a machine that like its four predecessors (PDP-4, PDP-5, PDP-6, PDP-7) was created by Gordon Bell. It was the first computer to take full advantage of major advances in integrated circuit technology. This gave it a tremendous boost in terms of delivering a significant level of processing power at an incredibly low cost—the machine was priced at only $18,000. DEC sold several hundred PDP-8 computers within the first year and more than 800 by the time of the company's initial public offering in 1966.

DEC's stock offering yielded $4.8 million. The PDP-8 continued to be a phenomenal success, and during the machine's decade-and-a-half manufacturing life more than 50,000 were produced and sold, making it by far the most popular computer of its era. By 1970, DEC, behind the success of the PDP-8, for a time moved into the position of the third largest computer manufacturer in the world, behind only IBM and Sperry Rand's UNIVAC division.[25] Around this time, William Norris, after a huge run up of CDC stock, became interested in purchasing DEC, but Olsen refused, just as he had done a couple of years after the advent of the PDP-8 when his firm was courted by Hewlett-Packard.

While many computers in DEC's growing PDP line (including the PDP-8E and PDP-8S) were sold for scientific applications, the market broadened beyond just academic computer centers and government agencies. DEC also moved into many areas of peripherals and services as the company expanded. While DEC had started a new segment of computing at the low end of the price scale, its brand was respected and it had considerable pricing power—its machines were never near the bottom for particular classes of minicomputers. In addition to achieving a degree of loyalty with many of its existing customers, DEC was always bringing new consumers into the computing area. Many small laboratories, schools, and medical facilities purchased PDP-8s as their first computers. More than ever, students were able to work with these machines, and in a far more direct manner than batch processing and mainframes of the past. The PDP-8 also had a number of manufacturing, industrial, and administrative applications, where the machines were used to automate particular processes, conduct design work, or handle clerical record processing. Creating a computer for process control in industrial settings was an early goal for DEC with the PDP-8, but the types of industrial and business applications of the machine went far beyond this. PDP-8s were

Digital Equipment Corporation's DEC PDP-8E, circa 1970. (Courtesy of Charles Babbage Institute, University of Minnesota, Minneapolis)

used to control the graphic displays on the scoreboard at Boston's Fenway Park and on a screen at New York's Times Square. While only a small number of individuals purchased the machines, increasingly, individuals used DEC PDP computers in work settings. With this, a hobbyist subculture began to develop among engineers and technicians, as well as students.[26]

Behind Olsen's leadership, DEC had fundamentally redefined

what a computer was and the number and types of organizations that could use stand-alone computing technology. It also changed the face of commercial computers as communication devices as the firm did pioneering work in peer-to-peer networking (with DECnet networking software) and was the first to integrate this with its operating systems and other products. DEC's achievements in creating computers that were priced at a small fraction of mainframes lent momentum to interactive computing, time-sharing, and networking, including work at a number of organizations contributing to the Department of Defense's IPTO-led ARPANET project (for more on this project see chapter 6).

In 1969, the term "minicomputing" first came into use to describe the new class of systems that DEC had created. Behind the PDP-8, the even more economical PDP-8S (a smaller machine, the size of a midsize file cabinet, that hit the market in 1966 and sold for less than $10,000), and the PDP-8I (a machine completed in 1969 that used medium-scale integration circuitry), the firm had grown to 5,800 employees and had sixty-eight locations around the world.[27] As with nearly any highly successful technological company in a new area, DEC's creation of the first mass-produced minicomputer led to a number of competitors during the second half of the 1960s and first half of the 1970s. DEC's competitors in minicomputing included new or relatively new firms such as Data General, Prime Computer, and Scientific Data Systems, as well as established computer industry companies that decided to try their hand in the new business, such as Hewlett-Packard and Honeywell. DEC in turn, continued to add new businesses and new business segments to hedge its bets as competitive pressures grew in the minicomputing field.

DATA GENERAL AND OTHER MINICOMPUTING COMPETITORS

Of its competitors, most upsetting to Olsen and other DEC executives was Data General. Not only did this firm grow into a rival, it did so behind DEC talent. Edson de Castro, a young engineer who led design efforts to bring Gordon Bell's PDP-8 to life, left with several other DEC engineers in 1968 to form Data General and build minicomputers. It is unclear if de Castro and others had worked on their first system for Data General before departing, but Digital Equipment's executives later made such claims. Olsen felt betrayed by de Castro's departure, an event that left DEC in a bind with designing its new 16-bit computer (the PDP-X). In contrast to the exodus of Sperry Rand engineers to form CDC, the parent firm, however, did not sue.[28]

De Castro and company did not venture far, setting up head-quarters by renting out a former beauty parlor in Hudson, Massachusetts. The firm started with $800,000 in capital. Like DEC's early years, most of the money went into the design and manufacture of computers rather than services. While service was fundamental to mainframe firms, and perhaps IBM's most distin-guishing characteristic, minicomputer manufacturers generally sold to customers willing to do their own programming and main-tenance, as long as they could get a good deal on a relatively in-expensive computer.

Data General came out with its first computer, NOVA, in 1969. It was similar in many respects to DEC's PDP-8 series. The NOVA, however, had advances in its circuitry that exceeded DEC's ma-chines and used a larger printed circuit board, reducing the amount of hardware necessary. Data General marketed it aggres-sively for the industry's annual trade show, the National Computer Conference—purchasing billboards nearby and distributing copies of the *Wall Street Journal* with inserts on the NOVA. The machine was a success as Data General shipped more than 200 NOVAs in the first several years and the company had recouped its design and development costs by only the second year. Throughout the 1970s, Data General would grow its revenues at an annual rate of more than 40 percent per year.[29]

DEC held about 80 percent of the minicomputer market at this time, but the aggressiveness of Data General and others led to the firm's greatest challenge since its initial success. Bell took the lead again, working with a new group of top designers, and developed the idea for the PDP-11, a machine the firm pre-announced par-ticularly early to reassure its customer base and maintain market share. Despite being two years behind on a 16-bit computer, DEC had weathered the storm of the exodus of de Castro and other skilled engineers. The new firm however, would continue to be a thorn in DEC's side. Behind Data General's rapid success with the NOVA and subsequent machines, the company was selling com-puters for the second highest margin in the industry after IBM. By the late 1960s and early 1970s, DEC, Data General, and other minicomputer manufacturers also were producing machines that competed against the lower-end computers of IBM's System/360 series, a trend that would continue with DEC's VAX and subse-quent minicomputers.

In the late 1960s and early 1970s, Hewlett-Packard (HP) also en-tered the minicomputing area. Formed in 1938 by David Packard and Bill Hewlett, with encouragement from Stanford University's Frederick Terman, this electronics company had a long record of success with various types of instruments, and by 1966, had come out with processors for instrument control. In 1972 the firm produced the HP 3000, a powerful minicomputer that for a time technically outperformed DEC and Data General machines. Innovations in the following several years led to an enhanced model that was successful at time-sharing and multiprogramming. During much of the 1970s, minicomputing represented roughly half of Hewlett-Packard's annual revenue.

Most of the other competitors in minicomputing during the 1970s were specialized firms, such as DEC and Data General, as opposed to giant companies like IBM and Hewlett-Packard that had just entered this new business. Though smaller than the aforementioned firms, Wang Laboratories, Prime Computer, Tandem Computer, and Stratus Computer all sold a significant number of minicomputers during the decade.

By 1978, Data General achieved the distinction of joining DEC in the Fortune 500. Innovation came quickly in the minicomputer field, however, and companies had to stay on top technologically. Behind the skilled computer architecture of Gordon Bell and his heuristic, or rule-based, model for building, DEC had come out with its VAX 11/780, a 32-bit computer that was labeled a "supermini." The computer achieved this distinction as a result of its significantly higher processing power relative to other minicomputers (16-bit machines). The VAX 11/780 sold for more than $100,000 and was a high margin product. This worried the engineers and management at Data General, and the firm immediately embarked to develop its own super minicomputer in less than a year, an unheard of pace even for the rapidly changing and hard-driving minicomputing sector. The initial VAX was part of a series of powerful minicomputers that would, despite a rough spell at DEC in the early 1980s, usher in a final decade of glory and substantial financial success, before the firm would experience the full effect of the shift of consumers to personal computers.

Data General formed a team led by computer engineer Tom West and others to build the ECLIPSE, a 32-bit super minicomputer. Journalist Tracy Kidder provides a fascinating inside look at the ECLIPSE development project in the Pulitzer Prize–winning *The Soul of a New Machine.* Not only is this book an insightful examination of a minicomputing company's efforts to compete with DEC, but it is also one of the most intriguing and well-written accounts of a twentieth-century technological development project to date. Both the VAX and the ECLIPSE could be interfaced with

IBM System/360 machines—further challenging IBM on its lower-end computers. This resulted in IBM trying to meet the competition from the minicomputer sector head-on by directly competing in this industry. In the mid-1970s IBM produced the successful 4300 mid-range series, and within a decade it had surpassed DEC in the minicomputing sector.[30]

By 1978 the minicomputer industry consisted of roughly fifty companies, though some were focused elsewhere and participated in the industry sector in only a modest fashion. This industry had gone through a quiet shakeout, as there were nearly one hundred minicomputer start-ups per year during part of the previous decade. Between 1968 and 1978 annual revenue for the minicomputing sector had climbed from approximately $150 million to more than $3 billion. By this time, however, the personal computer (PC) was beginning to gain more and more attention, and before the end of the next decade the PC would put substantial pressure on the minicomputer manufacturers.

SUPERCOMPUTING AND MINICOMPUTING IN PERSPECTIVE

Control Data Corporation and Digital Equipment Corporation both formed in 1957 and soon initiated two new segments of the industry, supercomputing and minicomputing. They would lead these areas for roughly two decades. Though both firms benefited substantially from individuals previously trained on government projects and received significant government contracts, they were formed with only modest venture capital. They both took advantage of and built upon cutting-edge technology (particularly transistors) to stand out in an industry that was in many respects still in its infancy and where future profitability was largely uncertain. They breathed life and excitement into the computer trade and instilled the industry with an entrepreneurial spirit that was somewhat lacking as large established office machine and electronics firms had come to dominate the new field. With minicomputing, this spirit and drive for commercial and technological leadership was extended to a number of new firms that competed against DEC, such as Data General.

In many respects, a new culture was created by DEC, Data General, and other minicomputing enterprises, a culture that was characterized by relatively small development teams, informal dress, and above all, a focus on innovative engineering and the thrill of creating something entirely new. In many ways, this was a cultural precursor to the start-up personal computer firms such as Apple Computer two decades later. The informality and commitment to innovation and change that existed at minicomputer firms stood in contrast to IBM where strategic planning was far more bureaucratic, change was an involved and difficult process, and the dark blue suit was almost a standard uniform for executive staff. Peter Delisi, who came from IBM to join DEC as product line manager for the Distributed Processing Group in 1977, noted the vast difference in the culture of the companies and how the two firms' products reflected these cultures. IBM's mainframes were symbolic of authority and centralization, while DEC's less expensive minicomputers and focus on time-sharing and networking were representative of individualism and freedom.[31]

There were a number of similarities in managerial style between William Norris and Kenneth Olsen. Like a number of chief executives both were strong visionary leaders who had served in the U.S. Navy, but in many ways eschewed bureaucracy and were risk takers. In contrast to most company chiefs, however, they also were introspective and concentrated less on being in the spotlight than creative stewardship of their firms. Both had deep moral convictions that helped guide their decision-making and structuring of their corporations, albeit in somewhat different ways (Norris and CDC having the broader philanthropic commitment and vision). Though they made all the large and difficult decisions, they also delegated substantial authority to a strong team of executives. Each was gifted at maintaining and extending his firm's position in its industry segment in spite of significant competition, especially Olsen given the rapidly expanding minicomputing sector and competition DEC faced in the late 1960s and early 1970s. In the end, both were reminders that even the strongest of technological innovators and visionaries typically fall prey to a life cycle defined by unforeseen change that results in others moving to the forefront to produce the "new new thing," much as they had both done in the past. DEC and CDC each fell back somewhat as subsequent technology provided other firms with different opportunities during the 1970s.

With DEC the cause of decline was not single-mindedness with regard to minicomputing to the exclusion of other businesses. The company had in fact competed in many segments of the computer industry outside of minicomputer hardware before the end of the 1980s, including mainframes, networking, workstation software, fault-tolerance, systems integration, management consulting, hardware repair, and semiconductors.[32] In the retrospective words of Gordon Bell, "by the mid-1980s DEC had become a classic well-run, vertically integrated company." The industry, however, was becoming increasingly fragmented. Such structure made it all the more difficult for the innovators of the past to be the innovators of the future.

In the case of CDC, its star engineer, Seymour Cray, left to form Cray Research, a firm that would become the leader in super-computing. While CDC continued to have some modest successes in other areas, such as producing peripherals and providing data and professional services, this success was far less impressive than the heyday of the 6600. Peripherals and business services were less exciting to Norris, who became increasingly focused on philanthropic work and education to help improve the poor neighborhoods of Minneapolis, as well as other cities that had major CDC facilities. This contrasted sharply with many computer firms, which at best took modest interest in social problems. Kenneth Olsen believed corporations and their managers should be focused on their fundamental endeavor of creating wealth and jobs, and repeatedly discouraged his management team from becoming involved in community affairs.

In the late 1960s, DEC Vice President Peter Kauffman did lead an effort to establish some new facilities in inner-city neighborhoods and institute training programs to bring inner-city workers to these plants. On this issue and others, Kauffman did not see eye-to-eye with Olsen, and this talented leader who some saw as a future DEC chief executive left the company in the late 1970s.[33] Though both Norris and Olsen were deeply respected leaders within and outside of their firms, the former tended to have smoother relationships with his top managers, while the latter's idiosyncrasies and outbursts at times made for tense situations at DEC.

Though DEC did not shift its resources to focus development on personal computing technology, something that with hindsight represented a strategic shortcoming, the firm was in many respects a contributor to this area by changing the nature and definition of how computers were used and who used them. Though far less affordable than the personal computer would later be, DEC's PDP-8 series greatly reduced the size and cost of computing and expanded the scope of computer installations and applications. A computer hobbyist subculture emerged, and many began to think about computing in new ways—as tools to automate routine industrial and business processes, as scientific instruments for individual scientists, as broad-based educational tools—not just as mysterious giant brains doing secretive complex calculations for a few government, corporate, and scientific elites. In short, while neither DEC nor CDC exist today as independent entities, and they were acquired or restructured in a period of relative stagnation rather than at the height of their success, they were part of an innovative and entrepreneurial spirit that helped shape computing technology in ways that are evident to this day. In doing so, they broadened the computer industry, and the businesses they engaged in resulted in IBM's share of the industry, though substantial, heading into a period of gradual, but ongoing, decline.

NOTES

1. As will be discussed in the chapter on the personal computer, IBM's competitors did have success at imitating and underselling IBM in personal computers in the 1980s and 1990s. In the mainframe field, RCA's Spectra 70 was the most successful IBM imitation (of the System/360 machines). Spectra 70's success, however, lasted only several years, and though it was profitable, its positive impact for RCA (given the relative small size of the firm's computer division) was modest, and the negative impact on IBM was minimal. Plug-compatible peripherals manufacturers, at times, had considerable success relative to the makers of compatible mainframe computers.

2. William C. Norris, interview by Arthur L. Norberg, July 28 and October 1, 1986, Minneapolis, MN (Charles Babbage Institute, University of Minnesota).

3. James C. Worthy, *William C. Norris: Portrait of a Maverick* (Cambridge, MA: Ballenger Publishing Company, 1987), 34–37.

4. William C. Norris to James J. Troy, September 12, 1957 (William Norris Papers, Charles Babbage Institute, University of Minnesota).

5. William C. Norris, interview.

6. William C. Norris to H. S. Forrest, September 6, 1957 (William Norris Papers, Charles Babbage Institute, University of Minnesota).

7. Summary and Conclusions of the 1961 Planning Meeting, Control Data Corporation Records (Charles Babbage Institute, University of Minnesota).

8. Paul Ceruzzi, *A History of Modern Computing* (Cambridge, MA: MIT Press, 1998), 126.

9. Boelie Elzen and Donald MacKenzie, "The Social Limits of Speed: The Development and Use of Supercomputers," *IEEE Annals of the History of Computing* 16, no. 1 (1994): 46–48.

10. Some have labeled Stretch, or the IBM 7030, a machine that preceded the CDC 6600 by several years, as a supercomputer. While this may be justified, the CDC 6600 was far faster, held onto the title of world's fastest computer longer, had more installations, and was more successful commercially. It also defined Seymour Cray as the world's leading supercomputer engineer.

11. "Computers Get Faster than Ever," *Businessweek*, August 31, 1963, 28.

12. Emerson Pugh, *Building IBM* (Cambridge, MA: MIT Press, 1995), 298.

13. Ibid., 236–237.

14. Ibid., 318.

15. Ibid., 296–299.

16. Vector processing is a single-instruction multiple-data parallel-processing technique. It contrasts with the traditional processing of the time, scalar processing, where one instruction acts on each data value.

17. Elzen and MacKenzie, *Social*, 50–51.

18. While the base for supercomputer customers grew substantially in the 1970s, by late in the decade, advances in the performance of micro-processors were beginning to narrow the gap between supercomputers and other types of mainframes, minicomputers, and emerging personal computing systems.

19. Worthy, *William C. Norris*, 83–106.

20. James Parker Pearson, ed., *Digital at Work: Snapshots from the First Thirty-Five Years* (Burlington, MA: Digital Press, 1992).

21. Martin Campbell-Kelly and William Aspray, *Computer: A History of the Information Machine* (New York: Basic Books, 1996), 223.

22. Glenn Rifkin and George Harrar, *The Ultimate Entrepreneur: The Story of Ken Olsen and Digital Equipment Corporation* (Chicago: Contemporary Books, 1988), 41–43.

23. Despite the wide range of applications of DEC machines, a number of customers benefited from the Digital Equipment Corporation User Society (DECUS), a group that shared software code and insights on using DEC equipment.

24. Batch processing was an innovation of the mid-1950s to economically manage the use of computer time. It involved running machines in batches, or parts.

25. DEC and Control Data held the distinction of being the computer industry's third leading firm at different times during the decade, and the minicomputing specialist made it to number two briefly in the 1980s and again in the early 1990s. Nevertheless the industry was undergoing a transformation as personal computers were becoming increasingly powerful and ubiquitous, and the seeds for DEC's decline were already sown by this time.

26. Ibid., 224–225.

27. Pearson, *Digital*.

28. Tracy Kidder, *The Soul of a New Machine* (New York: Avon Books, 1981), 15–16.

29. Ibid.

30. Alfred D. Chandler, Jr., *Inventing the Electronic Century: The Epic Story of the Consumer Electronics and Computer Industries* (New York: Free Press, 2001), 106–108. IBM's position in the minicomputing field depends on the classification of its many systems, something that becomes increasingly complicated as the performance characteristics of minicomputers and mainframes converge by the late 1970s.

31. Peter Delisi, "A Modern-Day Tragedy: The Digital Equipment Story," *Journal of Management Inquiry* 7, no. 2 (June 1998): 116–132.

32. Gordon Bell, "What Happened? A Postscript," in *DEC Is Dead, Long Live DEC: Lessons on Innovation, Technology, and the Business Gene*, Edgar H. Schein, and others (San Francisco: Berrett-Koehler Publishers, Inc., 2003), 296.

33. Rifkin and Harrar, *Ultimate*, 104–108.

——5——

The Rise of Software as a Service, Product, Business, and Industry, 1955–1975

The previous four chapters primarily focus on computer *hardware*—the only part of computing systems that existed as a substantial and defined business in the first decade of the computer industry. While ongoing advances in hardware—memory, processing, and input/output technology—were achieved during the 1940s, 1950s, and 1960s, using computers and extending the range of their applications required developing the less tangible element of computing systems: *software*.[1] Computer technicians who plugged and unplugged hundreds of cords to open and close particular electrical connections were the first to program mainframe digital computers. In retrospect, this task, often referred to as plug-board programming, was extremely inefficient. It could take hours or even days to set up a machine to calculate certain types of mathematical equations.

The group of six individuals hired to program the ENIAC at the University of Pennsylvania's Moore School of Electrical Engineering in 1945 were all women—Kathleen McNulty, Frances Bilas, Betty Jennings, Ruth Lichterman, Elizabeth Snyder, and Marilyn Wescoff—and became known as the "ENIAC girls." While engineering computer hardware was clearly seen as a male profession, programming was initially perceived as clerical—organizing and sorting various instructions, and plugging and unplugging cords like a telephone operator—and "women's work." As the stature of programming began to grow in the 1950s, more and more men moved into this area. Resources and compensation started to expand, and it became increasingly difficult for women to enter the

Electronic Numerical Integrator and Computer programmers Betty Jennings (left) and Frances Bilas (right). Bilas is arranging the program settings on the ENIAC Master Programmer, circa mid- to late-1940s. (Courtesy of Charles Babbage Institute, University of Minnesota, Minneapolis)

profession.[2] Nevertheless, early women programmers, and particularly those from the Eckert-Mauchly Computer Corporation such as Elizabeth Snyder and Grace Murray Hopper, left a substantial mark on programming tools and techniques.[3]

By the late 1940s and early 1950s, new computers using architecture based on the ideas of Institute for Advanced Study (IAS) mathematician John von Neumann were designed to store programs that contained both data and instructions. Selecting or compiling particular sets of sequences of binary code (machine instructions containing long lists of 0s and 1s to open and close electrical connections) and inputting this information (typically using stacks of punched cards and card readers) to be stored and retrieved was a great advance over plug-board programming. The von Neumann architecture enabled programmers to develop new tools to help facilitate and ease the difficult process of programming.

COMPILERS, ASSEMBLERS, AND PROGRAMMING LANGUAGES

Many types of basic machine code instructions were used repeatedly in the late 1940s and early 1950s. Grace Murray Hopper, a naval captain who had worked with Howard Aiken on the Harvard Mark I and joined the Eckert-Mauchly Computer Corporation in 1949, provided leadership in automating the task of compiling code for the UNIVAC.[4] Sets of instructions that automated the process of selecting and reusing code to create programs were soon referred to as compilers. Compilers, such as Hopper's A-0, which was one of the first when she completed it in 1952, consisted of instruction sets that could produce new programs to address particular tasks or problems.

A program that translated between a more recognizable assembly notation and machine code soon followed. Early on these types of programs were called assemblers. As both assemblers and compilers became more advanced, they were often referred to as programming languages. Between 1954 and 1957, IBM engineer John Backus led a team that created the highly successful programming language FORTRAN (FORmula TRANslation) for the IBM 704. FORTRAN's syntax, resembling algebra, was familiar to scientists and engineers. Like many programming languages, FORTRAN took far longer than expected to produce (nearly three years rather than the planned six months) and went through various modifications and refinements during the 1960s and 1970s. For decades it was the language of choice in programming for scientific applications. FORTRAN's success resulted from its flexibility (to either reveal or conceal complexity), its ease of use for its principal users (scientists and engineers), its origin with industry-leading IBM, and its relatively early availability—1957 in its first iteration. More generally, there were clear advantages for users in selecting one or only a small number of standard programming languages.

An equally prominent programming language was COBOL (COmmon Business Oriented Language). This language became the standard in business computing. The U.S. Department of Defense (DoD) insisted on having a standard programming language for commerce to avoid the problems and costs associated with system incompatibility (the inability to use specialized and expensive applications on different computer makes and models). In 1959, the DoD formed the Committee on Data Systems and Languages (CODASYL) to design COBOL. As with the A-0, software pioneer Grace Murray Hopper played a central role in its creation. COBOL, unlike FORTRAN, used full words and phrases in English. While

COBOL was much more user-friendly for new programmers, it often proved overly simplistic and limiting for scientists, engineers, and experienced programmers. To ensure it became standard, the government announced in 1960 that it would not purchase or lease any computers or systems that were not in compliance with COBOL. During its peak in the 1960s, roughly two-thirds of all programs were written in COBOL.[5]

Many thousands of programming languages have been developed over the years, but only a small number, such as FORTRAN, COBOL, ALGOL, C, C++, Pascal, and BASIC have remained prominent for decades.[6] The economic advantages resulting from setting and adhering to standards have been critical to the concentrated use of only a few major programming languages.[7] These languages greatly expanded the labor pool of potential programmers and made the programming process more efficient. In spite of these advantages, programming languages were only one necessary tool to address the high costs, complexity, and attendant problems of programming computers for an ever-growing number of applications.

SEEKING ECONOMIES AND THE EMERGENCE OF USER GROUPS: SHARE AND DECUS

Though software did not exist as a significant business in the first decade of digital computing, this was not indicative of the increasing resources that went into programming. These costs were considerable and incurred by computer manufacturers, and more often, their customers. IBM had a substantial number of programmers by the late 1950s and continued to bring in and train large numbers of individuals for this emerging profession. By the early- to mid-1960s, with the advent of the OS/360 project, IBM became the leading company in the world for training computer programmers, surpassing the System Development Corporation.[8] IBM endured many challenges in developing its compatible operating system, OS/360, for the System/360 series.

With software, cost overruns and late deliveries were common for IBM and other firms that had originated from the office machine industry (Sperry Rand, Burroughs, and NCR). Problems associated with software development were less evident at the two major start-up computer manufacturers of the late 1950s, Control Data Corporation (CDC) and Digital Equipment Corporation (DEC), but only because CDC and DEC initially targeted scientific users, many of whom did their own programming. Before the end of their first decade, DEC and CDC became heavily involved in software development, and they were not immune to the inevitable costs, and technical and managerial challenges of this activity.

While computer manufacturers of the 1960s took much of the responsibility and risk in developing new operating systems, such as IBM had done with the OS/360, customers did a substantial amount of their own applications programming. Programming was not only a challenging enterprise; it had become the single most expensive part of maintaining a computer installation. One technique computer users used to help mitigate these problems and costs was to band together in software user groups. Representatives from organizations and companies, some competing in the same industry, would meet regularly in these groups to create libraries of code to share. They would also discuss and strategize about common problems with programming, as well as set standards. IBM users who faced the prospect of switching systems from the IBM 701 to the new IBM 704 formed SHARE, the largest of the early user groups. Competing firms such as Lockheed Aircraft, North American Aviation, Boeing Airplane, and Hughes Aircraft first met on the neutral ground of the nonprofit RAND Corporation in 1955, and by the end of the year there were more than sixty-two SHARE members, a number that would expand rapidly.[9]

Around this time other mainframe user groups began to emerge, including Remington Rand's UNIVAC Scientific Exchange (USE). Four prospective scientific users of UNIVAC 1103A computers and Sperry Rand representatives met in Los Angeles in December 1955 to form USE. Early in the group's history, it developed a USE compiler and distributed an extensive library of programs to its members. In 1956, IBM formed a second user group, GUIDE, targeting corporate and institutional customers of its 650, 702, and 705 computers. GUIDE continued to grow over the years and eventually became the world's largest user group. During the early mainframe era, however, the user groups of other computer manufacturers were in the shadow of the more prolific SHARE.

SHARE's principal purpose was economic: to take advantage of the collective knowledge and work of IBM users and counterbalance the insufficient application programming services of the computer giant. The group also helped identify and began to define the emerging profession of programming. SHARE provided a means for different types of computer programming specialists to work together, network and expand their career possibilities, and better understand their evolving relationship with their corporate and government employers. The professional status of programmers had risen from the days of the first mainframes, but still was well below the level of computer engineers. SHARE initiated a dialogue that continued to evolve throughout the 1960s and 1970s and helped reduce the gap in the stature of these two professions.[10]

While SHARE was by far the largest and most visible, and instrumental to boosting demand for new IBM systems, other user groups were perhaps even more critical to the computer companies that provided less software than IBM did. Programming responsibilities for the Digital Equipment Corporation's (DEC) earliest computers lay almost entirely with DEC customers. To help address this challenge, DEC users formed a group called DECUS (Digital Equipment Corporation User's Society), an independent organization, but one with very close ties to the minicomputer manufacturer. DEC development groups would hold workshops at DECUS meetings to obtain feedback from customers on the most desired features of new hardware, software, and services. DEC provided DECUS with a media library as well as some of the firm's employees to help facilitate the distribution of "freeware," free software shared between the user group's member companies and organizations.[11] During the 1960s and 1970s, most significant computer manufacturers had customer user groups that met on a regular basis and engaged in some of the same activities as SHARE and DECUS. These two early user groups, however, were more influential than others, and provided a fundamental service that made systems of the leading mainframe firm, IBM, and the leading minicomputer company, DEC, all the more attractive.

THE EMERGENCE AND GROWTH OF THE COMPUTING SERVICES AND PROGRAMMING SERVICES SECTORS

In addition to computer manufacturers' development of programming languages, their efforts to build systems bundled to hardware products, and their customers' programming work and cooperative efforts within user groups, a fourth mechanism existed to advance the universe of software: purchasing programming services on the market. This business tended to grow out of earlier enterprises specializing in a full range of computer and data services. As the software services business grew, a small number of firms and new start-ups began to develop software products, or standardized programs that could be sold to multiple customers. The following sections examine early computer and data service firms that pioneered the move into programming services. They also examine the subsequent evolution of some of these firms, as well as start-up companies, to break new ground in developing and marketing software products.

HERBERT ROBINSON AND C-E-I-R, INC.

In 1953, Herbert Robinson and three of his associates took over a struggling nonprofit research organization, the Council for Economic and Industrial Research (C-E-I-R). C-E-I-R had formed the previous year in Washington, D.C., to perform operations research and to conduct model building for the United States Air Force. When Robinson and his associates took the helm, C-E-I-R had yet to complete any significant work on its $350,000 air force contract. In 1954, Robinson changed the organization into a for-profit corporation, C-E-I-R, Inc., and two years later this company purchased an IBM 650.[12]

In 1957 Robinson, who had doctoral degrees from both the London School of Economics and Oxford University (economics and mathematical statistics, respectively), changed the company's name to the Corporation for Economic and Industrial Research (keeping the acronym), and the firm bought an IBM 704. This machine and subsequent digital computers were critical to the firm's incorporation of modeling, simulation, and other computer-based analytical techniques to assist its government and corporate clients. Orchard Hayes was in charge of computing and programming services for the company, a difficult task at the time, as it was hard to find competent programmers. Hayes had to institute a training program and hire individuals to be programmers who had no experience with computers. Despite the challenges, by the late 1950s C-E-I-R became increasingly proficient in this area, providing a wide range of computer and programming services, such as business data processing and custom software development. Before the end of the decade C-E-I-R, Inc., had an initial public offering. The firm began to implement its plans to set up computer service operations in larger cities throughout the United States and Europe, often by taking over smaller firms such as General Analysis Corporation in Los Angeles and Data-Tech in Hartford, Connecticut.[13]

During the 1960s C-E-I-R's computing and programming services began to dwarf the other more traditional analytical services it provided. In 1961, the company surpassed $10 million in annual revenue for the first time, aided by developing major new systems such as a data processing system for Connecticut's motor vehicle registration and computer-based analytical tools to evaluate ballistic missile systems for the Defense Research Corporation. In 1967, Herbert Robinson reported to C-E-I-R's Board of Directors that for the past seven years the core of the firm's business had been repetitive data processing based on a combination of "computer time" (for profit leverage) and "talent know-how" (advanced applications programming to hold customers). It had engaged heavily in scientific and engineering computations, linear programming, critical path scheduling, bank data processing, business data processing, and leasing computer time.[14] The company had also begun to use time-sharing techniques to enhance the efficient use of computing resources. C-E-I-R recognized that time-sharing, and software exploited through proprietary control programs, would be critical to its future. Proprietary control programs could give C-E-I-R and other such companies advantages and even "near-monopoly" benefits previously only enjoyed by the leading hardware and telecommunication companies.[15]

While C-E-I-R endured some operating losses in the early 1960s as it invested extensively in computing equipment, including IBM 7090s and other powerful mainframes of the time, it achieved a net income of $1.57 million on sales of $16.36 million in 1964.[16] As it invested in more equipment and resources in national and global expansion in the coming years, and as competition for computing services intensified, its profit margins decreased. Creating new innovative software tools held out the possibility of controlling small segments of the market, but this proved elusive in practice as there were hundreds of processing and software services firms by the mid-1960s, and C-E-I-R held less than 2 percent of the U.S. field. Looking back, Herbert Robinson believed that the company had suffered from being a pioneer in many aspects of computer services, incurring large expenditures in charting unknown terrain upon which future competitors capitalized. Robinson and the other top executives reflected that they had jumped into a number of areas of computing services without a clear long-term strategy of how they would profit from them over the long-term. Profound swings in demand led to significant periods of idleness for C-E-I-R's professional staff.[17]

In spite of the business challenges C-E-I-R faced as a technological innovator, the software services sector looked increasingly bright in the 1960s. The proliferation of computers continued alongside the programming skill of many business customers. The software provided by mainframe companies continued to be inadequate to meet the ever-expanding need for application tools. The attractiveness of the software services sector, the past deficiency of Control Data Corporation in this area, and the recent financial struggles of C-E-I-R (and hence the declining market value of the company) did not escape the notice of the supercomputer manufacturer's CEO William Norris. In 1967, Control Data purchased C-E-I-R, Inc., to take advantage of the fast-growing computing and software services field. More specifically, CDC wanted to increase the profitability of its computer services work and obtain skilled personnel in business data processing and time-sharing.[18]

JOHN SHELDON, ELMER KUBIE, AND THE COMPUTER USAGE COMPANY

Computer Usage Company started in March 1955, two years after C-E-I-R, but immediately moved into software contracting and was likely the first firm in this business in the world. John Sheldon and Elmer Kubie, both of whom had worked at IBM's Technical Computing Bureau during the early 1950s, founded the company. Shortly before this, Sheldon had left IBM to attend graduate school in mathematical physics at Columbia University and Kubie had joined General Electric as an operations research consultant. Sheldon, having raised $40,000 in start-up funds from family and friends, approached Kubie, former head of IBM's Applied Science mathematical group, about forming a programming services company. Kubie was excited by Sheldon's plan and they quickly started the firm. Initially, the business was run out of Sheldon's New York City apartment, but within months they had brought in enough business to afford office space in Manhattan. During its first year of operation, Computer Usage earned revenue of $200,000 and profits of $10,000.[19]

Computer Usage rented an IBM 701 and in its first years obtained contracts from the California Research Corporation as well as NASA to program systems for technical applications. By the late 1950s, the company focused most of its work on systems and applications software and had contracts to do custom programming for a wide range of tasks, including nuclear reactor design, supersonic air flow, linear programming, inventory management, traffic analysis, cataloging, insurance accounting, and business data processing (payroll, sales analysis, inventory management, cost analysis, etc.). It also engaged in specialized programs to develop operating systems, compilers, assemblers, and programming languages for its clients.[20]

Computer Usage preceded but was similar to many subsequent computer service firms of the late 1950s and 1960s. It was a small operation that began with a few programmers and grew to employ several dozen within its first five years. It had multiple offices, opening up branches in Washington, D.C., and Los Angeles within its first decade, and in 1962 had a total of 140 employees, annual revenue of $2 million, and profits of $60,000. At the firm's peak in 1967 it had a dozen offices, 700 employees, and net income of $600,000 on $13,000,000 in revenue. The firm diversified from analysis and programming services into selling computer time, proprietary software as a support to hardware, and other areas. Computer Usage's diversification, however, brought many challenges and the firm experienced its first annual net loss in 1969, a deficit of $430,000.[21] This was followed by a number of up and down years before a series of major losses pushed the firm into bankruptcy in the mid-1980s.

COMPUTER SCIENCES CORPORATION

Like C-E-I-R, Computer Usage's profit margin was quite modest compared to the computer manufacturers of the time, especially IBM. Most of the early software service start-up firms were acquired or out of business within a decade. Computer Sciences Corporation, a firm founded in Los Angeles in 1959 by Fletcher Jones, Robert Patrick, and Roy Nutt, is one of the remarkable exceptions. Behind the business leadership of Jones, who had been a senior data processing manager with North American Aviation and a founding member of SHARE, and Nutt, who provided superior technical leadership, Computer Sciences contracted to produce a massive compiler, FACT, for Honeywell in 1959. Computer Sciences' portion of the FACT project, which took eighteen months and utilized seventeen programmer years of labor, was paid for by Honeywell in stages and thus obviated Computer Sciences' need for start-up capital—the company earned revenue of $300,000 for the first year of the project. Honeywell's experience, having to foot the entire bill for cost overruns, led to its reluctance to give open-ended time and materials contracts in the future. Nevertheless, this early compiler provided visibility for Honeywell in computing at a critical time and helped it build brand recognition for selling hardware.[22]

In retrospect, the FACT project helped Computer Sciences practice and refine its unparalleled skills in software development and project management, while receiving substantial income along the way. This gave it a tremendous competitive advantage over other early software services firms that struggled financially in their first years.[23] Though COBOL largely superseded FACT in the corporate marketplace, Computer Sciences Corporation never looked back.

It remains a successful company, has hundreds of facilities worldwide, tens of thousands of employees, and had annual revenue
exceeding $11 billion in both 2002 and 2003, and more than $14
billion in 2004.[24]

THE SYSTEM DEVELOPMENT CORPORATION

System Development Corporation differed from C-E-I-R, CUC
(Computer Usage Corporation), and Computer Sciences in that it
was originally formed as a division of the nonprofit RAND Corporation, and long remained a nonprofit entity. In 1955, the RAND
Corporation, which received most of its funding from the U.S. Air
Force, launched the System Development Division to conduct
computer programming work on the Department of Defense's
Semi-Automatic Ground Environment (SAGE) air defense system,
study human machine symbiosis, and provide systems training.
In 1957, the System Development Division was spun off and became the nonprofit System Development Corporation (SDC), but
this had minimal short-term impact on its operations. Almost all
of the roughly 1,800 employees remained, and the primary project, programming for SAGE, continued uninterrupted. By this
time, the employees of SDC outnumbered that of its parent, the
RAND Corporation.[25]

In the late 1950s, SDC had roughly 700 programmers, which
represented an estimated one-half of computer programmers in
the United States at that time. The SAGE program, in its first iteration, was completed in 1958. It contained 1.1 million lines of
code, 230,000 for the operating system and 870,000 for support
programs and utilities. Over the next couple of years the programming group produced many versions of the operating program that could handle different configurations. By 1962, the
SAGE system was complete and operational. It was the largest
programming project in the world to that point. Programming expenditures totaled $150 million, a tremendous sum, but less than
2 percent of the estimated $8 billion dollar cost of SAGE.[26] By the
mid-1960s many of the programmers who had worked for System
Development on SAGE went on to other programming jobs. The
programming work force was cut by two-thirds by the second half
of the 1960s and the nonprofit firm was doing a variety of smaller
scale work on DoD contracts and for a few large corporations.

In 1968, SDC became a for-profit enterprise and in 1980 it was
taken over by the Burroughs Corporation. After the early 1960s,
SDC never regained the level of importance it had achieved in programming SAGE. Nevertheless, SDC had trained many of the first

generation of computer programmers. It had also anticipated many of the challenges that would plague future large-scale software projects, particularly the difficulty of efficiently integrating the work of many different programmers and scaling up programming efforts. In short, it provided infrastructure for the emerging computing and software services industry, while other firms reaped the benefits of the foundation it helped lay.

H. ROSS PEROT AND ELECTRONIC DATA SYSTEMS

The most financially successful computing and programming services firms characteristically found niches where they became indispensable to large companies. No enterprise did this better than Electronic Data Systems (EDS), a firm founded by H. Ross Perot in 1962. By this time a substantial number of larger corporations had bought or leased computers for their data processing departments. Some of these firms soon found that maintaining these departments was a drain on resources and that many services could be obtained on the market for less. This was sometimes the result of poor performance of data processing departments, but more often was a matter of fluctuating demand resulting in frequent periods of excess capacity. Shutting down the data processing department, however, was not an attractive solution. These companies had invested in infrastructure they did not want to write off immediately and had data processing employees they preferred not to terminate. Perot came up with a highly successful strategy to capitalize on this. EDS would come in and take over a firm's data processing services for a fixed fee that was below the current cost of running the department. In managing these facilities, EDS would retain most or all of the existing employees. Because EDS could almost always use human and computing resources for work on other EDS projects or contracts, there was rarely excess capacity. Perot ran these departments for far less than EDS's customers had previously done, and most of the savings went to his firm. Perot's strategy soon brought imitators, but none were as successful as EDS, a first-mover that established a large base of loyal customers during the 1960s.

Likewise, Automatic Data Processing (ADP) of Clifton, New Jersey, demonstrated the strategic advantage of obtaining a leadership position in a niche of the computing and software services area. The firm was established in 1949, as Automatic Payrolls, and used mechanical accounting machines to do payroll services for corporations and other organizations. In 1961 the firm went public, purchased its first digital computer (an IBM 1401), and changed its name to Automatic Data Processing, Inc. (retaining the acronym). Under the leadership of cofounders Frank Lautenberg (CEO and chairman) and Henry Taub (chief planner and strategist), the company grew at a phenomenal rate. By 1970 it was processing the payroll of 7,000 firms. Lautenberg would go on to have a distinguished career as a four-term U.S. Senator from the State of New Jersey.[27]

While Computer Usage, C-E-I-R, and several other companies had been the earliest movers in computing and software services, and were somewhat diversified in the range of services provided, they had only modest success. EDS and ADP, on the other hand, came up with fairly simple, but unique, long-term strategies that they could employ with many corporate customers and enterprises worldwide. Another strategy to capitalize on volume was focusing on turning software into a product that could be mass produced and sold. In time, this would be a highly successful industry sector, and in the personal computer era, it produced one of the leading firms (in terms of capitalization and revenue) in the United States, Microsoft, and the richest man in the world, Bill Gates. (See chapters 7 and 8 for additional discussion on the personal computer software industry).

THE EMERGENCE OF SOFTWARE PRODUCTS

Software products had a long history prior to the existence of retail computer stores and electronics outlets selling ubiquitous Microsoft operating systems and applications, computer games, and other shrink-wrapped boxed software. The earliest software products came from computer and software service firms that recognized they could sell certain standard software programs instead of creating unique code for every client. Computer trade events, industry catalogs, and small sales forces were the primary mechanisms used to spread the word about new software products, prior to the emergence of retail outlets. This section will explore three early producers of software products: Applied Data Research (ADR), Informatics, and the Cullinane Corporation. ADR was the first service firm to market an important and widely used software product. Informatics was the service company that developed the most commercially successful product of the early software products era. And Cullinane Corporation was the first software products start-up company in the United States.

MARTIN GOETZ AND APPLIED DATA RESEARCH

In 1954, Martin Goetz responded to a Remington Rand advertisement in the *New York Times* for a relatively new profession: computer programmer. After attending the standard twelve-week training course, Goetz began an assignment seeking to obtain a major programming contract for Remington Rand from the Consolidated Edison Company. IBM beat out Remington Rand to contract with this client, giving Goetz his first exposure to the effectiveness of IBM's account control in both computer hardware and software services. Despite the challenges IBM posed for Remington Rand (and Sperry Rand), during the next half decade Goetz effectively worked on numerous projects to help program sorting routines, debugging aids, and other software tools for Remington Rand clients.[28]

In 1959, Goetz left Sperry Rand to help found a software services start-up firm, Applied Data Research (ADR) in Princeton, New Jersey. For its first several years, ADR was solely a programming service firm. It competed with companies such as Computer Usage and the Computer Sciences Corporation. In the early 1960s, ADR developed an operations software system for Radio Corporation of America (RCA); however, the electronics giant did not follow through with the project and ADR appeared to be stuck with the design cost. Believing it a successful system, ADR took the bold move of completing the development of the automatic flowchart generator and attempted to sell it to RCA's base of about 100 RCA 501 users. Attempting to sell a standard software system to multiple customers was unprecedented at the time. Though ADR only sold two licenses for its system (named Autoflow) to RCA customers, unconsciously, Goetz and others at ADR had initiated the software products business.[29]

In the mid-1960s, ADR, still a relatively small firm with three offices, roughly thirty employees, and less than a $1 million in annual revenue, went public and raised more than $6 million. This influx of capital allowed the firm to expand its Software Products Division, which was led by Goetz. ADR soon reprogrammed a version of Autoflow called 1401 Autocoder for the most popular computer of the time, the IBM 1401. Initially, using its software services sales personnel, ADR was able to sell a number of 1401 Autocoder systems to IBM customers. The company soon learned, however, that IBM was producing an inferior, but free, flowchart-generating software program, IBM Flowcharter. Prospective ADR customers of 1401 Autocoder began to press IBM for improvements to Flowcharter. IBM viewed its large programming staff and

118

significant capabilities in this area as an important advantage to tie customers to IBM hardware, its primary concern at the time. ADR realized that, given the nonlevel playing field resulting from IBM's extensive programming resources, marketing, and customer base, it was probably prudent to steer clear of producing software for IBM customers.[30]

ADR, and other emerging software products producers, however, did have another option: trying to level the playing field. In 1967, ADR and several other software companies brought a complaint to the U.S. Justice Department concerning IBM's pre-announcements, "free software," and other alleged anticompetitive practices used to maintain its dominance of hardware. The software companies also emphasized the negative impact of IBM's actions on the growth of the nascent software products industry. In April 1969, ADR sued IBM for using pre-announcements and other tactics that monopolized the software products trade. Two months later, facing active legal proceedings from ADR and likely future legal action from the Justice Department and various hardware manufacturers, IBM announced that it would "unbundle" its software (price and sell it as a separate product from its hardware) at the beginning of 1970.

ADR, having incurred extensive legal costs and having suffered many months of negative cash flow, settled the suit with IBM later that year, receiving $2 million and some other concessions. Specifically, IBM agreed to market Autoflow abroad, as well as to use Autoflow and ADR's Librarian software system internally. This, coupled with a major stock offering the previous year, provided ADR with much needed funds to continue to develop new products. By the start of 1969 there had never been greater enthusiasm for the future of software products as a business. ADR's market valuation was indicative of an exuberance that holds many similarities to that of the dot.com bubble of the late 1990s. ADR's stock peaked at $40 per share that year and the company's market valuation was just shy of $40 million. It would be a number of years, however, before software products would produce substantial and sustainable net income for ADR, and the company's stock declined to $1 per share during the following decade.[31]

MARTIN GOETZ'S EARLY LEADERSHIP IN PROTECTING SOFTWARE AS INTELLECTUAL PROPERTY

In addition to leading the way with software products, ADR and Martin Goetz provided leadership in efforts to protect software as intellectual property. Software was an atypical technology that presented some challenges with regard to protecting it. Most significantly, it had no physical presence other than the memory device that held the code. In 1967, Martin Goetz applied for a patent for Autoflow. Though many software products were pending, Goetz and ADR received the first software patent in April 1968. Key to receiving the patent, Goetz had to present Autoflow as a technique, analogous to a manufacturing *process*, rather than as a manufactured *product*.

Copyright law was also a potential means for protecting software as intellectual property, but it too presented practical difficulties. Back in 1964, the U.S. Congress had passed legislation that granted protection for a software program if it was deemed to be a "literary expression." While the law provided protection against making an exact copy of software code, it did not protect against the know-how contained in the algorithms of the program. Programmers could quickly extract this know-how from a program and reverse engineer it to be different in form—change the actual code, but essentially retain its intellectual process and structure.

Trademarks were also a means used by software firms to protect intellectual property through branding. This did not protect the actual code and structure, but it helped to strengthen bonds with existing customers, as well as attract new ones. While patents, copyrights, and trademarks were imperfect and only a partially effective early means to protect software as intellectual property, they did offer some hope that stronger protection might lie ahead.

WALTER BAUER, JOHN POSTLEY, AND INFORMATICS

Like ADR, Informatics was a company that engaged in software services for roughly a half-decade before making the jump to enter the field of software products. It did this a few years after ADR and did not have the same success in trying to patent its primary software product. It also did not have the high-profile victory over IBM that was achieved by ADR. Nevertheless, its role in setting trends for the early development of the software products trade was unmatched. It achieved this through the early entrepreneurial vision and skill of Walter Bauer in starting and leading Informatics, and the talented product development, promotion, and marketing management of John Postley.

In 1956, Ramo-Wooldridge Corporation merged with Thompson Industries to form Thompson Ramo-Wooldridge (TRW). At the time of the merger, the Ramo-Wooldridge Division increasingly concentrated its efforts on designing computer systems and developing custom programming services for military and corporate clients. In 1959, Bauer, who had received a doctorate in mathematics from the University of Michigan in 1951, became manager of the Ramo-Wooldridge Information System Department. It was the commercial counterpart to the Ramo-Wooldridge Division's Computation and Data Reduction Center of Space Technology Laboratories, a group of around 250 individuals that Bauer had previously managed. At the Information System Department, Bauer led efforts to develop the nation's first operational computerized automobile traffic control system (for Los Angeles), the "polymorphic" computer of the Transit Satellite Project, and computer programming for the Department of Defense Damage Assessment Center.[32]

In 1961 Bauer, who was well connected to many in the programming services area through his involvement in the Association of Computing Machinery (ACM), the American Federation of Information Processing Societies (AFIPS), and the International Federation of Information Processing Societies (IFIPS), decided to develop a plan to form a new company to specialize in computer applications, systems analysis and development, programming, and computer-time sales. Joined by two TRW colleagues, Werner Frank and Richard Hill, they sought venture capital for this new firm.

Around this time, Erwin Tomash, a former engineer with Engineering Research Associates and vice president of marketing for Telemeter Magnetics, Inc. (a manufacturer of computer memory systems), was also looking to start a new company with several partners, and he met with Bauer and Hill to discuss their mutual plans.[33] In February 1962, Tomash founded computer peripherals firm Data Products Corporation (soon thereafter Dataproducts Corporation) and agreed to fund Bauer's venture as a subsidiary that would support Data Product's hardware as well as generate independent business. Both Data Products and its subsidiary, Informatics, Inc., were operational by April 1962. In the early months, Informatics consisted of only the three founders. During August of that year it brought on Frank Wagner, a computer engineer from North American Aviation and past president of SHARE, as director of plans and programs.

Initially, Informatics struggled with small contracts before landing significant deals in the next couple of years to provide programming services to Rome Air Development Center, the U.S. Military Command Systems Support Center, and the U.S. Navy's Pacific Missile Range. While Informatics was doing well at building and maintaining a client base, Bauer became interested in expanding the company for faster growth. One fortuitous action Bauer took was acquiring the Advanced Information System (AIS) Division of Hughes Dynamics, and in the process, bringing on board AIS's John Postley, and the file-management program he had created, MARK III.

John Postley had been the director of computing at Northronics Division of North American Aviation, head of the RAND Corporation's Data Processing Group Logistics Department, and vice president of Advanced Information Systems, Inc., before the latter was acquired by Hughes Dynamics. He had known the principals of Informatics through the ACM, a connection that was likely influential when Hughes Dynamics put up the AIS Division for sale in 1964. Informatics received a great bargain—in fact Hughes Dynamics paid Informatics $38,000 to take over the division and its modest contractual liabilities.[34]

MARK III was actually a fourth-generation retrieval and listing or file-management system. Postley had been a leader on its earlier iterations: the Generalized Information Retrieval and Listing System (GIRLS) that AIS developed for Douglas Aircraft, MARK I, and MARK II. File management performed two primary functions: (1) handling routine data management and preventing the need for special file-management systems, and (2) generating specified reports. It could reduce programming tasks substantially and save users of large data sets enormous amounts of time and computing resources. While GIRLS, MARK I, and MARK II were moderately successful, they were also part of a fundamental learning process. When MARK III was used by the city of Alexandria, Virginia, in 1965 to process a five-year census and generate a number of specialized reports, the true worth of the system became evident. By this time, Postley already was committed to the idea of turning the next version of his file-management system into a product.

Postley provided estimates of $500,000 to turn Mark III, a system that was refined for each user, into an off-the-shelf product to be sold in standard form: Mark IV. At this time, $500,000 represented about 12 percent of Informatics' annual revenue. Bauer was reluctant to commit such a large sum, despite the fact that he favored the idea of moving into the software products area. The time was ripe, as IBM had just come out with its popular System/360 series the previous year. While IBM was potentially a formidable future competitor, the computer giant's new system meant that the hardware side had never been more standardized. By creating Mark IV for the IBM System/360 series, Informatics would have a ready market of thousands of potential customers and might reasonably be able to expect dozens of sales. Even with such prospects, Bauer believed the risk/reward pendulum seemed far too heavily weighted on the risk side. Thus, he came up with a different model, and asked Postley to find some sponsors.[35]

Companies that took on the role as sponsors of MARK IV would purchase the file-management software for their own use, but would also receive modest royalties from Informatics' sales of the program to other customers. Between November 1966 and July 1967 Postley secured five sponsors putting up a total of $451,000: Standard Oil of Indiana ($100,000), National Dairy Industries ($90,000), Allen-Bradley, Inc. ($100,000), Getty Oil ($110,000), and Prudential ($51,000). Tomash and Bauer agreed that they could come up with the last $50,000 internally if it were necessary.[36]

The Mark IV development project proceeded quickly. The project team decided upon the design features in the second half of 1967 and began programming in the latter part of the year. The team, which initially consisted of only a dozen individuals, focused on three key characteristics: (1) standard applications–oriented features to enable users to efficiently get results, (2) simplicity of use by noncomputer-oriented individuals, and (3) the accommodation of fixed-format files, chained files, hierarchical files, files with trailer records, and COBOL compatible files.[37] In addition to the programming, Informatics now had to concentrate on packaging, marketing, and product pricing.

At the time of the product launch of Mark IV in November 1967, Informatics had no model for pricing it. ADR had priced Autoflow at $2,400 per unit, but Mark IV was a more involved and versatile product that had cost far more to develop. It was not merely a system to make computing easier (like Autoflow); for many organizations it made computing possible. Postley thought that the market would bear $100,000.[38]

Like media products or pharmaceuticals, the marginal production cost of software is minimal—expenditures lie with the original cost of development, and to a varying and often substantial degree, the marketing and selling cost. In the end, Informatics hired a consulting company to conduct market research and went with a figure in the middle of this consulting firm's estimated range, setting the price at $30,000.[39] Bauer later remarked that potential customers were "astounded" at that amount. Most individuals and organizations, given past dealings with hardware firms, thought of software as something that was free. Despite these initial reactions, many customers paid this price. In the first eighteen months following Informatics' MARK IV product launch,

Table 5.1
Revenue and Profit Generated for Informatics by Mark IV
(in millions of dollars)

Year	Revenue	Profit	Profit Margin
1969	$2.8	($0.1)	--
1970	$2.8	$0.3	10.7%
1971	$3.4	$0.5	14.7%
1972	$4.1	$0.7	17.0%
1973	$7.5	$2.0	26.7%
1974	$8.2	$1.1	13.4%
1975	$8.4	$0.3	3.6%
1976	$11.1	$1.8	16.2%
1977	$13.0	$1.6	12.3%
1978	$15.5	$1.6	10.3%

Source: Richard L. Forman, *Fulfilling the Computer's Promise: The History of Informatics, 1962–1982* (Woodland Hills, CA: Informatics General Corporation, 1985), 9–40.

the firm sold more than 130 units. Mark IV generated far more revenue than any other software product in the succeeding decade, selling thousands of copies. It was the first software product to reach the cumulative $1 million, $10 million, and $100 million revenue levels (see Table 5.1). Postley led the effort to establish a sales force similar in style to IBM's, though far smaller. In fact, Postley intentionally kept the sales force small (under twenty sales representatives throughout the early 1970s) because he felt there were few individuals that possessed the technical ability and understanding to adequately represent his product.[40]

Informatics had a number of other software products, but none would be as important to the company, financially or otherwise, as MARK IV. Within several years it altered the nature of the firm. Prior to MARK IV, a substantial amount of revenue had come from sizable government contracts. By 1969, behind MARK IV, Informatics had become a major supplier of software products to industry. Informatics used its revenue to become more an acquirer of new software products than a designer. It had also established a substantial international base by this time. Nevertheless, even with the success with MARK IV and the firm's newfound commitment to software products, Informatics' primary business remained in software services.

When the economic recession of 1970–1971 hit, it was particularly devastating to software companies. Revenue from MARK IV helped Informatics weather the storm and offset operating losses from other areas of the company, including programming services. MARK IV's highest margins were achieved in the first half of the 1970s. More broadly, MARK IV, through its powerful file-management and report-generating functions, its ease of use, and the skill and persistence of its designer, John Postley, succeeded in helping to bring a number of organizations into the world of computers.

JOHN CULLINANE AND THE CULLINANE CORPORATION

While the Cullinane Corporation did not have an individual product that rivaled the success of Informatics' MARK IV, its contribution to the early software products business was equally strong. The Cullinane Corporation, founded by John Cullinane in 1968, was the first of the Wall Street–financed software products houses. Unlike Informatics, software products, rather than services, rapidly became the Cullinane Corporation's primary business. Shortly after the company's difficult start in 1968, it achieved thirteen consecutive years of annual revenue and profit growth of more than 50 percent. John Cullinane had a knack for selling—whether it was selling innovative ideas to financiers who backed his company or selling software systems to corporate executives of midsized to large companies. He was arguably the most skilled entrepreneur of the first wave of software products pioneers.

Cullinane grew up in Arlington, Massachusetts, and while attending Northeastern University he began working for Arthur D. Little in 1954. It was there he first became exposed to computer technology and upon graduating, was hired full-time as a computer operator for Arthur D. Little. He was sent to programming school, and shortly thereafter responded to an advertisement for a sales position with C-E-I-R. He soon became director of C-E-I-R's

Boston operation and brought a losing center to profitability. Always seeking new challenges, he moved on to Philip Hankins & Company. At this firm, he began to reason that software could effectively be made into a product rather than just sold as a service. The notion came to him after two banks both wanted a programming system for payroll. Philip Hankins & Company had developed a system for Marine Midland Bank of Buffalo, and soon thereafter a firm with the same hardware configuration, First National State Bank of New Jersey, wanted a similar application. Cullinane had sold the system to Marine Midland for $35,000 and worked out an agreement to pay this bank $5,000 for the rights to sell the identical system to First National State.[41]

Cullinane left Philip Hankins & Company to join the consulting firm, Auerbach, and run the company's Boston operation. By this time he was becoming increasingly concerned about obtaining an ownership stake in a firm and reaping the benefits of his successful management. This was not possible at Auerbach, as its founder, Isaac Auerbach, owned nearly all the equity in the firm. In 1968, with the memory of what he had done with the two banks while at Philip Hankins & Company still fresh in his mind, as well as his knowledge of the recent success of Autoflow and MARK IV, he decided to develop a proposal to start a firm that would market software products. Unlike any of the software product pioneers who preceded him, he did not have a service firm as a base. He sought to raise capital from Wall Street financiers for a dedicated software products company and came to them armed with non-binding letters of intent from potential corporate customers. This innovative strategy helped sway the financiers he met with to help him raise $450,000.[42]

The Cullinane Corporation's first product was a Program Library Update System, soon followed by a report generator named Culprit. These early products had some useful attributes, but overall the firm was losing money. This was in part the result of the challenge of a new firm in a new field, but also was influenced by a downturn in the economy and the market for software at the end of the 1960s and beginning of the 1970s. Cullinane had to make the difficult decision to cut his staff of nine people back to five, which included letting individuals go who were fundamental to the creation of both Program Library Update System and Culprit. He, however, learned that the smaller staff was more dedicated to serving customers, and his firm developed a new iteration of Culprit that included a file-matching capability, a popular feature absent from the original program.[43]

Because Cullinane recognized that some customers were using

Culprit for auditing purposes, he renamed it EDP Auditor and his firm added some audit routines, including statistical sampling and verification notices. While some customers understood how the program could be effectively used for auditing purposes, Cullinane recognized that others did not. He addressed this by starting an EDP user group. The first meeting included more than eighty customers. In addition to this, the Cullinane Corporation also provided strong individual technical support. All of a sudden the company was no longer primarily marketing to data processing departments, but instead was providing a product and support to auditing departments of banks and other major financial corporations. Essentially the same program the Cullinane Corporation had difficulty selling to data processing departments for $10,000 in 1971, it was easily selling to finance and auditing departments for $20,000 in 1972. In the process, it was creating pressure for data processing units to buy the product as well. This was the turning point for the Cullinane Corporation, and it began its unparalleled record of continuous and rapid growth in revenue and earnings.[44]

The Cullinane Corporation put some money in advertising, including an early full-page advertisement in the *Wall Street Journal* entitled "Why Re-invent the Software Wheel?" Though the ad paid for itself in obtaining some new customers, the firm achieved its greatest success through showing persistence in getting in the door to do demonstrations, impressing potential customers, adding them to its loyal base, and cross-selling. Key to this strategy was the firm's strong product development and unparalleled service and support.[45]

In the first several years, the software systems of the Cullinane Corporation had been developed in-house. Ironically, it was not until 1972 that the company, by accident, fell into engaging in what had been its original strategy: to purchase successful software applications developed for clients and then repackage them as products. A member of an ACM panel recommended to Cullinane that he sell BF Goodrich's IDMS (Integrated Database Management System) that had originated with General Electric's IDS (Integrated Database System). Shortly thereafter, the Cullinane Corporation acquired IDMS from BF Goodrich and expanded and refined the successful system, adding more than a few million lines of code to the original 30,000 instructions.[46] The firm's ability both to improve upon and fully support the software that it sold was critical. The Cullinane Corporation transformed itself into a one-stop shop for many types of business software that ran on IBM systems, and in the database field competed against such

127

powerhouses as IBM and software database specialist Cincom, a firm that had developed a highly popular database product named Total. Cullinane, with a workforce of fifteen people, was effectively coexisting, and at times taking business away from some of the giants in the early 1970s.

In 1978, Cullinane and his investors decided to capitalize on the firm's success and took it public. Soon thereafter IBM announced a new series of computers, the 4300 series. The Cullinane Corporation moved quickly to develop a compatible IDMS, and in the coming year developed a dictionary-driven database version of the program, a feature that IBM did not match. While Cullinane and his senior sales staff had marketed to data processing and auditing departments in the firm's early years, he now met directly with top executives and sold full packages for hundreds of thousands of dollars rather than individual systems for tens of thousands. The Cullinane Corporation's staff of fifteen had grown to exceed 1,000. In 1983, the Cullinane Corporation became the first software product firm to be listed on the New York Stock Exchange. The company was now under the microscope of financial analysts and had to be increasingly focused on quarterly results. Given this environment, Cullinane lost some interest and moved from CEO to chairman of the board. In this role, he took a far less active role in the management of the firm. Just prior to this, he renamed the company Cullinet. He wanted "his name back," but also wanted to assure the firm would be recognizable to past customers.[47]

The database software sector was also beginning to switch toward a new model, relational databases. This trend began as a result of technology developed at IBM by research scientist Edgar Codd. Cullinet suffered from not moving in this direction.[48] The shift to relational database software also gave rise to new entrants such as Larry Ellison's System Development Laboratories, which he founded in Belmont, California, in 1977. In 1982, Ellison renamed the company after its relational database product: Oracle. By this time, the Oracle Corporation had begun to perfect its originally "bug-infested" software, and had an initial public offering. In 1986, Oracle had software on more than 3,000 minicomputer and mainframe installations.[49]

According to John Cullinane, Cullinet became too tied to existing products and ways of doing things, and lacked the customer focus that had led to the firm's prior success. While the company was slow to recognize the importance of relational database software, the problems were broader in his mind. New managers made some acquisitions that did not work out and the staff had grown to 2,400, despite financial setbacks. Cullinane returned to do some cost cutting and repositioning of the firm, but in 1989 sold Cullinet to Computer Associates for $320 million.[50]

Computer Associates (CA) was a software company founded by software salesperson Charles Wang in June 1976. In the beginning, the firm had just one product, CA Sort. It sold 200 copies of this sorting program during its first year at $3,000 apiece. In the 1980s and 1990s, CA directly or indirectly acquired many of the companies and products that were instrumental to the early software products industry, including firms such as ADR, Cullinet, Pansophic Systems, and Uccel.[51] CA has been successful at selling a wide range of disparate business software products over the years (both acquired products and internally developed products) and remains one of the largest software companies in the world with a market capitalization exceeding $15 billion.[52] The company is a holder of hundreds of software patents and generates much of its revenue from licenses to customers. CA's success was achieved despite its failed attempt to gain a major position in the personal computer software field through acquisitions in the 1980s.

THE EMERGING SOFTWARE INDUSTRY IN PERSPECTIVE

In the early years of the software services business, companies such as Computer Usage, C-E-I-R, and Computer Science Corporation fought hard for relatively meager net income. They often depended on DoD and other government contracts in the beginning. Profit margins rarely exceeded 15 percent for such companies and were often limited to single digits. Service companies typically had a cluster of areas they focused upon to enable them to recycle some code, but often chose to move beyond their core area in order to obtain clients, and many jobs required considerable new programming to meet the demands of customers. Predicting costs was challenging, and effective estimates, bidding, and project management were critical to remaining profitable.

Marketing software products provided a different business model, one in which initial development costs remained high, but additional units could be produced with minimal cost. Marketing became ever more critical, and bidding and cost estimates were less important than having a good set of products and an effective sales force. Martin Goetz and ADR led the way in this new endeavor with Autoflow, and John Postley soon followed with

Informatics' even more successful MARK IV. Despite these important products, both firms were still primarily programming service companies for a number of years—and this never ceased to be Informatics' main business. Alternatively, the Cullinane Corporation focused on products from the beginning. After a rocky start, it had more than a dozen years of strong financial results prior to being bypassed by IBM and new entrants in the database and other fields.

The development of the early software industry was influenced by broader economic events of the time and internal dynamics within the larger business of computing technology and its strategic, legal, and social environment. IBM's decision to unbundle in 1969 was a critical event to the software industry, but did not bring the trade into being, and its impact was modest in the short term.

This decision extended from an IBM Unbundling Task Force, which began examining the issue in 1967.[53] Though still small, the emergence and growth of the software product sector was well in place by the time of IBM's decision. Both the decision and its implementation in the coming year lent momentum to the software products trade. Prior to this, software pioneers such as Martin Goetz and John Postley had to battle the strong and widely held perception that software was a free service properly provided by mainframe computer manufacturers. It was the superiority of the products of Informatics, ADR, and others that helped motivate IBM to invest more in software in the 1960s and that allowed software companies to sell some software products in spite of "free" IBM software.

With pending antitrust litigation alleging IBM's unfair practices to dominate computer hardware, IBM decided that unbundling was the prudent course of action. The firm's fears became reality in January 1969 when the U.S. Justice Department filed an antitrust case against IBM. The Justice Department was not concerned with giving a boost to an emerging software industry or with complaints by firms in this trade, but rather, was focused on limiting IBM's use of bundled software, pre-announcements, and other practices that gave the computer giant advantages and unrivaled power in dominating the hardware trade.[54]

Antitrust did not appear to be the sole factor for IBM in deciding to unbundle. An emulator, called Liberator, that allowed Honeywell computers to run software developed for the IBM 1401 in 1963, and two years later, the RCA Spectra 70 series that ran software of the IBM System/360 series, forced the computer giant to reflect on the fact that it was spending an increasing amount of resources on software that could run on competitors' hardware.[55] IBM's programming operations had grown to include nearly 4,000 employees and fifteen laboratories internationally by the late 1960s, and expenditures in this area were well over $50 million annually and expanding rapidly.[56]

When IBM unbundled software, the firm initially implemented a 3 percent reduction in the price of its hardware and thus was not assigning a cost to software in line with what many felt the firm was spending on this activity. IBM justified the 3 percent figure as the percentage of software development employees compared to hardware development employees. This included all manufacturing and engineering staff, the former being a fundamental activity on the hardware but not the software side. Nevertheless, the mere separation of software and hardware was a watershed event that, despite broader economic problems in the United States, would give a modest boost to the software industry during the half-decade before the emergence of the personal computer in the mid-1970s, and set the stage for rapid growth of the sector thereafter.

During the 1960s and 1970s, programming faced the constant challenge of keeping up with the real and perceived opportunities that arose from the development and implementation of ever smaller and more powerful integrated circuits. During this time, industry talk and trade press reporting of a "software crisis" was pandemic. The most common element of this so-called crisis was the frequent shortage of quality programmers and the often-related fact that projects were rarely completed on time or on budget.[57] While the shortage of programmers was quite real, the degree to which it represented a true crisis is debatable. Also, firms had to learn that adding more programmers was not always the solution to slow-moving major software development projects—scaling up in software is often far less effective than in many other areas of technological development.

The status of programmers was also an issue of controversy. There was indeterminacy and battles over the proper place of the programmer in traditional academic, occupational, and professional hierarchies.[58] While the status of programmers during the 1960s was higher than of the "ENIAC girls" in the mid-1940s, it remained uncertain and contested. At corporate and institutional computer departments, programmers' salaries were fairly high. Nevertheless, opportunities for advancement within the hierarchies of these organizations paled in comparison to that of computer engineers. Various organizations, including the ACM, the Data Processing Management Association (DPMA) and the National Machine Accountants Associations (NMAA), tackled the

Table 5.2
User Expenditures on Software Products, U.S. Software Trade
(in millions of dollars)

Year	Systems Products	Applications Products	Total Products	Total Products and Services	% Products of Total
1970	$150	$100	$250	$994	25.1%
1971	$210	$140	$350	$1,206	29.0%
1972	$270	$170	$440	$1,392	31.6%
1973	$330	$210	$540	$1,612	38.9%
1974	$390	$270	$660	$1,860	35.5%
1975	$490	$320	$810	$2,162	37.5%

Source: Martin Campbell-Kelly, *From Airline Reservations to Sonic the Hedgehog: A History of the Software Industry* (Cambridge, MA: MIT Press, 2003), 19–20. Dr. Campbell Kelly compiled data from INPUT reports.

issue. The latter developed a Certificate in Data Processing (CDP) in the early 1960s. Conflicts occurred over the value of this and other certificates, and the appropriate academic requirements for certification. The ultimate arbitrator of the value of a particular certificate was the marketplace, and the CDP often did not influence prospective employers.[59]

Reflecting the recognition of the higher status of computer engineers, elite programmers first began to use the term "software engineering" in the mid- to late-1960s. In 1968 it became part of common vernacular following a famed NATO Conference on Software Engineering held in Garmisch, Germany, in October.[60] Despite the many challenges of programmers and the software trade, the industry continued to grow substantially, although somewhat unevenly at differing times with regard to software services and software products.

To gain a fuller macroeconomic picture of industry change, existing aggregate economic data on the trade is useful, but unfortunately, is also limited and incomplete. Leading computer and software historian Martin Campbell-Kelly's presentation of financial data compiled by market research firm INPUT, represents the best public data on the industry and a major advance over what was previously available in the public domain. A small portion of this data (on the early years of the software business) is presented in table 5.2. This indicates that the growth of software products was significant during the first half the 1970s, but it had yet to make major inroads to match or begin to displace software services. It was not until 1981, the year IBM came out with the PC, that software product expenditures first exceeded that of software services. While the services business has remained important, software products have become fundamental to rapid industry growth during the personal computer era and will be explored in chapters 7 and 8. First, however, it is important to examine the underlying forces that led to the radical transformation of computing and software technology, and that led the computer and software industries to propel personal computing and networking to the forefront.

NOTES

1. The term "software" was coined in the late 1950s and came into widespread use during the early- to mid-1960s.

2. Phillip Kraft, "The Routinization of Computer Programming," *Sociology of Work and Occupations* 6 (1977): 139–155.

3. Elizabeth Snyder, one of the earliest and most talented computer programmers, is commonly referred to by her married name of Betty Holberton.

4. Grace Murray Hopper, "Keynote Address" in *History of Programming Languages*, ed. Richard L. Wexelblat (New York: Academic Press, 1981), 7–20. Hopper was influenced by some early programming tools, particularly those developed by Eckert-Mauchly Computer Corporation's Elizabeth Snyder (Holberton). Snyder developed the Sort-Merge Generator in the late 1940s. This programming tool handled sorting and merging as well as managed input and output of various tape units, and helped give rise to a number of generators. In addition to Wexelblat's informative volume consisting of edited transcripts from the Association of Computing Machinery (ACM) SIGPLAN (Special Interest Group for Programming LANguages)-sponsored History of Programming Language Conference, June 1–3, 1978, Jean E. Sammett provides a significant resource of the technical and organizational history of approximately 120 programming languages in her *Programming Languages: History and Fundamentals* (Englewood Cliffs, NJ: Prentice-Hall, 1969).

5. Robert L. Glass, "COBOL" in *Encyclopedia of Computers and Computer History*, ed. Raul Rojas (Detroit, MI: Fitzroy Dearborn Publishers, 2001).

6. The use of C, C++, and versions of BASIC have held up better than FORTRAN in the MS-DOS, Unix, and personal computing era of the 1980s and 1990s.

7. Many highly specialized programming languages are used by small groups of individuals and organizations, but the number of programming languages receiving widespread use has always been relatively small.

8. Nathan Ensmenger and William Aspray, "Software as Labor Process" in *History of Computing: Software Issues*, eds. Ulf Hashagen, Reinhard Keil-Slawik, and Arthur L. Norberg (Berlin: Springer-Verlag, 2002), 142. Between 1956 and 1961, SDC trained an estimated 7,000 programmers and systems analysts. During the early- to mid-1960s, as the number of new military systems declined and IBM initiated the OS/360 Project, the computer giant surpassed SDC as the largest trainer and employer of programmers.

9. Paul Ceruzzi, *A History of Modern Computing* (Cambridge, MA: MIT Press, 1998), 88. SHARE held both national and regional meetings. About half of the original seventeen member corporations, organizations, or divisions came from the aerospace industry. Representatives from different areas of the country were present, but nearly half came from the Los Angeles area.

10. Atsushi Akera, "Volunteerism and the Fruits of Collaboration: The IBM User Group, SHARE," *Technology and Culture* 42, no. 4 (2001): 710–736.

11. Edgar H. Schein and others, *DEC Is Dead, Long Live DEC: The Lasting Legacy of the Digital Equipment Corporation* (San Francisco: Berrett-Koehler Publishers, 2003), 74.

12. Herbert W. Robinson, interview by Bruce H. Bruemmer, July 13, 1988, Bethesda, MD (Charles Babbage Institute, University of Minnesota).

13. C-E-I-R, Inc., *Annual Report: 1964* (Charles Babbage Institute, University of Minnesota).

14. Memorandum from Herbert W. Watson to C-E-I-R, Inc., Board of Directors, May 1, 1967 (Charles Babbage Institute, University of Minnesota).

15. C-E-I-R, Inc., "Computer Services Strategy Document," n.d., likely from 1967 (Charles Babbage Institute, University of Minnesota).

16. C-E-I-R, Inc., *Annual Reports: 1959–1966* (Charles Babbage Institute, University of Minnesota).

17. Herbert W. Robinson, interview.

18. Ibid.

19. Elmer C. Kubie, "Recollection of the First Software Company," *Annals of the History of Computing* 16 (1994): 65–71; Martin Campbell-Kelly, *From Airline Reservations to Sonic the Hedgehog: A History of the Software Industry* (Cambridge, MA: MIT Press, 2003), 51–52.

20. Ibid.

21. Ibid.

22. Campbell-Kelly, *Airline*, 53–54.

23. Ibid. In 1962, FACT was believed to be the most extensive compiler in existence. After its first iteration, Honeywell took over the project that eventually included four years of work between the two companies, 100 programmer years, and 223,000 lines of code (compared to 18,000 for the original FORTRAN compiler).

24. Computer Sciences Corporation, *Annual Report*: 2003; Computer Sciences Corporation, *Annual Reports*: 2002, 2003, and 2004.

25. Claude Baum, *The System Builders: The Story of SDC* (Santa Monica, CA: System Development Corporation, 1981), 31–44.

26. Campbell-Kelly, *Airline*, 39–40.

27. Frank Lautenberg, interview by Paul Ceruzzi, May 3, 2002, Washington, DC (Charles Babbage Institute; University of Minnesota).

28. Martin Goetz, interview by Jeffrey R. Yost, May 3, 2002, Washington, DC (Charles Babbage Institute, University of Minnesota); Martin Goetz, "Memoirs of a Software Pioneer: Part I," *IEEE Annals of the History of Computing* 24, no. 1 (2002): 43–56.

29. Ibid.

30. Ibid.

31. Ibid.

32. Richard L. Forman. *Fulfilling the Computer's Promise: The History of Informatics, 1962–1982* (Woodland-Hills, CA: Informatics General Corporation, 1985), 1–10.

33. Tomash and others at Telemeter Magnetics were dissatisfied after Ampex Corporation acquired the firm in 1960.

34. Forman, *Fulfilling*, 9–10.

35. Ibid.

36. Ibid.

37. Ibid., 9–24.

38. Ibid.

39. Ibid. In the coming years, modified versions of Mark IV were sold at different prices ranging between $15,000 and $50,000.

40. Campbell-Kelly, *Airline*, 100–109.

41. John Cullinane, interview by Jeffrey R. Yost, July 29, 2003, Boston, MA (Charles Babbage Institute, University of Minnesota).

42. Ibid.

43. Ibid.

44. Ibid.

45. Ibid.

46. Ibid.

47. Ibid.

48. Relational databases had the advantage of being able to handle more complex queries than traditional hierarchical databases.

49. Campbell-Kelly, *Airline*, 188.

50. John Cullinane, interview.

51. Charles Wang, "Unbundling Software: The Emergence of the Software Product," address at Conference of the Charles Babbage Institute at Xerox PARC, Palo Alto, CA, September 23–24, 2000 (Charles Babbage Institute, University of Minnesota).

52. Computer Associates, *Annual Report*: 2003.

53. Watts Humphrey, "Unbundling Software: The Emergence of the Software Product," address at Conference of the Charles Babbage Institute at Xerox PARC, Palo Alto, CA, September 23–24, 2000 (Charles Babbage Institute, University of Minnesota).

54. Steven Usselman, "Unbundling: Economic Analysis," from "Unbundling Software: The Emergence of the Software Product," address at Conference of the Charles Babbage Institute at Xerox PARC, Palo Alto, CA, September 23–24, 2000 (Charles Babbage Institute, University of Minnesota).

55. Ibid.

56. Watts Humphrey, conference.

57. Richard Canning, "The Persistent Personnel Problem," *EDP Analyzer* 5, no. 5 (May 1967); American Federation of Information Processing Societies, "The State of the Information Processing Industry," report presented at the Spring Joint Computer Conference (1966); Barry W. Boehm, "Software and Its Impact: A Quantitative Assessment," *Datamation* (May 1973): 48–59.

58. Nathan L. Ensmenger, "The Question of 'Professionalism' in Computer Fields," *IEEE Annals of the History of Computing* 23, no. 4 (October–December 2001): 56–58.

59. Ibid., 65–68.

60. Peter Naur and Brian Randell, *Software Engineering* (Brussels: Scientific Affairs Division, NATO, 1969).

—6—

The Infrastructure for Long-Term Change, 1962–1974

By the mid-1960s the mainframe computer industry was well established. The IBM System/360 series, and its backward compatible operating system, OS/360, had brought a degree of standardization to a previously disparate set of IBM computers. The success of this system led to RCA's production of a clone, the Spectra 70 series, adding to the trade's standardization around the OS/360 platform.[1] The modest though real movement toward standard systems also facilitated a more conducive environment for the software business. Software services had already begun to thrive, and a small number of insightful programmers and entrepreneurs, including Martin Goetz, John Postley, and John Cullinane, led an emerging software-products sector of the industry. IBM's unbundling at the start of the 1970s lent additional momentum to the software products trade.

Despite significant growth in software services and moderate growth in software products, hardware still dwarfed these businesses during the 1960s. The implementation of integrated circuits into new computing systems during the decade resulted in third-generation mainframes far more powerful than their first- or second-generation ancestors, and led to the creation of supercomputers. It also initiated a shift toward smaller and cheaper machines that led to the birth and rapid growth of the minicomputer sector. With minicomputing, many midsized corporations and smaller laboratories began to use computers. This class of machine also contributed fundamentally to time-sharing, a development that allowed users seemingly to have their own computer, and avoid the long delays of batch processing.

Despite this environment of change, computing was also remarkably tied to traditions of the past. Programming languages had provided programmers with tools to ease their burden and expand their field, but the task of creating new software was still complex and primarily limited to a relatively small group of individuals—a group sometimes referred to as a "priesthood" based on their specialized knowledge, and their efforts to erect barriers and control access to the computing domain.[2] While the digital computer had evolved from merely an advanced calculating machine during the late 1940s into a more diverse business data processing tool by the mid-1950s, ideas framing the nature of the technology and its range of uses and users appeared to change only modestly during the following decade. The government continued to be an important market for computing technology, but with the exception of SAGE and Project Whirlwind during the 1950s, it only seemed to be supporting evolutionary change, not the revolutionary type of research and development that had brought the digital computer into being in the mid-1940s.

During the 1960s and early 1970s, however, seeds were quietly being sown for a fundamental transformation of computing technology. The work of a small number of visionaries, coupled with expanded Department of Defense (DoD) research appropriations and organization, began to lay the foundation for computing to depart from its existing path. This departure would extend primarily from two organizations: ARPA's IPTO and Xerox's PARC (Palo Alto Research Center). On the surface the organizations were quite different, but common personnel led to common perspectives, practices, and goals. In time, the people working at or funded by these organizations would not only profoundly alter the nature of computing technology, but also the possibilities for and composition of the computer industry.

INFORMATION TECHNOLOGY IN A CHANGING POLITICAL ENVIRONMENT

As the Cold War intensified during the late 1940s and 1950s, the U.S. government and the American people continued to see the advancement of science and technology as critical to ensuring the nation's defense. While a minority of individuals questioned the further development of nuclear weapons and nuclear power, most were comforted by the fact that the United States had been the first to reach key technological plateaus, including the development of the atomic bomb and the hydrogen bomb. This relative complacency, born from America's unwavering belief in its continuing technological leadership, was shaken on October 4, 1957, when the Soviet Union successfully launched its Sputnik I satellite.[3] Sputnik caused the U.S. government and many Americans to question not only the national efforts in the race to space, but also the country's military strength and, more broadly, its position in and commitment to science and technology. In 1958, as a direct result of Sputnik and its early aftermath, the Eisenhower administration formed an agency within the DoD to further research and development in science and technology, the Advanced Research Projects Agency (ARPA). It was part of a multifaceted response that included radically expanding space and aviation research with the initiation of the National Aeronautical and Space Administration (NASA).[4]

While the immediate focus of ARPA was also on aerospace and weaponry, there were other areas of technology the agency considered important. One such field was information technology. Code-breaking machines had been critical to the Allies' success in defeating Germany in World War II. Shortly after the war, digital computer calculations became fundamental to the development of thermonuclear weapons, advances in radar, and many other military applications. The U.S. government perceived efficient and reliable command-and-control systems as essential to its ability to achieve success in future conflicts and wars, and information and communications systems were at the heart of effective command and control.[5]

J.C.R. LICKLIDER AND ARPA'S INFORMATION PROCESSING TECHNIQUES OFFICE

The Department of Defense sought to initiate an organized and broad-based research program with ARPA. The key idea behind the agency was to fund both mission-oriented research and development—projects in existing high-priority areas such as ballistic missile defense and nuclear test detection systems—as well as to support higher risk (less certain) basic research that *might* lead to important military applications down the road.[6] With regard to information technology, both types of research were perceived as significant, but initially the focus tended to be on basic research. To facilitate projects of this kind, ARPA decided to form a specialized administrative office. In 1962, it created the Information Processing Techniques Office (IPTO) and named J.C.R. Licklider as the director.[7]

J.C.R. Licklider, born in St. Louis in 1915, was a creative, intellectually gifted, and personable individual. He had wide interests in the physical sciences, the behavioral sciences, and mathematics, which were demonstrated by his completion of a triple major in physics, psychology, and mathematics at Washington University (1937). During the following year, he received a M.A. in psychology from this school, and in 1942, completed his doctorate in psychology at the University of Rochester.[8] This university had one of the nation's leading research programs on auditory regions of the brain, a topical area that had captivated Licklider and the general subject matter of his dissertation.[9]

After a postdoctoral year teaching at Swarthmore, Licklider began to work as a researcher at Harvard University's Acoustical Laboratory. At this laboratory, he focused on how distortion in radio and telephone signals could affect a listener's ability to comprehend sounds, an area of great importance to military communications. In 1950, he left Harvard to accept a faculty post at nearby Massachusetts Institute of Technology (MIT) in the Department of Electrical Engineering, where he proceeded to set up a psychology program within the department. Licklider became a member of MIT's Research Laboratory of Electronics and the school's Acoustics Laboratory. He also took part in Project Charles, an air-defense study, and became codirector of Project Lincoln's radar-display development group.[10]

Licklider's move across Cambridge did not represent his first introduction to the MIT community. For several years he had participated in weekly Tuesday night dinners organized by the Institute's renowned mathematician Norbert Wiener. Wiener held these dinners to bring together leading researchers from MIT, Harvard, and other Boston-area schools to discuss cybernetics, or the science of communication and control. Licklider contributed to many of the discussions, and these informal events helped further his strong ideas about the benefits of studying the interaction between humans and machines, particularly computers. He understood computers as versatile, general-purpose tools and thought that they could be invaluable to expanding knowledge of complex systems such as the human brain. In addition to the weekly cybernetics meetings, his research in psychology and acoustics at MIT lent additional momentum to his growing interest in human-machine interaction.[11]

In 1957, Licklider became a vice president of Bolt Beranek and Newman (BBN), a firm that MIT Acoustics Laboratory faculty members Richard Bolt and Leo Beranek had formed nine years earlier. Licklider's group at the company, roughly a dozen individuals in-

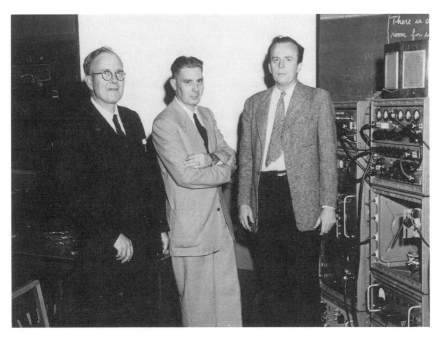

MIT psychology professor and future IPTO Director J.C.R. Licklider (right) with Walter Lawrence (left) of Signals Research and Development Establishment, Christchurch, England, and Northeastern University's Martin W. Essigmann (middle) at MIT's symposium on "Engineering Applications of Speech Analysis" in November 1953. (Courtesy of MIT Museum)

terested in computing technology, purchased one of the first Digital Equipment Corporation PDP-1 minicomputers, and designed and built one of the nation's earliest time-sharing systems. During Licklider's first years at BBN, he refined his long contemplated ideas on computing into a seminal article, "Man-Computer Symbiosis."[12] This article challenged some of the common notions of computing and artificial intelligence of the time by emphasizing the importance of humans and computers *interacting* to solve problems.[13] He saw computers as tools that could aid humans in critical ways by automating routine information retrieval tasks and freeing people up to spend more time and energy on substantive scientific thought.[14]

Licklider viewed human-computer interaction to be at the heart of command and control and wasted no time in conveying this to his superiors at ARPA. The dominant computing paradigm in the early 1960s was batch processing, a practice Licklider felt was incompatible with human computer interaction.[15] He believed time-sharing networks held out much greater possibilities. The conflict between the two processing mechanisms reached a head in Licklider's first days at the Pentagon's IPTO. ARPA had an existing $6 million command-and-control computer research commitment to the System Development Corporation (SDC). Though Licklider saw some useful aspects to SDC's research and development in the database area, this firm's scientists and engineers were using their Q-32 computer as a batch processor—something he felt was at odds with the DoD's goals to improve command and control. Licklider proceeded to make some strategic cuts to SDC's funding on this project and also insisted that its focus shift from batch processing to time-sharing. At first, this did not go over well at SDC, but after Licklider and a colleague brought some of the great minds in computing (Marvin Minsky, Alan Perlis, and Fernando Corbato) in for a presentation on time-sharing, opinions among the leadership of SDC quickly changed.[16] This was one of many examples of Licklider's skills as a manager—his ability to bring people together, but at the same time stand firm on his agenda and beliefs.

In general, Licklider and future IPTO directors were given a great amount of autonomy, based in part on the overwhelming attention ARPA's leadership devoted to mission-specific projects on defense systems.[17] Looking back on the early years of IPTO, Licklider recalled that he did not "feel much pressure to make a military case for anything."[18] While there were reporting requirements, he considered most DoD officials he communicated with to be supportive.[19] Licklider used his relative autonomy and support to concentrate nearly all IPTO funds on projects seeking to create more harmonious human-computer interaction or human-computer symbiosis. Following the cuts to SDC, he had most of his more than $10 million annual budget unrestricted during his two years as director. He used this money on projects to help build infrastructure at a small number of leading university centers and departments.[20]

Licklider's selection criterion for awarding funds was primarily based on the existing expertise, competencies, and commitments of individuals and groups of scientists and engineers. He began by distributing funds to several universities that had a solid background in computing. With IPTO's support, these schools became leading centers of computing research: MIT, University of California at Berkeley, and Carnegie Institute of Technology (later Carnegie Mellon University). All three schools had done research in areas of artificial intelligence (AI). Behind MIT's SAGE, Project Whirlwind, and MULTICS (Multiplexed Information and Computing Service), as well as Project Genie at the University of California, Berkeley, the first two schools had also contributed substantially to time-sharing. Additionally, MIT, unparalleled among universities in receiving DoD support for computing (and many other areas of technology) during the 1950s, had a strong background in early graphics work. For more than a decade and half following the formation of IPTO, it was the largest funding source in the world for AI research, and a major source of funds for research on computer graphics and time-sharing.[21]

Forever modest and always de-emphasizing his personal role, Licklider later reflected that a key factor in IPTO's success was that "it . . . organized itself into a community, so that there was some competition and some cooperation, and it resulted in the emergence of a field [computer science]."[22] As James Morris, chair of computer science at Carnegie Mellon University later put it, "Lots of very smart people made a career decision to go into a field that didn't exist yet, simply because ARPA was pouring money into it."[23] While the funding was critical, Licklider's vision, personality, and leadership skills also won people over, and helped to bring many talented scientists and engineers on board.[24]

Though Licklider's first tenure as the director of IPTO was only for two years, he earned tremendous respect within the computing community. In this short time, he left an indelible imprint that shaped the organization for the next decade and a half. He built a community of individuals that IPTO continued to draw upon for its future leadership. This was enhanced through annual meetings of IPTO-funded individuals and organizations. Though subsequent directors had their own styles and unique interests, they all shared Licklider's dream of advancing computing technology in a way that augmented human capabilities. Licklider's successors would extend his practice of developing and continuously funding centers of excellence in computing research by supporting top universities with talented personnel in computing, adding institutions such as Stanford University, UCLA, University of Michigan, and Rutgers University.

FUNDING EARLY RESEARCH IN COMPUTER GRAPHICS

Graphics was central to Licklider's notion of human-computer symbiosis. It was a potential tool that could ease the process of using a computer, as well as provide the basis for many new operations and applications. Like Licklider, a number of top military personnel recognized the need for user-oriented computing systems. Graphics was an important potential tool to achieve a user-orientation or user-friendliness. As one U.S. Air Force report put it in the early- to mid-1960s, "there is an urgent requirement to develop computer-based data processing systems which can be used directly and modified as desired by military and technical specialists who are not themselves computer specialists."[25] Not all air force leaders, however, recognized the importance of this goal, and some outside advisors, including the RAND Corporation's director of computer science, Willis Ware, emphasized the many components of the software development process and the need to be realistic about what programming tools could achieve in the near term.[26] The proposed GENISYS (GENeralized Information SYStem) of the early 1960s, a project to focus broadly on user orientation, was not funded as planned because some air force leaders believed user-orientation would soon be achieved on its own by industry, and others felt it lacked clear definition.[27] Given the focus of computing firms on business data processing, and the existence of a computing priesthood at many corporate computer departments, user-friendly graphics would not be at the top of the agenda in the IT industry for many years.

In contrast to the military branches, Licklider's IPTO funded a number of basic computer graphics projects in the early- to mid-1960s, following his general model of leveraging the office's resources to build upon existing expertise. In 1949, Charles Adams and John Gilmore had developed the first animated computer graphic image as part of MIT's Project Whirlwind. They built circular phosphorescent-coated Cathode Ray Tube (CRT) screens and applied electron beams to excite small regions of phosphor picture-elements or pixels to produce on-screen images. SAGE scientists used these monitors with "light guns" to produce an interactive graphics system. MIT's Douglas Ross, in turn, used a light gun to produce a computer-aided design (CAD) system. Behind this pioneering work, a number of agencies, including the National Science Foundation (NSF), National Institutes of Health (NIH), and NASA, funded graphics work at MIT at various times and to varying degrees during the 1950s and 1960s. Though time-sharing remained center stage, Licklider made graphics one of the priorities at IPTO. He provided substantial funding for MIT in this area, as well as built upon early air force–funded research at the RAND Corporation to support this organization's construction of the RAND Tablet (another computer-image creation device) and the development of GRAIL, a graphic input language.[28]

Licklider made many trips back to MIT as IPTO's director, and he became well acquainted with one of the school's star doctoral students in computer research, Ivan Sutherland. In 1962 Sutherland, who was working under Claude Shannon for his doctorate, developed Sketchpad at MIT's Lincoln Laboratory. This system enabled operators to interactively make line drawings on a CRT screen, and Sutherland's dissertation on Sketchpad was the first in the field of computer graphics. In the early part of 1964, when Licklider decided to leave IPTO to return to MIT, he pushed for Sutherland to be his successor. While some in ARPA's leadership and the computing community thought him young (twenty-six years old) for the position, he had already built up an impressive research program and was named IPTO director without any serious opposition in June 1964.

Sutherland recruited Robert Taylor to be his deputy director, a talented administrator who would take on a great amount of leadership responsibility during his two years in the position. Taylor would go on to succeed Sutherland as IPTO director in 1966, when Sutherland joined the faculty of Harvard University. Prior to IPTO, Taylor had been a program officer at NASA. While he possessed strong management experience, Taylor lacked a doctorate—having only completed an M.A. in psychology from the University of Texas. This caused some in the research community to doubt his scientific and technical competency for such an important position, but Sutherland and others helped secure the directorship for him.[29]

Under the tenures of both Sutherland and Taylor, IPTO was highly committed to the field of graphics—carrying on and accelerating the funding precedent established by Licklider.[30] Sutherland viewed graphics as a means to advance human understanding and emphasized that the ability of people to construct, manipulate, and observe complex pictures of digitized phenomena could radically change their ability to grasp complex ideas.[31] This belief led him to form a targeted initiative at IPTO, "Graphic Control and Display of Computer Processes," in order to fund a number of different institutions and "build tools necessary for controlling a wide variety of computations graphically."[32] Sutherland provided substantial support for graphics research to Lincoln Laboratory, the University of Michigan, and along with NASA, a small center at Stanford Research Institute (SRI) in Menlo Park. SRI's Augmentation Research Center was founded and directed by Douglas Engelbart.

DOUGLAS ENGELBART AND SRI

Douglas Engelbart, born in Portland, Oregon, in 1925, was a strong student and attended Oregon State University for two years prior to being drafted into the U.S. Navy in 1944. He was stationed at Manila Bay for the remainder of the war. Subsequently, he returned to Oregon State to complete his electrical engineering degree. Upon graduation, Engelbart began working as an electrical engineer for NASA Ames Research Center.

In 1950, however, Engelbart had an epiphany. As he was driving alone along the Pacific Coast one day, he started reflecting on his life. He had completed school, was recently married, and had a solid job. He questioned what came next and focused on how the world was rapidly changing and how a growing number of complex problems now plagued society. He pondered how technology might help aid this situation. The more he reflected, the more he became convinced that the computer could be an effective tool to help solve human problems.[33]

In 1951, Engelbart enrolled in a doctoral program in electrical engineering at the University of California, Berkeley (UCB), having been impressed by Professor Paul Morton's talk on the school's navy-funded CALDIC, or California Digital Computer.[34] Engelbart studied computing and symbolic logic at UCB, substituting philosophy courses on logic for the mathematics curriculum typical for his program. He remained driven to understand how computers might augment human thought and solve human problems. This was accentuated in the early 1950s when he read Norbert Wiener's *The Human Use of Human Beings: Cybernetics and Society*.[35] In 1956 Engelbart completed his Ph.D., but neither of the two traditional job paths, academe or working for a corporation, appealed to him. As a creative and independent individual who was interested in the social and philosophical side of technology, Engelbart did not want to conform to either of those settings. Instead, he started his own company, Digital Techniques, with the hope of developing computing systems that could augment human intellect. Instead, he was blindsided by the switch to integrated circuits in the late 1950s and his firm collapsed. In the summer of 1957, Engelbart accepted a job at Stanford Research Institute (SRI).[36]

SRI was an independent industrial-research organization that sought to build a close relationship with Stanford University, and conduct economic, management, and social science research. At SRI, Engelbart initiated his Augmentation Research Center, based on his belief that computers should and could take human thought to a higher level. Engelbart was eccentric, often quiet and contemplative, but a charismatic visionary. He inspired a small group of talented scientists and engineers to work at his center.

Engelbart's perspective on computer technology was similar to that of Licklider's and Robert Taylor's. When Robert Taylor was an administrator for NASA in 1963, he helped provide a small amount of funding to keep Engelbart's struggling center open. After Taylor became director of IPTO in 1966, he started funding Engelbart in a far more significant way, providing a $500,000 annual grant that allowed the Augmentation Research Center to occupy an entire wing of SRI's headquarters.[37] With these additional resources, Engelbart and his team delivered strong results. They developed an unprecedented interactive graphics system that he referred to as NLS, or oNLine System. It consisted of monitors and software to facilitate interactive computing. The system included a device made out of wood that used two small wheels on its underside and could roll on a flat surface. The wheels communicated motion to sensors, which in turn instructed the computer to move the position of a cursor on the screen. In other words, Engelbart and his team had invented the computer mouse. This invention, which occurred in 1964, proved more efficient and easier to use than existing graphics-control devices of the time, including the joystick and the light pen or light gun.

At the 1968 Fall Joint Computer Conference in Chicago, Engelbart and his colleagues put on a ninety-minute multimedia show to demonstrate NLS. The presentation included split-screen graphics, superimposed text and images, and the use of a "window," by cutting a "hole" in the screen to display an image in space. Engelbart controlled the entire show using his computer mouse. Even more prescient to future computing, Engelbart and his assistants demonstrated how a user could select a word in the text and shift the display to a relevant portion of a different document. This was a demonstration of hypertext, a technology that more than two decades later would provide much of the basis for the World Wide Web.

CREATING A NEW CENTER OF EXCELLENCE: UNIVERSITY OF UTAH AND COMPUTER GRAPHICS

By the late 1960s, IPTO had been critical to advancing influential computer research projects at MIT, Carnegie Institute of Technology (Carnegie Mellon University), University of Michigan, University of California at Berkeley, the RAND Corporation, SRI, and other university departments/centers and research institutions. The universities that IPTO supported were among the first to initiate departments of computer science. The influence of IPTO funding on the nation's computer research infrastructure was undeniable. At the same time, all the aforementioned institutions had at least some prior history in the area. This, however, was not true of the University of Utah.

At the University of Utah, ARPA brought a true center of excellence in computer graphics into being at an institution that did not have a significant base in computing and was not generally considered a leading research institution. The direct impact of IPTO's funding of computer research projects at other schools was substantial, but on a relative basis more difficult to discern given the multiple funding sources that typically existed. In contrast, at the University of Utah all the early sponsored funds were from IPTO, and thus, the impact far more transparent.

In 1966 the University of Utah hired David Evans, a researcher who had worked on the University of California at Berkeley's Project Genie. Though Project Genie was much smaller in scale than MIT's MULTICS, it was nevertheless an important time-sharing project and Evans was a gifted researcher. Upon joining Utah, Evans initiated a graphics program and applied for a modest IPTO grant to fund his research. Robert Taylor chose to radically expand this contract and turn the University of Utah into one of the nation's leading centers for the study of computer graphics. Not only was he impressed with Evans, but he also believed that isolation from the traditional centers of computing research might lead to greater originality and creativity to advance this important field of computing.

In 1968, Ivan Sutherland left Harvard to accept a one-third-time post at the University of Utah, and he and Evans cofounded Evans and Sutherland, a graphic systems company. Despite lacking a pre-existing base, behind Evans, Sutherland, and a small number of others, the program thrived, exceeded IPTO expectations, and made major contributions to computer graphics in the late 1960s and early 1970s. These accomplishments included the creation and manipulation of three-dimensional models in a computer database, the development of algorithms for hidden-surface removal and shading, and the development of CAD/CAM vector-graphics displays. The University of Utah also produced a number of quality graduate students who contributed to computer graphics within both academe and industry. University of Utah computer science graduates in graphics went on to faculty positions at Carnegie Mellon University and the University of Texas, Austin, as well as filled top executive posts at Pixar and Adobe Systems.[38]

DEVELOPING THE ARPANET

Under Licklider's leadership, IPTO showed an early and strong commitment to time-sharing—an area in which he had witnessed pioneering research at MIT's Project Whirlwind, and had conducted work at BBN. Licklider was drawn to time-sharing because it provided more possibilities for human-machine interaction than batch processing, and helped to make costly computer resources more accessible and efficient. By early 1963, Licklider was beginning to contemplate and articulate a more expansive networking concept that could potentially connect computing resources at great distances. He referred to his system as an "Intergalactic Computer Network." In April 1963, Licklider sent a memo to some colleagues, or "members and affiliates of the Intergalactic Computer Network," to speculate on a strategy to connect individual computers and time-sharing systems throughout the nation.[39]

That Licklider's early vision of a major computer network was present by the latter days of his first tenure as IPTO's director is clear from this memo, but in many respects it seemed to be more playful musing on his part than a serious attempt to start a new initiative. At the time, the office was primarily supporting local networked systems through time-sharing projects. Time-sharing continued to be a fundamental area of IPTO support with his successors, even as Ivan Sutherland strongly pushed computer graphics. In 1965, however, Sutherland, and particularly Robert Taylor, began to look at networking in a new light after seeing a demonstration of a unique type of computer by an IPTO-supported engineer, Wesley Clark, at Washington University.

Wesley Clark led a project at MIT in the early 1960s to build a laboratory computer that would work interactively and would be responsive to an individual user. In concept, it bore significant resemblance to how we now think about and use personal computers. By 1964 Clark's team had completed a laboratory computer named LINC (Laboratory INstrument Computer). During the second half of the 1960s there were more than 1,200 LINC installations being used by scientists.[40] Dissatisfied with the environment at MIT, Clark led his small team to Washington University in St. Louis. With IPTO funding, Clark and his colleagues began to develop "macro-modules" allowing users to tailor interactive LINC computers to their particular scientific research needs.

When Sutherland and Taylor visited Clark in St. Louis for a demonstration of LINC in 1965, they found the computer striking. Taylor was particularly impressed at the level of interactivity between the user and machine. Clark believed that time-sharing had been an unfortunate, but understandable mistake. He thought that sharing resources of a central mainframe was limiting to a user's interaction with a computer. After witnessing LINC, Taylor began to agree with Clark's assessment.[41] At his office at the Pentagon, Taylor had to use a number of different teletype machines to connect to the different ARPA-funded time-sharing systems. Increasingly, he came to see the centralization of computer resources, incompatibility of systems, and the attendant limits of both interactivity and efficient communication, as fundamental problems. When he took over IPTO in June 1966, he pushed the office in a new direction. He initiated a project to connect all of IPTO's contractors through a computer network called the ARPANET. This would bring about a different type of networking than time-sharing that would not be subject to the same limits with regard to interactive computing.

Such a large-scale network would differ not only technically, but also managerially, from anything that the Information Processing Techniques Office had done in the past. It would need to be administratively controlled by IPTO. With smaller-scale individual projects, IPTO merely granted awards and then monitored progress to decide on future allocations. In contrast, with the ARPANET a top down approach had to be used to ensure cooperation between a number of people and organizations, and compatibility between different machines and software systems. Furthermore, IPTO's annual budget, which had grown to exceed $15 million by the mid-1960s, was already committed. Taylor had to go to ARPA to seek additional funds, and despite his initial concerns, was successful. A mere fifteen minutes after entering ARPA Director Charlie Herzfeld's office, Taylor had received his request for $1 million to get the project started.[42]

Once Taylor had the initial funding, his next task was to ensure the proper leadership for the project. He quickly decided that MIT's Larry Roberts, a Ph.D. who had worked under Licklider, was the best person for the job. Roberts, however, was quite content with his research position at Lincoln Laboratory and politely declined. Unbeknownst to Taylor, back in 1964, Roberts had been Sutherland's first choice to succeed him as director of IPTO. Roberts, however, lacked interest in this bureaucratic opportunity and turned it down. To work under Taylor appealed to Roberts even less. This forced the IPTO director to play hardball. Taylor reminded the head of Lincoln Laboratory that more than half of the lab's funding came from IPTO. With pressure from above, Roberts accepted the position to direct the ARPANET project. Despite his reluctance to accept this job, he did believe in the aims of the project. His underlying rationale for the importance of developing the ARPANET focused on the benefits it could provide for scientists to share hardware, software, and data.[43]

In taking on the leadership of the project, Roberts had a couple of fundamental hurdles to address: developing the best means to network the computers of ARPA contractors, and doing this in a way that ensured that the different computer hardware and software systems would be compatible. The solution to the first problem had been achieved several years earlier, but was not known to Roberts at the time. It was a development called packet-switching, a technology that had been invented simultaneously and independently by two principal individuals: Paul Baran of the RAND Corporation and Donald Davies of the National Physical Laboratory (NPL) in Teddington, England.

In October 1967, at the ACM Symposium on Operating System Principals in Gatlinburg, Tennessee, Roberts attended a talk by the National Physical Laboratory's Roger Scantlebury on Davies' telecommunication research group at NPL. Davies, who ironically was inspired in his research by a conversation with Licklider and Roberts at a conference two years earlier, proceeded to outline a decentralized networked communication system that involved many different switching stations (places where information was retrieved and resent).[44] As part of the system, digitized data was broken into small packets that could be sent by different routes (go through different switching stations) and reassembled as a whole at the final destination.

Concurrent to the work at NPL, Paul Baran of the RAND Corporation had also developed a packet network system. He had joined the RAND Corporation in 1959 and worked on computing within RAND's Mathematics Department. During the early 1960s, Baran was interested in designing a new communication system that had much greater survivability than existing systems in the event of a nuclear attack. With the extreme lack of trust between the Soviet Union and the United States, Baran knew that a survivable communication system could be critical to the prevention of an accidental nuclear war. Detection systems were imperfect, and if the survivability of communications did not exist, then a decision for a "retaliatory strike" would have to be made based on information from detection systems prior to the strike rather than real information after a strike—a false positive could result in disaster. Baran reasoned that a system highly redundant with many distribution paths and switching stations would offer far more security—it would buy time. He developed his ideas into eleven research memos on a distributive computing system in 1965, and that summer the RAND Corporation made a preliminary proposal to the air force. It involved the use of radio transmission of data and cryptographic controls to ensure secrecy.[45]

After hearing Scantlebury's talk, and engaging in subsequent communications and interaction with both NPL and the RAND Corporation, Roberts' problem of how to structure the network and transmit information had largely been solved. In addition to packet-switching being a key factor to an efficient and operational computer network, Baran's focus on survivability had provided a clear justification to the Department of Defense for building such a system—something that would be significant in the changing DoD funding environment that developed over the next several years. Packet-switching represented the single most significant technological development underlying the ARPANET and later the Internet.[46]

The other major problem facing Roberts was compatibility. All the ARPA contractors used different makes and models of computers and had a range of operating systems. Roberts, influenced by the ideas of Wesley Clark, decided to use identical minicomputers at all the different ARPA contractor locations, or nodes of the network, to handle the transmission and receipt of information. These minicomputers, which would exist between the network and the different computing systems of the ARPA contractors, would be called Interface Message Processors (IMPs). IPTO would only have to develop common software for the IMP, rather than specialized software for each different system on the network. Each of the ARPA contractors would be responsible for developing the software to communicate between their computing systems and the IMP. Graduate students did most of this programming, many of whom would go on to become leaders in computer networking.

In 1968, Roberts succeeded Taylor as the director of IPTO. That summer he initiated a $2.5 million project to connect four nodes and actually create the ARPANET.[47] He put out a call for proposals for the primary contractor to develop the software and oversee the implementation of the system. Though many larger companies, such as Raytheon, made proposals, the intellectual talent and horizontal management structure of tiny Cambridge-based BBN appealed to Roberts, and this firm received the contract. BBN also had an additional advantage, a highly knowledgeable engineer in packet-switching technology: Robert Kahn.

In 1969, the IMPs and associated software were in place and the first four nodes of the network were connected: University of California at Los Angeles, University of California at Santa Barbara, University of Utah, and SRI. Within two years there were twenty-three different nodes, and the number would continue to grow. Roberts was pleased with ARPA's response to this technical achievement, but hoped that the computer networking concept would move into a broader arena. To help achieve this, he organized a major public demonstration at the first International Conference on Computer Communications, an event held in Washington, D.C., in the fall of 1972. More than a thousand delegates attended the three-day event and were able to use computers attached to the different ARPA contractors' systems. This event created large-scale interest within the academic world; many more universities wanted to join the network, and by 1974 there were 111 nodes.[48]

Ironically, many nodes rich with computer resources were infrequently tapped by networked users—calling into question Roberts' primary initial justification for developing the ARPANET: resource sharing. At the same time, following upon BBN programmer Ray Tomlison's development and modification of a mail program, e-mail rapidly became the ARPANET's most popular and influential application. In spite of the fact that it was not an original goal, Roberts and ARPA director Stephen Lukasik promoted e-mail heavily and it became critical to creating an ARPANET community. The development of e-mail as a primary function of the ARPANET highlighted the importance of user communities in shaping new technologies.[49] Meanwhile, the DoD was starting to grow weary of financing this network that was widely available, given that the original aims had been resource sharing for scientists and military communications. This issue was resolved by the creation of a separate military network, Milnet, which was completed during 1982.[50]

By this time, other computer networks had been developed, such as NSFnet, sponsored by the National Science Foundation. IPTO funded the development of common protocols by Vinton Cerf and Robert Kahn that allowed various networks to be interconnected: Transmission Control Protocol and Internet Protocol (commonly referred to as TCP/IP).[51] The National Science Foundation was the chief administrator of this networking during the 1980s. In that decade, several hundred networked systems were connected through use of these common protocols. Many users of networks during the 1980s were associated with universities and government. This began to change in the early 1990s as public and commercial interest in computer networking broadened. Before these developments could occur, however, people needed to have greater access to computers, and these machines had to be far more user-friendly than in the past. The work of a leading industrial research laboratory was fundamental to making this possible.

ROBERT TAYLOR'S LEADERSHIP AND THE CONTINUATION AND EXTENSION OF INTERACTIVE COMPUTING AT XEROX PARC

As the U.S. involvement in the Vietnam War escalated, ARPA became increasingly focused on funding mission-specific research and development and shifting funds away from basic research. While IPTO's budget continued to rise at the end of the 1960s and throughout the 1970s, the amount of money for basic research declined. This was formalized in the Mansfield Amendment that was attached to the 1970 Fiscal Year Defense Department appropriations bill. Although only officially in place that fiscal year, the amendment stated that there had to be a "direct and apparent" connection between all DoD expenditures and military functions, and it changed the culture within the DoD. As a result of this change, military funds for basic research were scarce during the 1970s. Further emphasizing this changing environment, in 1972 the DoD changed the name of ARPA to DARPA, the *Defense* Advanced Research Projects Agency. IPTO was not immune to these broader changes at DARPA. Substantial IPTO funding for the ARPANET continued into the 1970s because it was still easily justified as a redundant and survivable military communications infrastructure. Funding in other areas, including some work in graphics and artificial intelligence, was more difficult to justify as having a mission-specific DoD function. Furthermore, some scientists were turned off by changes that had occurred at the former ARPA and by the Vietnam War. Many of these scientists did not want to try to come up with direct military justifications for their research. Given this situation, a great number of talented people in computing who had long been supported by IPTO, seemingly had nowhere to turn to continue their dedicated research. One organization in particular, would take advantage of this situation.

At the end of the 1960s Xerox was thriving. It had held a monopoly in the photocopier business for roughly a decade, successfully commercializing technology acquired from the Haloid Corporation that extended back to the work of inventor Chester Carlson during the mid-1940s. Xerox was generating more than $1 billion a year, primarily based on this technology. By the late

1960s, Xerox management recognized their stranglehold on copier technology was destined to be challenged and that the company needed new capabilities to best maintain its document-reproduction business. In the ambitious words of Xerox CEO Peter McColough, the firm needed to "control the architecture of information."[52]

This fueled McColough's interest in purchasing one of the existing computer companies. Most of the firms in the industry were outside of Xerox's reach however, as they had no interest in becoming a division of the photocopier giant. Xerox ended up with only a single alternative, Max Palevsky's Scientific Data Systems (SDS), a firm that had built the successful SDC 940 time-sharing computer. Xerox's past difficulty with acquiring a computer firm led McColough to move quickly. He did not involve the firm's financial team, and came to an agreement with Pavelesky to pay more than $920 million in stock for SDS in February 1969.[53] It was a fateful decision. Time-sharing, a strength of SDS, would not be the model for computing that some expected, and SDS had never exceeded $10 million in annual revenue.

The problems with SDS were not just its high purchase price and its relatively low revenues, but the fact that it did not demonstrate the capacity to be a future innovator. The acquisition, and McColough's statement about "controlling the architecture of information," however, did leave the door open for Jack Goldman, the head of research for Xerox, to try to push the company forward and build a greater infrastructure for innovation.[54] He developed a twenty-one-page proposal for a "Xerox Advanced Scientific & Systems Laboratory" to help compensate for SDS's lack of ability in research, and to boost research and development throughout the firm.[55] He proposed a lab that would be world-class in basic research along the model of AT&T's Bell Laboratories, and would exist for Xerox's long-term interests rather than short-term needs. Though Pavelesky, Xerox's largest stockholder after the SDS acquisition, was opposed, McColough and others sided with Goldman, who now had the green light to initiate a new laboratory. This laboratory, which would be at a site to be determined, would do basic research in computing and physics, and complement the existing photocopier-focused research operation of the firm that was located at Webster Research Park near Rochester, New York.

Goldman soon convinced George Pake, a senior administrator at Washington University in St. Louis and former physicist at Stanford University, to direct the new research laboratory, a facility that would plan to employ more than 300 scientists and engineers.

Initially, Goldman had favored New Haven, Connecticut, as the location for the laboratory, but the interest of scientists, engineers, and administrators at Yale University to build synergies with such a lab was absent. Given this situation, Pake convinced Goldman to accept a location Pake knew well, Palo Alto, California. Palo Alto had the strong appeal of possessing two top-notch universities nearby: Stanford University (in Palo Alto itself) and the University of California, Berkeley. Following the tradition started by Frederick Terman and the creation of Hewlett-Packard, Stanford University had long had a reputation for supporting collaboration with industry. While certain economies could have been achieved if the new lab had been built on the Webster Research Park infrastructure, both Goldman and Pake knew that Xerox's existing facility was too tied to document-reproduction technology, and a new setting was absolutely imperative to innovate in other areas.

The facility would include laboratories for both physics and computing. As a physicist, Pake had very little knowledge of the field of computing and its leading researchers. He immediately sought to contact the one individual he knew who seemed to be connected to everyone in the field, Robert Taylor. Taylor had left IPTO when the DoD forced the office to concentrate on mission-oriented research. In 1969, following Ivan Sutherland's lead, he headed to the University of Utah to work for the computer science department that he and Sutherland had funded into being with IPTO grants to David Evans. Pake invited Taylor to Palo Alto, originally just seeking to learn about people in the field, but soon recognized his skill in assessing talent and decided to offer him a job as associate manager of PARC's Computer Science Laboratory (CSL), a position in charge of hiring the first wave of researchers, including the laboratory manager. PARC did not hire a CSL manager until after Taylor had hired a number of key researchers and established a horizontal management structure in the laboratory with everyone reporting directly to him. Taylor orchestrated the hiring of Jerry Elkind of MIT as the lab's manager, a past doctoral student of Licklider's. Although there were conflicts at times, Taylor continued to have a great deal of authority within the laboratory.[56]

The newly formed Xerox PARC secured a facility on Porter Drive, not far from Stanford University.[57] Taylor soon started a search to staff the facility, but took his time. Given DoD cuts in basic research in computing and physics, and the recession in the early 1970s, it was a buyer's market for talent from industry, universities, and government laboratories. Companies were going under frequently, and Taylor showed great patience and insight in not moving too quickly, but taking advantage when opportunities arose. Like IPTO in the past, PARC could afford to pay considerably more than faculty positions at universities, and to many researchers, the possibility of doing research full-time (with no teaching responsibilities) was appealing.

A number of specific events led PARC to secure many of the best and the brightest in computing research, a number of whom had directly or indirectly been supported by IPTO previously. The Berkeley Computer Corporation was a firm that developed out of IPTO-funded Project Genie at the University of California. In 1970 the company fell on hard times and seven of its best engineers, including Butler Lampson, Charlie Thacker, Charles Simonyi, and Peter Deutch, were hired by Taylor to join the PARC team. The group caused tension with Xerox's top management and the SDS division when it requested to buy a DEC PDP-10, a time-sharing machine that competed directly against a new model developed by SDS, Sigma 7. PARC further aggravated the situation when, rather than providing the requested justification for why a Sigma 7 would not suffice, Lampson, Thacker and others went ahead and built a PDP-10 clone called MAXC that was completed in 1972.[58] The name, based on SDS founder and Xerox board member Max Pavelesky, added more salt to the wounds of SDS, and aggravated Xerox's central management.

Robert Taylor drew upon key researchers from a couple of other past IPTO projects. He had been struck by Engelbart's development of NLS and his presentation of this networked graphics system in 1968. IPTO had provided much of the funding for Engelbart to expand his center at SRI and make this development possible. In 1971, Taylor sought to hire individuals working under Engelbart and to bring this technology and skill to PARC. He did not seek Engelbart himself, as he felt he would be difficult for others to work with in the laboratory. Taylor instead targeted William K. English, a gifted engineer who had been at the Augmentation Research Center from just after its formation and who had been fundamental to engineering the computer mouse. Not only did English accept Taylor's offer to join and try to bring the NLS technology to PARC, but he soon convinced about a dozen of the key researchers from the Augmentation Research Center to sign on with him.[59] Although the specific attempt to recreate NLS was unsuccessful, bringing this talent had substantial positive impacts on future developments in graphics and networking at PARC.

Taylor, having been sold years earlier by Wesley Clark on the merits of dedicated individual computers, also hired the leading doctoral student out of the IPTO-supported University of Utah

Computer Science Department: Alan Kay. In 1969, Kay had completed his dissertation, "The Reactive Engine," a study that explored technology underlying a personal computer. Kay would later refer to this machine as "Dynabook." In 1972 Kay began working with Butler Lampson and Charlie Thacker to build a personal computer that would become known as "Alto."

Thacker, an extremely talented engineer, finished the design of the Alto in November 1972, a mere three months after he began work on it. He benefited from Robert Taylor's insight in establishing fundamental design features, Kay's ideas from his proposed Dynabook, and the assistance of a number of PARC scientists and engineers. It was a streamlined machine that lacked the power of the MAXC minicomputer, but benefited from some underlying concepts extending from this machine. This included using the central processing unit (CPU) to take over the functions of all the peripherals, a design feature that allowed for prioritizing and fuller use of the power of the CPU. The Alto also used a rudimentary "bitmap," or a block of memory that corresponded to dots on the monitor in order to achieve the most advanced graphics possible given its modest 128K of memory.

For an early demonstration some CSL members programmed the Alto to display an image of Sesame Street's Cookie Monster smiling and holding a cookie. In its initial form, the Alto fulfilled two of Taylor's primary three ingredients for moving human-computer interaction forward: building a computer designed for an individual user and incorporating a graphical display that made it easier to use.[60] For most tasks it could respond to its user faster than a time-shared DEC PDP-10 minicomputer, and, perhaps more important, its response time was highly predictable, not based on the fluctuating number of time-sharing users competing for memory and processing power. The anticipated cost of the machine was $10,500, just over half of what it cost to build a MAXC. Modifications were made on prototypes of the hardware during the following year, and work was conducted on debugging its software. By the end of 1973, Thacker and his team were ready to construct the thirty Alto units to fulfill the computer needs of the CSL.[61]

The final goal Taylor had for interactive computing was that computers not only be personal and easier for most to use (single users and graphic displays), but also distributive—that they exist as part of a decentralized network that facilitates communication. An Alto on a distributive network would take advantage of the best aspects of time-sharing, collaboration, communication, and building a community of users. At the same time it would avoid the primary drawback, shared processing and memory resources that limited its operations and interactivity. Independently, another former IPTO-funded researcher at PARC was achieving the task of building the required networking capabilities for such machines.

Robert Metcalfe was an applied mathematics doctoral student at Harvard who was fascinated with computing and had more interest in developments at MIT than his department at Harvard. He spent the latter part of his time in graduate school working at MIT on the ARPANET as a researcher for J.C.R. Licklider's Project MAC.[62] After failing to pass his dissertation defense, which was more on practical computer networking than on theory (his professors wanted a more theoretical study), he accepted Robert Taylor's offer to come to PARC to work on networking Xerox's MAXC to the ARPANET and reformulate his dissertation. He also worked on research in conjunction with the University of Hawaii's Alohanet, an ARPANET-type system that used radio waves rather than wires. As Metcalfe thought about networking the MAXC, and subsequently the Alto, he reflected on what he had seen with Alohanet. He decided to develop a local area network that would be based on the principles of Alohanet, and then would feed into the larger ARPANET.[63] Files were separated into packets and transmitted by radio on this local network. This appealed to Metcalfe because the medium—radio—was passive and merely carried the signals. All of the individual computers and software did the processing, queuing, and routing of data—it was a decentralized or distributed system. While the sea separated the computers or nodes of Alohanet on the Hawaiian Islands, nodes were separated merely by office walls and short distances at PARC. The data moved through empty space, or for physicists, "ether," leading to the name "Ethernet." All of a sudden many "smart" interactive terminals could replace the model of "dumb" terminals connected to a central mainframe. The Ethernet was implemented in 1979 by Digital Equipment Corporation on its VAX minicomputers in conjunction with Xerox and Intel, and would be very influential in later PC-era networking.[64]

In 1974, PARC followed the Alto and the Ethernet with some influential software developments that included Dan Ingalls invention of "BitBlt," a display algorithm that was a precursor to the graphical user interface of the Apple Macintosh a decade later. Charles Simonyi, and Tim Mott and Larry Tesler, created "Bravo" and "Gypsy" respectively. These programs would combine to make the first user-friendly word processing program. This text program was unique in that its graphical display presented what could be translated to a printed page—an early fulfillment of "what you see is what you get," or WYSIWYG.

Xerox did move forward with the creation of the System Development Division (SDD) to produce and market some PARC technologies in 1975. It did so, however, in a conservative fashion. Xerox produced a line of office equipment products (including word processing machines, fax machines, and printers).[65] Over time, the division had some successes, but it lacked the unified management and corporate backing to take full advantage by boldly moving into the computing field during the mid-1970s. PARC did not fit in with the broader corporate culture of Xerox, something that had been accentuated a couple of years before the formation of SDD when Stewart Brand wrote an article on Xerox PARC for *Rolling Stone*. The article, entitled "Space War: Fanatic Life and Symbolic Death Among the Computer Bums," highlighted some revolutionary achievements of PARC researchers, but presented the scientists and engineers at PARC as radicals. It focused on PARC's most eccentric, and perhaps greatest visionary scientist, Alan Kay. The article's images of PARC scientists in T-shirts and sandals contrasted sharply with the formal corporate culture of Xerox's headquarters in Stamford, Connecticut.[66]

In August 1977, Xerox made the decision not to market the Alto, a machine that cost roughly $18,000 per unit in the relatively modest volume it was produced. Over time, hundreds were built, and though some made their way outside of PARC, including a small number that went to the White House and the U.S. Congress, most were just used internally at the center.[67] The experience of Wang Laboratories gives some perspective on the missed opportunity. Wang, a calculator firm that recognized its primary product was becoming a commodity by the early 1970s, transitioned to become a minicomputer firm. After some initial missteps, the firm came out with the Wang Word Processing System (WPS), a minicomputer geared toward word processing and office users. Selling at $30,000, a price point that the more advanced and graphically impressive Alto likely could have met, WPS and its successors sold well enough to propel the firm from forty-fifth in data processing revenues to eighth by 1983. However, Wang Laboratories, hurt by the rapid growth of cheap personal computers and shrink-wrap word processing programs, went bankrupt during the 1990s.[68]

Though PARC had developed much of the technology that in subsequent forms would become influential to personal computing and networking, it did not commercialize this technology in a timely manner. It was not until 1981 that Xerox's SDD completed a revised version of the Alto that it called the Xerox 8010 Star Information System, or simply, Xerox Star. This machine was the most graphically advanced personal computer of its time when it was announced at the National Computer Conference in Chicago that year. While it stood out as a technological achievement, it was priced at around $17,000, and failed to become a star in the marketplace. Lesser personal computers—priced nearly five times less—had some of the same functionality, albeit with less graphical style.

Given subsequent events, many have chosen to present Xerox PARC as a tremendous technical success and an unparalleled business failure: "fumbling the future," as the title of one book put it.[69] While the former is justified, the latter is not. Starting PARC was an insightful and opportunistic decision that brought together an incredible collection of computing research talent. History, however, shows that it is extremely difficult for established corporations that lead in one area of technology to transition to become a major player in another. Furthermore, it is only with hindsight that personal computing can be seen as a great business opportunity. Taking prototype technologies to the product stage and marketing them is extremely expensive and risky in an uncertain market. The subsequent development of the personal computer and networking technology, largely extended from former PARC scientists and engineers. This, however, was not always smooth, and many developments went through a number of iterations. Some technologies benefited from the interaction of many firms before they became commercially successful. Xerox, like many established firms of the 1970s, had a relatively closed structure, and did not follow the model of collaborating with a number of outside individuals and firms.[70] Furthermore, during the first half of the 1970s, it was impossible for top management at Xerox to think of computing outside of SDS, a firm it had paid $918 million to acquire, but one that did not have the structure, personnel, market share, or innovative culture to thrive in the rapidly evolving computer industry. SDS resulted in an $84.4 million write-off for Xerox in 1975.[71]

That Xerox neglected to capitalize on many of the early PARC technologies, led to a common myth that the research center was a losing investment for the firm. This was not true. Future revenue from laser-printing technology alone would pay for Xerox's investment in PARC many times over.[72] Ironically, George Starkweather originally conceptualized this product while he was at

Xerox's Webster photocopier research facility. Nevertheless, it was only when he transferred to PARC in 1971 that he had the resources and the environment to actually develop it as a product.

IPTO AND PARC REVISITED

Much of the research and early training of PARC scientists and engineers was made possible by the prior support of ARPA's IPTO. Once this office shifted away from supporting basic research at the end of the 1960s, PARC picked up the torch. This was not only in an engineering and science sense, but also in a managerial one. Robert Taylor was educated as a physiological psychologist just like J.C.R. Licklider, and the former was deeply influenced by the latter. The two had a common vision for the possibilities for computing technology to augment human capabilities. They both not only showed insight in and were influential to what computing later became, but achieved this in large measure because they had the skill to bring the right people together and create a community conducive to achieving results. Licklider started the practice of having regular meetings of IPTO's contractors to produce an extended community of innovators. Taylor's subsequent work at IPTO, and particularly his effort in pushing the development of the ARPANET forward, furthered this interactive community. Similarly, Taylor's leadership at PARC's CSL resulted in the creation of an unprecedented team of engineering talent and an environment of creativity. Xerox's decision to create PARC was insightful, and its response as a market leader in one technology to forego a risky venture in another was understandable. Like most large established corporations, it took a conservative route, and it would be former rather than current PARC employees, as well as others, that would commercialize much of the center's computing research. As a result, PARC's work in the 1970s provided the basis for much of the technology that led to the ubiquity of personal computer hardware, software, and networking in the 1980s and 1990s.

NOTES

1. Most of the standardization around this platform in the trade was the result of the substantial volume of sales/leases of IBM mainframes compared to their competitors.

2. In addition to programmers, computer operators at centralized computing centers were also sometimes referred to as a "computer priesthood." Some experienced programmers favored more complex languages, at times, to reinforce distinctions between themselves and less experi-

enced programmers. For discussion of the "priesthood" by a pioneering programmer, see John Backus, "Programming in America in the 1950s: Some Personal Impressions," in *A History of Computing in the Twentieth Century: A Collection of Essays*, eds. N. Metropolis, J. Howlett, and Gian-Carlo Rota (New York: Academic Press, 1980), 125–135.

3. Eight years prior to Sputnik, the United States discovered that the Soviet Union had developed and tested an atomic bomb. This also surprised and disturbed many Americans, but unlike Sputnik, it did not define or symbolize the Soviet Union as a technological leader.

4. This built upon and greatly expanded the existing National Advisory Committee for Aeronautics (NACA).

5. For an illuminating discussion of computing, and command and control within the context of the Vietnam War, see Paul W. Edwards, *The Closed World: Computers and the Politics of Discourse in Cold War America* (Cambridge, MA: MIT Press, 1996).

6. Arthur L. Norberg and Judy O'Neill, *Transforming Computer Technology: Information Processing for the Pentagon, 1962–1986* (Baltimore, MD: Johns Hopkins University Press, 1996), 6.

7. Licklider was simultaneously overseeing allocation of ARPA funding for behavioral science research. Increasingly, this research coincided with IPTO research in areas related to artificial intelligence, including robotics. The initial budget was combined for the two areas when he came on as director of IPTO.

8. M. Mitchell Waldrop, *The Dream Machine: J.C.R. Licklider and the Revolution that Made Computing Personal* (New York: Penguin Books, 2001), 12–13.

9. Joseph Carl Robnett Licklider, "An Electrical Investigation of Frequency-Localization in the Auditory Cortex of the Cat" (Ph.D. diss., University of Rochester, 1942). Specifically, this work examined mapping neural activity on the auditory cortex by conducting experiments on the responses of cats to electrical stimuli.

10. Waldrop, *Dream*, 105–107.

11. Ibid., 22.

12. J.C.R. Licklider, "Man-Computer Symbiosis," *IRE Transactions on Human Factors in Electronics HFE-1* (March 1960): 4–11.

13. AI research of the late 1950s and the 1960s tended to either focus on broad attempts to achieve generality of "thinking" machines or efforts to produce computing systems with powerful, but narrow, areas of expertise. Frequently the primary goal of AI researchers was to attempt to try to meet or exceed human intelligence, not to focus on how computers and humans could effectively work together.

14. Ibid.

15. J.C.R. Licklider, interview by William Aspray and Arthur Norberg October 28, 1988, in Cambridge, MA (Charles Babbage Institute, University of Minnesota). The inherent time lag of batch processing rendered it highly problematic for command and control.

16. Ibid.; Waldrop, *Dream*, 207–208.

17. Norberg and O'Neill, *Transforming*, 17; J.C.R. Licklider, interview.

18. J.C.R. Licklider, interview.

19. Ibid.

20. Ibid.; Norberg and O'Neill, *Transforming*, 17–20.

21. Ibid., 197.

22. Ibid.

23. Waldrop, *Dream*, 258.

24. Ibid., 7.

25. Science Advisory Board, "ESD Computer Technology Development Plan," December 1963, quoted in J.F. Egan, "White Paper on GENISYS," July 28, 1965; System Development Corporation, "GENISYS Compared with Manufacturer-Supplied Programming and Operating Systems," Technical Memo TM-L-2471, June 24, 1965 (RAND Corporation Archives).

26. Willis Ware to Paul G. Galentine, Jr., March 10, 1965 (RAND Corporation Archives). Colonel Galentine was Director of Computing for the U.S. Air Force's Electronic System Division.

27. Various correspondence and reports quoted in J.F. Egan, "White Paper on GENISYS," July 28, 1965 (RAND Corporation Archives).

28. Norberg and O'Neill, *Transforming*, 123–125. Both projects at RAND were overseen by Keith Uncapher. The RAND Tablet used a wire screen beneath the surface in conjunction with a stylus to enable finely detailed drawings. GRAIL concentrated on making efficiency subordinate to "the user's needs."

29. Sutherland did seek to get Lawrence Roberts to be named as his successor. Roberts did not want the position, but several years later would be the leader of IPTO's ARPANET project as well as director of IPTO.

30. During Sutherland's second year Taylor had taken on much of the active management of IPTO.

31. Norberg and O'Neill, *Transforming*, 129.

32. Ibid., 128.

33. Howard Reingold, *Tools for Thought* (New York: Simon & Schuster, 1985), 176–178.

34. CALDIC was one of the early computers built to the von Neumann architecture in the mid- to late-1940s.

35. Norbert Weiner, *The Human Uses of Human Beings: Cybernetics and Society* (Boston: Houghton Mifflin Company, 1950).

36. Thierry Bardin, *Bootstrapping: Douglas Engelbart, Coevolution, and the Origins of Personal Computing* (Stanford, CA: Stanford University Press, 2000), 4–10, 12–15.

37. Michael A. Hiltzik, *Dealers of Lightning: Xerox PARC and the Dawn of the Computer Age* (New York: HarperBusiness, 1999), 63–64.

38. Norberg and O'Neill, *Transforming*, 137–138, 143.

39. Waldrop, *Dream*, 5.

40. Ibid., 261–263.

41. Ibid.

42. Ibid., 264–265.

43. Janet Abbate, *Inventing the Internet* (Cambridge, MA: MIT Press, 1999), 96.

44. Waldrop, *Dream*, 275.

45. The system that Baran developed and RAND proposed to the air force was very large and ambitious. It included 400 Switching Nodes, servicing 100,000 simultaneous users via 200 Multiplexing Stations. While Baran's initial system focused on radio transmissions, Davies' system was based on wired communications. Paul Baran, "Cost Estimate" RM-3766-PR (1965); Brownlee Haydon to RAND Management Committee, memorandum M-5313, August 1665 (RAND Corporation archives).

46. "Internet" here is not to be confused with the World Wide Web, a subsequent development that exists on the Internet backbone and is based on some key software developments.

47. Martin Campbell-Kelly and William Aspray, *Computer: A History of the Information Machine* (New York: Basic Books, 1996), 290–293.

48. Ibid.

49. Abbate, *Inventing*, 106–108. Being able to send messages easily to long lists of people was fundamental to the creation of a real community of early ARPANET users.

50. Campbell-Kelly and Aspray, *Computer*, 290–293.

51. Robert Kahn and Vintin Cerf developed Transmission Control Protocol (TCP) in the mid-1970s in conjunction with a group of early network users that made up the Network Working Group. In 1978, TCP was split between breaking data into packets and reassembly (which remained TCP) and Internet Protocol (IP), which routed individual data packets. TCP/IP won out over the rival International Standards Organization (ISO) protocol in the early 1980s. The ISO model was more abstract and unproven, whereas TCP/IP was a tested workable technology developed by many of the nation's leading researchers in networking.

52. Hiltzik, *Dealers*, 29. This vague phrase was later used by a number of researchers at the firm to justify projects.

53. Ibid., 26–29. The final price was later slightly adjusted to $918 million.

54. Ibid., 29.

55. Ibid.

56. Ibid., 48–50, 119–123. George Pake gave Taylor the green light to hire Jerry Elkind, a MIT Ph.D. who had worked under Licklider and was head of computer research at BBN immediately prior to accepting the position of director of PARC's CSL.

57. In 1975, it would be moved to its permanent headquarters at 3333 Coyote Hill Road, Palo Alto.

58. Waldrop, *Dream*, 350–351.

59. Hiltzik, *Dealers*, 65–66.

60. Ibid., xxiii, 169–172.

61. Waldrop, *Dream*, 369–370.

62. Project MAC was MIT's longstanding computer research laboratory that had concentrated on research in time-sharing and personal computers.

63. Robert M. Metcalfe, "How Ethernet Was Invented," *Annals of the History of Computing* 16 (1994): 81–88.

64. Paul Ceruzzi, *A History of Modern Computing* (Cambridge, MA: MIT Press, 1998): 292.

65. Hiltzik, *Dealers*, 243.

66. Stewart Brand, "Space War: Fanatic Life and Symbolic Death Among the Computer Bums," *Rolling Stone*, December 7, 1972.

67. Campbell-Kelly and Apray, *Computer*, 269.

68. Ceruzzi, *History*, 256.

69. Xerox's "failure" in computing has been perpetuated by books such as Douglas K. Smith and Robert C. Alexander's *Fumbling the Future* (New York: Morrow, 1988). Other books that show more insight and balance, such as Michael A. Hiltzik's *Dealers of Lightning: Xerox PARC and the Dawn of the Computer Age* (New York: HarperBusiness, 1999), continue to emphasize Xerox's lost opportunity with PARC rather than the inherent challenges any large-scale firm has in transitioning into a new area.

70. Henry W. Chesbrough, *Open Innovation: The New Imperative for Creating and Profiting from Technology* (Boston: Harvard Business School Press, 2003), 1–20.

71. Hiltzik, *Dealers*, 259.

72. Ibid., xxvii.

—7—

The Personal Computer and Personal-Computer Software, 1975–1990

IPTO-funded projects, and subsequent research at Xerox PARC, anticipated many critical aspects that, in time, would make personal computers, software, and networking broadly appealing and useful. In contrast, during the early- to mid-1970s, the first personal computers were difficult to operate and had limited functionality. Initially, these machines were only attractive to a small subset of American consumers. Declining costs, fascination with video games, and most significantly, ongoing advances in the power of hardware and functionality and user-friendliness of software, began to change this as the 1980s progressed.

While certain similarities can be seen between the informal culture and enthusiasm of the researchers at Xerox PARC and the first wave of individuals to create the personal computer and personal computer software industries, the differences are more profound. PARC researchers were leading scientists and engineers who showed vision and insight into what computing could potentially mean for society. Many had been direct or indirect beneficiaries of IPTO support, and following the ideological lead of IPTO directors J.C.R. Licklider and Robert Taylor, were concerned not only with human-computer interactivity in the basic sense of individuals having their own computer, but more importantly, the nature of this interactivity and the augmentation of human capabilities. On the other hand, the first-movers in personal computers and personal computer software were less educated, following their *own* interests and, at least initially, targeting their *own* subculture of electronic/computer hobbyists. The ones who survived and thrived had, or quickly developed, more of a business sense, brought on some experienced managers, and took some well-calculated risks to rapidly grow their firms. Also, timing and circumstance played a significant role.

Much has been written of a "personal computer revolution" that occurred between the mid-1970s and mid-1980s, but the personal computer did not achieve a revolutionary impact until the following decade.[1] This occurred when technologies of the past (the ARPANET/Internet) were integrated with new technologies (hypertext markup language, browsers, and URLs) to transform the personal computer into a ubiquitous communication device. This chapter will explore a number of the key developments that led to the emergence and early growth of the personal computer and personal computer software industries. The following chapter will then examine the widespread transformation of this technology into the communications field, and the contribution, position, and strategy of individual firms in this revolution and its early aftermath.

INTEL, THE MICROPROCESSOR, AND MAKING THE PERSONAL COMPUTER FEASIBLE

In 1965 Gordon Moore, a founder of Fairchild Semiconductor and director of the firm's Research and Development Laboratories, wrote a soon to be famous article in the journal *Electronics* speculating on the future of integrated circuits and computing technology. Moore presciently stated, "Integrated circuits will lead to such wonders as home computers—or at least terminals connected to a central computer—automatic controls for automobiles, and personal portable communication equipment."[2] More importantly, he also predicted that the number of circuits per chip would double every eighteen months. This prediction, from a different vantage point, meant the cost of integrated circuits of a given capacity, or computer processing power, would be cut in half every eighteen months. The press soon christened this idea as Moore's Law, a law that held considerable predictive power for several decades.[3]

In 1969 Moore, Robert Noyce, and others left Fairchild to form a new chip company, Intel Corporation, in Santa Clara, California. Intel was initially only interested in producing standard memory chips. The firm, however, occasionally took on specialized contract work, and in 1970 was approached by Busicom, a Japanese calculator manufacturer seeking a logic chip. Intel engineer Ted Hoff proposed a general-purpose (programmable) logic chip rather than the specialized one Busicom initially requested. Intel's management backed Hoff's idea, though it saw no commercial pay-offs beyond the Busicom application.[4] In early 1971, Intel delivered the 4004 microchip, or microprocessor, to Busicom. At this time, Busicom held the rights to the design. Intel, however, reconsidered the future possibilities that a microprocessor, or "a computer on a chip," might have, and fortuitously renegotiated to give the Japanese firm cheaper unit costs in exchange for rights to market the chip to non-calculator customers. Intel began to develop new logic chips, and as foreign competition heightened in the memory chip field, soon focused much of its efforts and resources on microprocessors.

Intel followed the 4004 with the more powerful 8008 in 1972 and the 8080 in 1974. It was a small step from these microprocessors to a personal computer, but there were no significant personal computers developed until mid-decade. Before that time, no one saw a use or market for such devices. Even when this began to change, the first personal computers tended to be cheap kits that only appealed to a small group of people: computer hobbyists.

EDWARD ROBERTS AND MITS AND BILL GATES AND MICROSOFT: SERVING A GROWING HOBBYIST MARKET

Much like radio hobbyists of the early twentieth century, the growing visibility and decreasing cost of components led to the emergence of computer hobbyists in the early- to mid-1970s. Most of these hobbyists were middle-class white males in their late teens or twenties who had been exposed to computing technology at work, school, or through family or friends.

Recognizing this small but emerging market of computer hobbyists in 1974, Edward Roberts, who ran a small radio and model airplane firm in Albuquerque, New Mexico, Micro Instrumentation Telemetry Systems (MITS), moved into the personal computer field. He was not the first to design or build a personal computer, but he was the first to gain much attention. Roberts and his team designed a computer kit, the Altair 8800, built around the new Intel 8080, a microprocessor that, in roughly adhering to Moore's Law, was twenty times more powerful than the 4004. Roberts succeeded in getting *Popular Electronics* (*PE*) to feature the, as yet incomplete, Altair. The story appeared in the January 1975 issue with a cover photograph of an assembled, but largely empty and nonfunctional version of the machine.[5] MITS struggled to finish and ship the Altair kits to meet the rapidly growing demand created by the article. At a price of $397, the kit was not much more than what an Intel 8080 chip would cost an individual consumer.[6]

The Altair had an attractive price, but also many drawbacks. The kit was essentially just a box with switches and lights (the input/output system), a circuit board (containing the 8080 chip), and a power supply unit. Programming the Altair involved laboriously flipping switches to code in machine language. Sometimes, once constructed, the Altair did not even work. Nevertheless, MITS received many hundreds of orders in early 1975, and though it advertised delivery within sixty days, few kits were shipped before midyear because of the small staff and the firm's lack of experience in running such an operation.

One early reader of the Altair story in *PE* was William (Bill) Gates, a Harvard University freshman from Seattle who came from an upper-middle class family. Gates was intrigued with computer technology and had learned to program in BASIC on his high school's minicomputer time-sharing system back in 1969. BASIC (Beginners All-purpose Symbolic Instruction Code) was a relatively simple programming language developed by John Kemeny and Thomas Kurtz at Dartmouth in 1964. In the late 1960s and early 1970s, it became popular in the educational market and with computer hobbyists.

Gates and his friend, Paul Allen, almost immediately recognized that, just like minicomputer time-sharing systems, the Altair would need a BASIC translator to be more readily programmable. Gates and Allen quickly formed a company called Micro-soft, contacted Roberts, and developed a BASIC translator that the firm delivered during February of 1975.[7] Gates, demonstrating business acumen from the start, insisted on retaining the rights to the code, licensing rather than selling it to MITS. While Gates was the prototypical hobbyist in some regards, his desire to sell and profit from software clashed with the ethos of some early hobbyists who believed software code was something to be shared rather than sold.[8]

MITS received over $1 million in orders for the Altair during the first half of 1975. The firm continued to have some production and quality problems throughout the year, and though it had demonstrated that personal computing could be a business, other personal computer companies that sold assembled computers, such as IMS Associates Inc. (IMSAI), soon surpassed MITS. IMSAI would be the first to take advantage of a microcomputer operating system, a system built by a firm called Digital Research.

In the mid-1970s Digital Research's founder, Gary Kildall, had

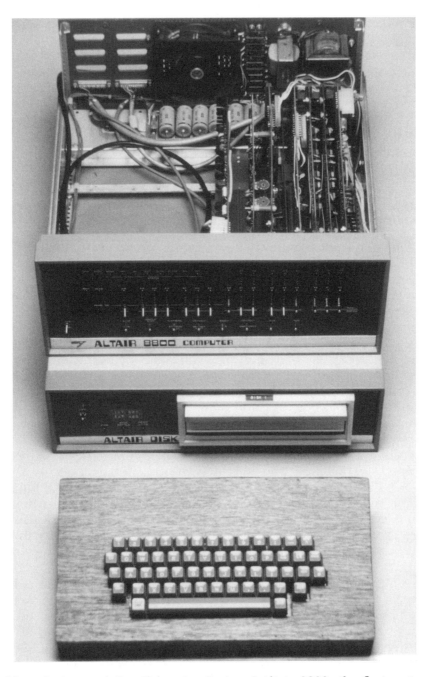

Micro Instrumentation Telemetry Systems' Altair 8800, the first major personal computer kit, 1975. (Courtesy of Charles Babbage Institute, University of Minnesota, Minneapolis)

developed an operating system, CP/M (Control Program/Monitor) on a DEC-PDP-10 with hopes of selling it to Intel, but the microprocessor manufacturer lacked interest. IMSAI, seeking an operating system for its new personal computer, soon approached Digital Research. Kildall split apart the original CP/M to separate out the parts that interfaced with different hardware into his Basic Input/Output System, or BIOS. What remained in CP/M could be used on all different types of computers. With this development, Digital Research became the leading personal computer operating systems company, a distinction that it would hold for more than a half-decade before being displaced by Microsoft.

PLAYING GAMES

One unmistakable draw for many early computer hobbyists was video games. Back in the fall of 1961, the first DEC PDP-1 was delivered to Massachusetts Institute of Technology. This Digital Equipment computer represented the start of the new field of minicomputing. It was the computer that J.C.R. Licklider did his early time-sharing work on at Bolt Beranek and Newman. It was also the machine upon which MIT artificial intelligence researcher Steve Russell created a short program called Spacewar. Spacewar was a two-player video game that allowed each player to control a spaceship and fire missiles. Russell saw no commercial opportunities for his program and allowed anyone at MIT to copy it. During the next several years the game spread, and a number of university and military minicomputer installations around the nation had a copy of Spacewar. Other games from other programmers soon followed and stirred a growing interest during the 1960s. By 1971, Computer Space, the first coin-operated video game machine, was built. The following year, Nolan Bushnell founded a video game company, Atari, and launched the legendary Pong, the first video arcade hit. Magnavox followed with a black-and-white soundless home paddle-hockey game that same year.[9]

A number of the individuals who would become early leaders in the development of personal computers were dedicated players and programmers of video games. Apple cofounder Steve Jobs was a video game designer for Atari in the mid-1970s, and games were frequently discussed within early computer hobbyist groups. More generally, during the early years of the personal computer trade, games would be a fundamental application that sparked interest in these machines. Code for games was published in trade magazines, and many programmed their own games to play, share, trade, and sell.[10]

In 1978 Atari, which had been sold by Bushnell to Warner Communications two years earlier for $28 million, came out with its commercially successful VCS (2600), a console that connected to televisions, included paddle and joystick controllers, and a "Combat" cartridge that allowed players to battle with tanks or planes.[11] Additionally, the first video game to become a large cultural phenomenon came out that same year: Space Invaders.

In 1980, Atari also succeeded in getting one of the great minds in computer graphics to head its new research laboratory, Xerox PARC's Alan Kay. With Kay's unparalleled reputation and connections, he was able to put together a strong team of computer graphics specialists. This contributed to Atari's continued success in the video game field. During the 1983 Christmas season alone, Atari sold more than 400,000 VCS (2600) machines. The firm soon claimed more than 75 percent of the home console video game market.[12] Concomitant to the launch of the Atari 2600, the firm also came out with two computers, the Atari 400 and the 800, but these machines were not very powerful, lacked compelling software, and were not successful in the marketplace.[13]

While game console makers had a tough time breaking into the personal computing field, they nevertheless had substantial impact on creating interest in computer technology. Arcade games had become a huge hit by the early 1980s with Space Invaders, Asteroids, Pac-Man, and other titles. In 1981, roughly $5 billion was spent on arcade games at malls, convenience stores, and other locations. Computer manufacturers selling lower-end machines, such as Commodore, were slashing prices on their computers to tap into the market and compete with the Atari 2600 as well as Mattel's Intellivision, which was launched in 1980. Around this time, Japanese video game houses Nintendo and Sega started exporting popular arcade games to the United States. Behind a successful character, Mario, that made his debut in the arcade machine game Donkey Kong in 1982, Nintendo built a brand that thrived for many years. In 1983, there was a major recession in the video game trade, and following this downturn, Nintendo and other Japanese firms took the lead in the American home console market. In 1990, Nintendo's game Super Mario 3 became the biggest home hit to date, grossing more than $500 million.[14]

The market for game consoles has had its ups and downs, but in the past decade has been fueled by more powerful systems (developed by Nintendo, Sega, Sony, and Microsoft) and more graphically intricate software created by many different firms. The pastime of playing games on computers has continued and is gaining new energy in the era of widespread computer networking. In 1993, a new game by Id Software called Doom was developed. Portions of the game, which involved a lone U.S. marine out to combat demons in outer space, were being shared on the Internet prior to the game's official release. Id subsequently sold more than 150,000 full versions of the software.[15]

Video game hardware and software is not only a huge business, but has profoundly impacted the broader personal computer and personal computer software industries. In the period generally thought of as the takeoff point of the personal computer, 1981 and 1982, more than four times more video game consoles were sold than personal computers. The value of consoles and game software/cartridges more than doubled that of home computers in both of these years.[16] While the console market and cartridges represented different businesses from arcade games and home computer games, the business and technological boundaries were often porous and cross-pollination of design talent and products occurred. It is difficult to assess the number of people (especially children) who were primarily introduced to computers through video games, and the number of home computer systems that were purchased, at least in part, as a means to play games. Nevertheless, given the vast quantity of games that have been sold, traded, and pirated, coupled with the hours spent playing and talking about the games (including highly controversial ones such as Sega's Mortal Combat), the economic and cultural impact on the broader computer industry has clearly been substantial.

BUILDING AN INDUSTRY: STEVE JOBS, STEPHEN WOZNIAK, AND APPLE COMPUTER

A number of early hobbyists had strong political agendas and gained attention as "computer liberationists," or individuals believing in the possibility of computers helping to create a freer society. Many of these individuals were influenced by the broader counterculture of the time. As some hobbyists espoused radical notions, many, and likely most hobbyists, were just interested in using the technology, not the politics of the machine.

Electronic enthusiasts Fred Moore and Gordon French formed one of the earliest and unquestionably the most famous of the computer hobbyists groups in March 1975. The first of the monthly meetings was held in French's garage in Menlo Park, California. While discussions of the computer as a possible tool of liberation occurred at some meetings, often the dialogue was about computer hardware, getting home machines up and running, buying components, starting companies, and applications software—particularly games.[17]

Meetings of the group soon grew to include hundreds of participants and were held at schools and other locations. The group decided on the name "Bay Area Amateur Computer Users Group—Homebrew Computer Club."[18] More than twenty of the attendees of the club's early meetings would go on to form computer companies. Many of these would not survive, but one would become, and for a few years hold the position as the leading personal computer company in the world: Apple Computer.

Steve Jobs and Stephen Wozniak, both from Cupertino, California, were close friends from high school and attended a number of the early Homebrew Computer Club meetings. Wozniak fit the model of most computer hobbyists, having an early interest in radio, and later minicomputing. Jobs spent some time drifting in and out of education, traveling, and studying Eastern religion before settling into a job as a game designer for Atari. In 1976, Jobs and Wozniak teamed up to form Apple Computer to build and sell personal computers—initially out of Jobs' garage. Earlier, Wozniak had been unsuccessful in trying to convince his employer, Hewlett-Packard, to manufacture personal computers. Wozniak was technically gifted, and Jobs understood the importance of growing the firm quickly to stand apart from the many emerging personal computer companies. Jobs succeeded in using an Atari connection to secure venture capital from Mike Markkula, a former engineer at Fairchild Semiconductor and executive at Intel. The original computer that Wozniak designed, the Apple, did not include a keyboard, or even a case for the circuits, and was not a success.

In February 1977, the firm moved out of Jobs' garage into a 2,000 square foot office in Cupertino. At this time, Wozniak was perfecting the Apple II. This machine included a 1 MHz 6502 processor, a built-in keyboard, a cassette recorder storage device, eight expansion ports, and game paddles. The Apple II, more advanced and refined than the machines of its primary competitors, hit the market in April 1977 at a list price of $1,298.[19] It contained a full-size keyboard, unlike calculator firm Commodore's PET, and had more peripherals than Radio Shack subsidiary Tandy's TRS-80. It also used Apple's internally designed and programmed operating system, rather than Digital Research's CP/M. As a result of Wozniak's design and programming skills, and the fact that Jobs had secured the talented Silicon Valley public relations

175

strategist Regis McKenna, the Apple II achieved considerable early success. It, however, would take a compelling application for this machine, and for Apple Computer, to grow into a powerhouse.

VISICALC: THE FIRST "KILLER APP"

Steve Jobs' focus on quickly establishing Apple's position in personal computing pushed the company to build new models and gain important brand recognition. This resulted in numerous amateur and professional programmers designing software specifically for Apple computers.[20] While software developers created products to help people with personal finances, foreign languages, and other educational and business areas, the largest field of applications was games. One amateur programmer, twenty-six-year-old Harvard MBA student, Daniel Bricklin, would help alter this balance and make a substantial mark on the trajectory of the personal computer and personal computer software industries.

In 1979, Bricklin conceived of using a personal computer for financial analysis, and conceptualized a spreadsheet program. Spreadsheets were not new to computing, but previously had only been developed for minicomputers and mainframes. The freedom of having a personal machine to "run the numbers" was a real breakthrough. Bricklin, more of a software designer (a developer of major concepts and structure rather than the actual code), collaborated with his friend and skilled programmer, Bob Frankston, to form a company called Software Arts.

One of Bricklin's finance professors put him in contact with a former student who had gone into the software field, Dan Fylstra. Fylstra had founded Personal Software, a company that, like many software product firms of the time, specialized in games (MicroChess was its primary product). Despite this focus, Fylstra's background in business school helped him to recognize quickly the potential of Bricklin and Frankston's concept. Fylstra loaned Software Arts the personal computer he was most impressed with for running his games, an Apple II.[21] Frankston proceeded to program a spreadsheet called VisCalc, short for visible calculator, and Fylstra struck a deal whereby he would publish the software (reproduce and market it) for a 37.5 percent royalty. Following his practice with computer games, Fylstra sold software products to retail outlets rather than original equipment manufacturers (OEMs). VisiCalc was an instant success and not only made great sums of money for Fylstra, and Bricklin and Frankston, but also for Apple Computer.[22]

For a year this first killer application, or "killer app," was only sold on the Apple II platform.[23] This distinguished the capabilities of the Apple II from the typical CP/M-based systems on the market. Apple, which previously had focused exclusively on the home and educational area, suddenly found its way into the business market. Fylstra had the rights to the program for other systems; and after a year, Software Arts was programming versions of Visi-Calc for other prominent personal computer platforms. Based on the importance of VisiCalc, Fylstra renamed his firm VisiCorp.

VisiCalc would become the leading spreadsheet program for many other makes and models of personal computers, including for a brief time, IBM's first entry into the personal computer field. Despite the importance of VisiCalc to Apple, especially in that first year when it only existed for that platform, VisiCalc would generate more revenue from its IBM version than from any other. This, however, would be short-lived. Conflict between Software Arts and VisiCorp led to counterproductive management of the product. This was exacerbated by a series of lawsuits and counter-lawsuits between the two firms, and a new competitor's even more prolific, killer-app spreadsheet for IBM. In the end, the conflict and outcome demonstrated the potential risks that exist when both a software producer and a software publisher are dependent on the success of a single product.[24]

It is ironic that spreadsheet programs were the first killer apps. Spreadsheets previously had been specialized, expensive tools for more powerful computers, while typewriters and the demand for typed text, were ubiquitous. Early personal computers, however, did not have lowercase character output capabilities, and affordable printers lacked speed and quality. Also, word processors were not perceived as new and exciting. Dedicated word processing machines had been around for years, and unlike minicomputer spreadsheet systems, some had become relatively affordable. Despite these factors, there nevertheless was a significant initial demand for word processing software, and its early impact might have been even greater if the industry leader in this area had not faltered.

Mainframe software programmer Seymour Rubinstein developed an early interest in the possibilities of personal computers and became software product marketing manager for IMSAI in 1977. The following year he left IMSAI to form personal computer software firm, MicroPro. Based on Rubinstein's general design and former IMSAI programmer Rob Barnaby's code, MicroPro came out with a word processor that soon evolved into WordStar. WordStar, which sold hundreds of units a month from the start, and had sold more than a million copies by mid-decade, quickly gained two-thirds of the word processing software market.[25] Following a heart attack in the early 1980s, Rubinstein signed over controlling interest in MicroPro, leaving authority to a venture capitalist. Rubinstein deeply regretted this decision, WordStar ceased to be the firm's focus under MicroPro's new management, and consequently, the word processing program WordPerfect surpassed WordStar in the mid-1980s.[26]

THE IBM PC

IBM had not been the first mover in mainframe computing. It carefully surveyed the market, developed technical know-how as the primary computer contractor for SAGE, and when the trade appeared to offer opportunity, moved quickly to enter the field and become the industry leader. Its enormous capital, cash flow from punch-card and tabulation equipment, large customer base, and unparalleled sales and service capabilities facilitated this success. Throughout IBM's history, it has at times been a technological innovator, but has rarely been the most technologically innovative company in the industry. IBM made powerful computers, but Control Data and Cray Research made more powerful computers. IBM eventually expanded its product line to include minicomputers, but Digital Equipment Corporation and others made more cost-effective minicomputers. This did not prevent IBM from using its base, sales and service skills, brand— and according to competitors, anticompetitive practices—to maintain its overall industry leadership. When IBM entered the personal computer arena, it did so in a new way and created some new opportunities. Ultimately, however, IBM's focus on earlier types of technology, coupled with some miscalculations, handcuffed its ability to hold on to its leadership position in personal computing and challenged the mighty Big Blue in a way it had not been previously challenged.

IBM long followed the classic model that leading business historian Alfred Chandler has emphasized with regard to integration. Much like Ford, General Motors, General Electric, and other large companies, when IBM had the opportunity to vertically integrate, it did. IBM showed greater similarity to Ford than General Motors, in that it usually integrated through building and expanding internal capabilities rather than engaging in external acquisitions. When it came time to enter the personal computer field, it broke with the past and opened an opportunity, but only took advantage of it in part, and for only a limited amount of time. While it did not acquire a firm, an action that typically requires great skill to integrate quickly and benefit from in the fast-paced high technology field, it did outsource technological know-how and key components.

Once VisiCalc and the Apple II had demonstrated that a personal computer could be a viable business machine, IBM moved quickly the following year to develop its personal computer, the IBM PC. The development team, the Entry Systems Division in Boca Raton, Florida, was far from the traditional bureaucratic culture that existed at IBM's New York facilities. The Entry Systems Division developed a proposal in July 1980 led by laboratory manager Bill Lowe. He pledged to finish the project in a year, knowing he would achieve this by breaking with IBM's tradition of internal development in favor of outsourcing nearly all the components and software. After getting the green light from IBM's top management, Lowe was promoted and Don Estridge took over the project. The key to the Entry Systems Division's success in producing the PC was that it was run as an independent business unit and did not suffer from the "not invented here" syndrome.

IBM had originally wanted Digital Research's CP/M operating system, but in one of the great examples of the importance of timing, there was miscommunication and Digital Research's Gary Kindall missed the meeting with IBM. IBM's team proceeded from California to the Seattle area to visit Microsoft, where they hoped to get a version of BASIC for the machine. According to Gates, he convinced IBM to go with a 16-bit (an Intel 8088) processor instead of the typical 8-bit processor being used by other personal computer firms. There, however, were no 16-bit operating systems on the market, though Digital Research had its 16-bit CP/M-86 under development. Similarly, Seattle Computer Products was also completing a 16-bit operating system, and Gates took a risk in buying the rights for this system, QDOS (Quick and Dirty Operating System), for $50,000—a substantial sum for Microsoft at this point. With no guarantees he could ever sell QDOS, which Gates renamed MS-DOS, he made a sales trip to Boca Raton and was successful. IBM purchased rights to use MS-DOS, which it packaged as PC-DOS, and a BASIC interpreter from Microsoft.[27] Gate's gamble established a relationship between the two companies' products that has continued ever since—and more importantly, as the IBM platform became the industry standard, Microsoft controlled the standard operating system.

The IBM Personal Computer (PC) was launched in August 1981 and listed for $2,880.[28] IBM did not have the sales force to sell these machines and did not want to confuse existing customer relationships for its more expensive and more powerful mainframe and minicomputers, so it utilized retailers, including Computerland and Sears. The firm was uncertain about the proper way to

IBM Personal Computer with keyboard and monochrome display, 1981. (Courtesy of Charles Babbage Institute, University of Minnesota, Minneapolis)

market the machine, but in naming it the Personal Computer it was covering the home market, while the IBM name and brand alone would indicate its appropriateness for business. The company benefited from a successful advertising campaign that featured Charlie Chaplin's Little Tramp.[29] Both the business and home markets responded well, and the machine, after gaining momentum based on a new killer app, legitimized personal computers as standard office equipment.

LOTUS 1-2-3: TAKING KILLER APPS TO THE NEXT LEVEL

Bricklin and Frankston's version of VisiCalc for the IBM PC, like that for other computers, was based on the original for the Apple II. It did not take advantage of the greater memory capacity of the PC. Prior to the launch of the PC, VisiCorp, recognizing that the original VisiCalc was becoming dated, concentrated on some new programs. One was Visiplot/VisiTrend, programmed by Mitch

Kapor and Eric Rosenfield. Visiplot/VisiTrend could plot data on graphs and had far more functionality than VisiCalc. Kapor, who had become head of the software business for VisiCorp, anticipated that the soon-to-be released IBM PC would become the standard—both IBM's hardware and the operating system, PC-DOS (Disk Operating System). Kapor decided to leave VisiCorp, and risk his own capital to found Lotus Development Corporation around a powerful spreadsheet program based on PC hardware and PC-DOS. Kapor not only developed an impressive product in Lotus 1-2-3, but also showed insight by initiating a heavy advertising campaign that extended beyond the trade publications into popular news magazines. Lotus 1-2-3, at a retail price of $495, sold 850,000 copies in its first eighteen months, making it by far the most successful software application program of its time.[30] All of a sudden, Lotus Development was the leading personal computer software company in the world. Lotus 1-2-3, in turn, became the killer application that helped IBM rapidly surpass Apple and contributed to *Time Magazine* naming the IBM PC "Man of the Year" in 1982. More significantly, Lotus 1-2-3 was a major force behind establishing IBM as the standard hardware platform and DOS as the standard operating system.

Lotus 1-2-3 continued to be a big seller for the firm throughout the mid-1980s, but other product rollouts were far less successful. In 1984, Microsoft sought to acquire Lotus Development. Kapor was in favor of selling the firm, but the company's new leader, Jim Manzi, opposed the offer. In some respects, Lotus seemed a victim of its own success. The initial product, Lotus 1-2-3, was such a hit that the company had difficulty seeing beyond it. As a Microsoft competitor, the firm was slow to adopt a version of Lotus 1-2-3 for Windows and was surpassed by Microsoft's spreadsheet program: Excel. Lotus Development, however, did come up with another big product, Lotus Notes, a groupware program that allowed people to share and access data. This is the product that led to IBM's interest in the firm, and in 1995, it acquired Lotus Development.[31]

In contrast to Lotus, Microsoft continued to thrive throughout the 1980s and was a much larger firm than Lotus by decade's end, surpassing it in revenue during 1987.[32] Gates had successfully captured the operating system market with MS-DOS and would continue this stranglehold with Windows. During the 1980s, the company built a full range of basic software, bundled it as Microsoft Office, and became the leader in spreadsheets (Excel), word processing (Word), and other common types of applications. Microsoft had grown from three employees with

$16,000 in revenue in 1975 to roughly 1,000 employees and $140 million in revenue a decade later. In 1990 it would cross the $1 billion revenue mark and have more than 5,600 employees.[33]

BRING ON THE CLONES

Like Mitch Kapor's insightful decision to focus on the IBM PC from the beginning, Bill Gates also showed great insight in acquiring QDOS and retaining the rights to market versions of PC-DOS (called MS-DOS) to other firms. These actions were critical to setting the stage for personal computer firms to incorporate an imitation strategy.

IBM believed that publishing and obtaining a copyright for its ROM-BIOS (Read Only Memory–Basic Input/Output) code would provide legal barriers against imitators. ROM-BIOS served the function of connecting the generic operating system to the specific hardware. IBM also thought that its purchasing power as a volume customer of components would prevent imitators. Finally, just as IBM had been cautious to avoid precipitating a decline in demand for its mainframes when it grew its minicomputing business in the 1970s, the firm wanted to assure that sales of its personal computers did not have a negative impact on its minicomputer and mainframe revenue. The notion of "creative destruction," developing innovative new products that would cannibalize existing lines, was not part of IBM's culture. IBM was a large bureaucratic firm that wanted to maintain its place in the industry by protecting existing revenue streams.[34]

On the first two counts IBM was wrong in its assumptions, and on the third, it miscalculated the future importance of personal computers. The way around IBM's copyright was to reverse engineer ROM-BIOS by recreating all of the functionality, but with different code. IBM was right that customers would have to pay higher prices for components, but failed to grasp that the higher overhead of its large infrastructure would more than offset the difference.[35] With regard to failing to cannibalize existing products in the minicomputer area, IBM failed to grasp how the personal computer business had its own set of characteristics. IBM had been able to move successfully into and come to lead mainframe computing despite the other firms that preceded it into this area. The customers, however, were largely the same as those for IBM's pre–digital computer tabulating machine business. With personal computing, a whole new set of customers was in the marketplace, and IBM had no unique infrastructure (other than its brand) providing competitive advantage in selling its machines. IBM would continue to ride the initial wave of success throughout much of the 1980s, but its market share in the personal computing field would continually decline and contribute to severe financial problems for the firm. IBM, after more than seven decades (which included the Great Depression) of consecutive positive annual net earnings would suffer a series of annual net losses in the early 1990s.[36]

Compaq was the first company to overcome what were in retrospect only modest hurdles and successfully implement an imitation strategy against IBM in personal computing. This Houston-based firm, founded by three former Texas Instrument managers, Rod Canion, Jim Harris, and Bill Murto, reverse engineered ROM-BIOS and cloned the IBM PC during 1982. In its first year in business, Compaq's revenue from its PC clone exceeded $100 million. In the early- to mid-1980s many personal computer companies followed Compaq's lead to make IBM clones. The computer firms that continued to build their own hardware and software systems, for the most part, did not survive. The notable exception was a company that had built a considerable base, had strong marketing, and implemented a successful differentiation strategy that yielded significant, but varying levels of success in the coming years: Apple Computer.

A COUPLE OF DAYS IN THE PARC: THE APPLE VISITS AND THE LISA AND MACINTOSH PROJECTS

Apple was dethroned from its leadership in the personal computing field by the IBM PC in 1982, but it was still faring better than the computer giant's other competitors and was engaged in a development project to take computing technology to a new level. Back in 1979, the Xerox Development Corporation (XDC) had invested $1.05 million for 100,000 shares of Apple stock. XDC was interested in further investing in Apple, and, as part of the deal, Apple was granted its request to send a small team to Xerox PARC to observe technological developments at PARC's Computer Science Laboratory. PARC had let visitors in before to see its technology, but letting Jobs and others from Apple in was different. PARC Computer Science Laboratory associate manager Robert Taylor, who was out of town at the time of the Apple visit, later remarked that he "would have told him [Jobs] to get out."[37]

The Apple group included Apple president Mike Scott, Steve Jobs, Bill Atkinson, and five others. They were given the standard tour. Jobs and the others came back a few days later unannounced wanting to see more details on certain technologies, particularly PARC's Smalltalk, software that might help them with the interface for their Lisa computer that was under development. Adele Goldberg and other PARC researchers were reluctant to provide any details, but Xerox headquarters backed the XDC's request, and the PARC researchers had to oblige.[38] Larry Tesler later remarked that he was struck by the quality of the questions he received.[39] Behind Jobs' strong backing, Apple was focused on the Lisa project and the firm had hired a number of engineers away from Hewlett-Packard and Digital Equipment Corporation to work on the project.

Atkinson, the chief programmer for the Lisa, was amazed by the sophistication of the work at PARC. In addition to the technology the Apple team saw in those two days, Apple also wound up with some of PARC's personnel. Several months after the visit, Larry Tesler, frustrated that PARC's important computing developments were not getting out to consumers, left the center to join Apple Computer. Other PARC engineers, including Owen Densmore and Steve Capps quickly followed Tesler over to Apple. In the early 1980s, Taylor became very frustrated at the mass exodus of top PARC scientists and engineers, and in 1983, after being insulted by the new PARC director, he too left, which led to an even more rapid draining of PARC research talent.[40]

Nevertheless, Apple was not merely copying or replicating PARC technology. It was borrowing and integrating numerous ideas, but was also modifying certain methods and functionality. For instance, the ability to drag and resize windows with a pointer was conceptualized by Bill Atkinson and was not present at PARC.[41]

Despite the fact that Apple had considerable technical talent, and was soon joined by some key PARC personnel such as Tesler, it was years rather than months before Apple could produce a computer with a graphical user interface (GUI) based on icons, overlapping windows, and a point-and-click system. This computer, Lisa, was completed in 1983 and had a price tag of around $10,000. Given this high price compared to other personal computers, it suffered from the same problem as the technologically impressive Xerox Star: it was too expensive to create much demand. Apple had a concurrent, similar project, Macintosh, and Jobs influenced the designers to keep the primary functionality and attributes of Lisa, but to cut out many of the costs. In January 1984, Apple unveiled its Macintosh computer to the public in a now famous two-minute advertisement during the Super Bowl that incorporated an Orwellian motif and presented the machine

Apple Computer's Lisa 2 (left) and Macintosh personal computers featuring 32-bit microprocessors, high-resolution bit-mapped graphics, and mouse point-and-click devices. (Courtesy of Charles Babbage Institute, University of Minnesota, Minneapolis)

as revolutionary—declaring that with the introduction of the Macintosh "you'll see why 1984 won't be like *1984*."

The advertisement created a stir and Apple benefited from a great deal of free advertising in the succeeding days and weeks as portions of it were replayed and discussed on television and written about in the print media. The Macintosh was a success in the marketplace; it represented roughly 10 percent of personal computer installations nationally, but failed make a big impact in the lucrative business market. The president Jobs had brought in, former PepsiCo executive John Sculley, and Apple chair Mike Markkula, questioned Jobs' management decisions. In 1985, Jobs was relieved of any active management responsibility, and left the firm soon thereafter.[42] While the Macintosh was user-friendly, its small screen and one-piece design (excluding input/output technologies such as the keyboard and mouse) made it appear more of a toy than a business tool to some.

APPLE AND MICROSOFT: APPLICATIONS AND WINDOWS OF OPPORTUNITY

The Macintosh had a major impact on the second leading personal computer software firm of the time: Microsoft. Bill Gates had a strong drive to make Microsoft the number one software firm.

Despite its monopoly on PC-platform operating systems, the success of Lotus 1-2-3 had propelled Lotus Development past Microsoft. Gates became increasingly interested in his firm's software applications products. This division of Microsoft had been formed in 1979, after the firm attracted a top Xerox PARC software engineer, Charles Simonyi, who, like Tesler and many others, had been frustrated by Xerox's lack of commitment to commercialize computing technology. Simonyi headed the division and influenced Gates with his concept of a "metaprogrammer," or a person who developed basic design features and left coding to a team of programmers. Microsoft, being a large and growing organization by this time, instituted a hierarchy of metaprogrammers, to create what Gates saw as a software factory.[43] As Microsoft increased its focus on applications in the mid-1980s, the Macintosh provided a test bed to try out and refine products, particularly its word processing program, MS Word, insulated from the competition of WordStar, WordPerfect, and other programs that concentrated on the PC-compatible platform.

The other impact of the Macintosh on Microsoft was that it led the firm to place an increasing focus on developing a graphical user interface (GUI) for the PC platform, one with similar features to the Macintosh GUI (windows, icons, point-and-click, etc.). The Xerox Star had led Microsoft, Digital Research, VisiCorp, and others to begin researching a PARC-style GUI, but the Macintosh is what inspired and pressured these firms to follow through on developing such an operating system. Gates had visited Steve Jobs back in 1981 and saw the Macintosh under development, which led to his decision to initiate a GUI development project. The technical problem was immense. Microsoft and others could abandon MS-DOS and be free to develop a system as Apple had done, but this would render all MS-DOS platform software applications unusable. Alternatively, it could place a GUI structure on top of MS-DOS. This was problematic because it required a lot of memory that pushed existing personal computers to their limit. Gates went with the latter strategy. Though Digital Research and others came out with GUI operating systems first, high prices and technical problems plagued these systems. Microsoft won the competition, but its system was slower and less visually appealing than that of the Macintosh.

Microsoft used graphics similar to that of the Macintosh on Windows and signed a licensing agreement with Apple Computer in November 1985. In late 1987, Microsoft came out with a new version, Windows 2.0, which had graphics that were nearly identical to those of the Macintosh. In March 1988, Apple sued Microsoft for copyright infringement.[44] This was an important case that continued for several years, but was eventually dismissed. Microsoft had met the challenge to maintain its leadership in operating systems software in the dominant PC segment of the market, and it had launched an application software division that it refined on the Apple platform before successfully transferring it to PC compatible machines. As time passed, Microsoft bore more and more resemblance to IBM. It was becoming a large international firm with near monopolies in some fields, it had a commitment to bring new technologies to market even if these technologies were not as sophisticated as that of its competitors, and it was becoming increasingly adept at using its strength in some segments to help it in others.

CONTINUITY AND CHANGE: PERSONAL COMPUTERS AND PERSONAL COMPUTER SOFTWARE

On the surface, the personal computer appeared to emerge as a revolutionary new technology and product extending entirely from a new group of individuals: computer hobbyists. The first hobbyists, however, seemed primarily focused on serving themselves and their fellow hobbyists, and only a select few began to recognize and help facilitate the broader interest developing around the personal computer with games, spreadsheets, word processors, and other applications. The hobbyists who survived in the computer business, such as Steve Jobs, benefited greatly from the venture capital and public relations infrastructure in Silicon Valley. Likewise, many of the important "new" ideas in personal computing and personal computer software had precursors in IPTO and other DoD-funded research of the 1960s, as well as PARC and other industry-funded research of the 1970s. The graphical user interface of the Macintosh had precursors in IPTO-funded SRI work and its subsequent refinement at Xerox PARC. Even the technology that made the personal computer feasible, microprocessors, extended from a long series of developments in semiconductor technology (from Bell Laboraties to Shockley Semiconductor to Fairchild Semiconductor to Intel), some of which was funded by the DoD.

Microsoft, which got its start selling BASIC translators, made some insightful and timely decisions and benefited from fortuitous circumstances. During the 1980s this firm solidified its near monopoly on personal computer operating systems, expanded into leadership in word processing and spreadsheet software, and arguably benefited substantially from ties created between systems and applications. Certain commonalities existed between Microsoft's position and strategy in the personal computer software industry and that of IBM's past. Alongside these connections, the impact of personal computers was beginning to touch more and more individuals. The proliferation of personal computing and widespread application of networking technologies (a mixture of both new and old technology) during the following decade would take the impact of computing to an entirely new level and result in new information technology (IT) segments, rapid growth, and in retrospect, irrational expectations for the future.

NOTES

1. In addition to the popular use of the term "personal computer revolution" within the press during the 1980s, *Time* magazine broke with its practice of naming actual human beings "Man of the Year," in a January 1983 issue the magazine bequeathed this honor to the IBM PC; Peter H. Lewis, "The Computer Revolution Revised," *New York Times* (August 7, 1988); J. C. Dvorak, "Nerds, Women, Radicals, and the Ironies of the PC Revolution," *PC Computing* 4, no. 8 (August 1991): 58. Anthropologist Bryan Pfaffenberger, in "The Social Meaning of the Personal Computer: Or, Why the Personal Computer Revolution Was No Revolution," *Anthropological Quarterly* 61, no. 1 (January 1988): 39–47, examined "meaning frameworks" and argued that the personal computer failed to empower people and revolutionize work, education, or other areas. This article, of course, preceded the advent of the World Wide Web.

2. Gordon E. Moore, "Cramming More Components onto Integrated Circuits," *Electronics* 38, no. 8 (April 19, 1965): 82–85.

3. In recent years, the doubling of circuits per chip has taken longer than eighteen months, but the expansion of computer processing relative to cost remains rapid.

4. Discussion of the possibility of a programmable logic chip had occurred in some technical circles for several years, but this was the first time such an endeavor was attempted.

5. H. Edward Roberts and William Yates, "ALTAIR 8800: The Most Powerful Minicomputer Project Ever Presented—Can Be Built for Under $400," *Popular Electronics* (January 1975): 33–38. The ALTAIR 8800 was referred to as a minicomputer, but bore all the characteristics of personal computers to follow (use of microprocessors, low cost, created for home use and for individual users, etc.). While it was more powerful than other personal computers that had used the Intel 8008 chip, it was not as powerful as many minicomputers on the market at the time. One portion of the article was continued in the February 1975 issue of *Popular Electronics*. An editorial on page 4 of the January 1975 issue of *Popular Electronics* proclaimed in its title, "The Home Computer Is Here."

6. MITS was able to offer this price because it negotiated a special deal with Intel to buy the chips for only $75 apiece.

7. The firm's name was soon changed from Micro-Soft to Microsoft.

8. Martin Campbell-Kelly and William Aspray, *Computer: A History of the Information Machine* (New York: Basic Books, 1996), 245.

9. J. C. Herz, *Joystick Nation: How Videogames Ate Our Quarters, Won Our Hearts, and Rewired Our Minds* (Boston: Little, Brown and Company, 1997), 5–7, 14–15.

10. Early video game programmers would place classified advertisements in computer trade publications and sell games via mail.

11. Martin Campbell-Kelly, *From Airline Reservations to Sonic the Hedgehog: A History of the Software Industry* (Cambridge, MA: MIT Press, 2003), 275.

12. Ibid., 275.

13. Herz, *Joystick*, 83.

14. Ibid., 21.

15. Ibid., 84.

16. Campbell-Kelly, *Airline*, 276.

17. Steven Levy, *Hackers: Heroes of the Computer Revolution* (New York: Doubleday-Anchor, 1984), 194–197; Paul Freiberger and Michael Swaine, *Fire in the Valley: The Making of the Personal Computer*, 2nd ed. (New York: McGraw-Hill, 2000), 118–124. Because computer-liberationist Lee Felsenstein took on the role as moderator at these at times chaotic meetings, the political nature of the overall group has likely been overemphasized. Also, the more radical members of the club were generally not the ones who initiated firms and impacted the computer industry.

18. Generally only the last part of the name ("Homebrew Computer Club") was used.

19. The Apple Museum, specification page for Apple II: http://www.theapplemuseum.com/index.php?id am&page=personal&subpage=apple 2_2&skin=specs.

20. Apple had unique operating systems while many computers of other manufacturers used CP/M.

21. Dan Fylstra, "The Creation and Destruction of VisiCalc," unpublished paper distributed by the author at "PC Software: The First Decade," a conference held in Boston, MA, on May 6–7, 2004.

22. Ibid. At its peak, VisiCorp, Personal Software's new name after it became the firm's primary product, was paying $1 million a month in royalties to Dan Bricklin and Bob Frankston's Software Arts.

23. "Killer application" is a term used to refer to a software program that achieves such popularity that it convinces many consumers to purchase hardware to run the software, and in the process becomes a major commercial success.

24. Ibid. Personal Software sued VisiCorp for VisiOn Calc, a product that it argued was derivative of VisiCalc. VisiCorp sued Personal Software for not maintaining development of the product as was stipulated in the original contract. Software Arts assets were sold to Lotus Development Corporation in 1985, a competitor that discontinued the VisiCalc product.

25. Campbell-Kelly and Aspray, *Computer*, 262.

26. Seymour Rubinstein, interview by Jeffrey R. Yost, May 6, 2004, in Boston, MA (Charles Babbage Institute, University of Minnesota).

27. Robert X. Cringely, *Accidental Empires: How the Boys of Silicon Valley Make Their Millions, Battle Foreign Competition, and Still Can't Get a Date* (New York: HarperBusiness, 1996), 131–134.

28. Campbell-Kelly and Aspray, *Computer*, 257.

29. Emerson Pugh, *Building IBM* (Cambridge, MA: MIT Press, 1995), 314.

30. Campbell-Kelly and Aspray, *Computer*, 262–263.

31. Cringely, *Accidental*, 323–324.

32. Paul Freiberger and Michael Swaine, *Fire*, 395.

33. Michael A. Cusumano and Richard W. Selby, *Microsoft Secrets: How the World's Most Powerful Software Company Creates Technology, Shapes Markets, and Manages People* (New York: Touchstone, 1995), 3.

34. Kenneth Flamm, *Creating the Computer: Government, Industry, and High Technology* (Washington, DC: The Brookings Institution, 1988), 238. Personal computer consumption (in terms of revenue) first exceeded mini-computers in 1982.

35. Cringely, *Accidental*, 171–173.

36. Pugh, *Building*, 323–324.

37. M. Mitchell Waldrop, *The Dream Machine: J.C.R. Licklider and the Revolution that Made Computing Personal* (New York: Penguin Books, 2001), 450.

38. Michael Hiltzik, *Dealers of Lightning: Xerox PARC and the Dawn of the Computer Age* (New York: HarperBusiness, 1999), 329–345. This source provides the most detailed, and likely the most accurate account of the Apple visit to PARC.

39. Steven Levy, *Insanely Great: The Life and Times of Macintosh, the Computer that Changed Everything* (New York: Penguin Books, 1994), 78–79.

40. Waldrop, *Dream*, 451. Taylor resigned from PARC in late 1983 and by 1984 had arranged to launch and become director of Digital Equipment Corporation's System Research Center in Palo Alto. Butler Lampson, Charles Thacker, and thirteen other PARC scientists soon followed. Prior to Taylor's departure Larry Tesler and others left for Apple Computer, Alan Kay for Atari, and Charles Simonyi for Microsoft.

41. Levy, *Insanely*, 91.

42. Cringely, *Accidental*, 196–200. Jobs held the chair position and Sculley was hired as president once Markkula retired from the position in 1983. Markkula went on to become Apple's chair. Sculley formally had been an executive at PepsiCo. Jobs likely chose Sculley in order to have someone he thought he could control—something he was able to do at first, but less so once Sculley learned more about the computer business.

43. Ibid., 110–111.

44. Campbell-Kelly and Apray, *Computer*, 279.

—8—

The Computer Networking Revolution and the Computer Industry, 1990–2004

By the second half of the 1980s, the personal computer had become a standard tool for many office workers, a growing number of individuals had purchased personal computers for their homes, and the use of these machines by educational institutions was becoming increasingly common. Following upon Robert Metcalfe's development of the Ethernet at Xerox PARC, local area networks (LANs) were beginning to proliferate within corporations and other organizations. This was facilitated and accelerated when Metcalfe founded the Santa Clara–based 3Com Corporation in 1979 and commercialized LAN technology, and also by 3Com's emerging competitors.[1] During the 1980s, local computer networks typically made it possible for individuals in a particular facility, office, or department to communicate, exchange data, and share expensive peripheral devices such as laser printers. In spite of these developments, personal computer networking was still in its infancy. During this decade, many personal computers in peoples' homes were not networked at all, and personal computers that were part of LANs generally were not networked with other LANs, the ARPANET, or the emerging Internet.

Technological developments occurring in a world-renowned particle physics laboratory, CERN (Centre Européen de Recherche Nucléaire), as well as in corporations and universities, altered this environment during the 1990s. Together, these developments spawned a revolution in the use of computing technology, transforming personal computers from stand-alone devices into unprecedented information and communication tools. With this, the computer industry broadened beyond the computer and software businesses to include the important new sector of networking. Computer networking companies developed the hardware and specialized software that facilitated the connection of different individual computers, LANs, and WANs (wide area networks, or multiple connected LANs). In addition to computer networking equipment and software companies, other new sectors of the computer industry emerged, including, Internet service providers (ISPs) and electronic commerce (E-commerce) firms. While new opportunities emerged and information technology enthusiasm reached new heights, some individuals and groups became increasingly concerned about social issues surrounding these developments. Two of the most fundamental issues were, and remain, the potential for heightened social stratification based on differential access to computer networking (the so-called Digital Divide), and security risks posed by the widespread use and exchange of data over computer networks.[2] This chapter will survey the state of the computer industry from the late 1980s to the present, the technological developments in networking that transformed computing technology during this period, and the associated new segments of the computer trade. The chapter (along with a discussion in the conclusion) will also briefly examine some related societal impacts and ethical issues.

WINTEL: AN INDUSTRY STANDARD AND MARKET DOMINANCE

During the latter part of the 1980s, Microsoft had met the technological bar set by the Apple Macintosh graphical user interface (GUI) operating system with its own GUI-based Windows. On a different front, Microsoft's key applications, Word and Excel, had become the leading word processing and spreadsheet software, respectively. Windows was not an improvement on the Macintosh operating system, but it had the advantage of running on top of and being compatible with MS-DOS, the system on more than three-quarters of existing personal computers in the United States.[3] Likewise, Word and Excel were not necessarily better products than other word processors and spreadsheets on the market (such as WordPerfect and Quattro Pro), but the firm benefited from its relationship as a supplier of operating systems to original equipment manufacturers (OEMs)—personal computer firms—as well as from the Microsoft brand.

Meanwhile, Intel, after inventing the microprocessor, continually worked to innovate its design and manufacturing processes to place more circuits on each chip and create ever more powerful microprocessors relative to cost. Competitors arose, such as Advanced Micro Devices (AMD—a firm that was formed in Sunnyvale, California, in 1969 and entered the microprocessor business in 1975), but it and other companies generally were a step behind.[4] Andrew Grove, Intel's chief executive, frequently reiterated his belief that "only the paranoid survive," an often-quoted remark that became an unofficial motto for the firm, and a motivator for its scientists, engineers, and executives. Intel clearly recognized that competition would increase in the future, and the firm had to stay at the top of its game in developing new generations of microprocessors, as well as additional products.[5] Intel, and other semiconductor manufacturers such as Motorola and National Semiconductor, also benefited from the ever-growing market for embedded computer processors in a vast range of technological devices, from fax machines and cameras to automobiles and cellular phones.

With Intel as the largest value-added OEM supplier of hardware components for personal computers and Microsoft as the leading producer of operating system software, the term "Wintel" (a combination of Windows and Intel) emerged and gained currency to refer to the dominant, near monopoly position that had been achieved by the two firms. In the early 1990s, Intel, like Microsoft, sought to capitalize on its brand to differentiate itself from competitors, even though its microprocessors were often only modestly different from others that worked with the Windows platform by this time. With the firm's "Intel Inside" campaign, it advertised this slogan broadly and had its computer manufacturing customers place it on the consoles of all their computers. This strategy helped differentiate Intel-based computers in the minds of many end-market users and influenced purchasing decisions of Intel's primary customers, name-brand computer firms.[6] The "Intel Inside" campaign was not the first time a component supplier to OEMs had marketed broadly to the public, but it was the most extensive, visible, and prolific. It also demonstrated and contributed to the notion that the microprocessor (along with software) was what was important, not the particular clone manufacturer that was often just assembling identical or near identical components. One personal computer firm, however, incorporated a new path to differentiation and achieved widespread attention, imitators, and long-sustained market success.

MICHAEL DELL AND DELL COMPUTER: A DIFFERENT TYPE OF INNOVATION

Compaq took the lead as the first firm to successfully reverse engineer IBM's ROM-BIOS and produce IBM PC clones. With successive personal computers, IBM was no longer a leader that competitors mimicked. IBM's personal computer business, like many other personal computer producers, was increasingly just assembling the components and software that Intel, Microsoft, and others produced. The term "box maker" became common to describe personal computer firms, as the press and consumers recognized that these companies increasingly were simply assembling, packaging, marketing, and through retailers, selling personal computers.[7] A new computer company and its visionary leader, however, saw value in differentiating itself on these more mundane business processes, as well as in an area that was fundamental to mainframe computing, was evident and significant in minicomputing, but up until the early- to mid-1980s, had been rare in the personal computing industry: service.

In 1983 Michael Dell, a nineteen-year-old freshman at the University of Texas at Austin, recognized a potential business opportunity arising from the fact that IBM PC computers were priced at $2,880 retail, but were composed of off-the-shelf components and software totaling roughly $600 or $700.[8] The following year, Michael Dell created Dell Computer Corporation and hired an engineer, Jay Bell, to build Dell's first Intel 286–based computer. Michael Dell realized that while retailers did not add much to the computer buying experience, they took a substantial cut of the profits. Instead of using retailers in the early years, Dell became the first significant enterprise to sell PC-based computers by mail directly to customers. Michael Dell understood the importance of home users as well as the significance of building and maintaining strong relationships to the business, government, and educational markets. The company that Dell had begun in a 1,000-square-foot office space in 1984 moved into a 30,000-square-foot facility the following year and was generating more than $70 million in annual revenue.[9]

Through seeking out and integrating the latest components, Dell assembled computers that often had higher performance characteristics than IBM personal computers and other clones.[10] Dell received favorable reviews in many trade publications, which helped the firm get a foothold in the industry. In 1988, Dell Computer went public and raised $30 million. It was expanding rapidly, but in retrospect, had few controls in place. In 1989, a decrease in demand, excessive inventory resulting from technological change (from standard 256K memory to 1 megabyte memory), an overly ambitious computer project (Olympic), and a misguided move into selling through retail channels, resulted in Dell's first stumble. Despite the financial setback, it quickly regrouped (abandoning Olympic) and returned to profitability the following year.[11] In 1994, after extensive analysis, Michael Dell concluded that even though the firm was generating substantial revenue through using retailers, this mechanism was not adding to the bottom line. Dell took quick action to abandon the retail market to concentrate exclusively on direct sales—a decision that, along with other factors, set the company apart for faster growth than its peers. The problems at the end of the 1980s also taught Michael Dell and his team a valuable lesson about the importance of inventory management. This was a major focus of the firm entering the 1990s and became a key element of Dell Computer's competitive advantage.

Dell Computer rapidly became more skilled than other firms at using technology to coordinate its business and its supply chain. Through more effective market-segmentation analysis, it could forecast demand more accurately than its competitors. Dell pioneered the use of information technology to coordinate its strategy for mass customization, and thereby created a system where customers could choose the specifications of their computer, have it delivered quickly, and due to Dell's high volume and savings from avoiding retail-related expenses, still get a relatively low price.[12] Dell capitalized on its direct relationship with customers to institute an unparalleled after-purchase service program, which provided ongoing assistance to consumers whether they were individuals, small businesses, corporations, or nonprofit organizations. In 1996, Dell emerged as the industry leader in providing customized direct ordering and twenty-four-hour service on the World Wide Web, and along with memorable and effective television advertising, including the "Dude, You're Getting a Dell" campaign, surpassed Compaq to become the leading personal computer firm in the U.S. market in 1999.[13] It had grown from revenue of $3.48 billion and net income of $149 million in 1994 (when it began to refocus on direct sales), to $31.89 billion in sales and profits of $2.31 billion in 2001.[14]

In spite of the fact that Dell lost its leadership position in the U.S. personal computer market after the 2002 merger of two primary competitors, Hewlett-Packard and Compaq, Dell continues to be the benchmark against which others in the personal computer trade and many manufacturing and direct marketing firms from a range of industries, measure themselves. Unlike other areas of consumer electronics, Japanese brands such as Hitachi, Sony, and Toshiba, have had only modest success in the U.S. personal computer market. Dell's direct sales, leadership in logistics, and strong service, coupled with the pressure these have imposed on other U.S. personal computer manufacturers, has been critical to the continuing competitiveness of U.S. firms in the domestic market. Of the different competitive advantages held by Dell, its leadership in direct marketing has been the most critical to the firm's long-sustained higher margins. In the late 1990s, Compaq Senior Vice President Mike Winkler estimated that the retail markup, cooperative marketing costs, and price protection that manufacturers had to provide retailers added more than 10 percent to the cost of personal computers.[15]

TIM BERNERS-LEE AND THE WORLD WIDE WEB: FACILITATING A SEA CHANGE IN COMPUTER NETWORKING

Vannevar Bush outlined the basic concept of hypertext back in 1945, and Douglas Engelbart demonstrated a hypertext system at the Fall Joint Computer Conference in Chicago in 1968. During the 1970s, Xerox PARC had conducted research similar to that of Engelbart's (hiring some of Engelbart's colleagues), as well as provided leadership in certain networking developments, particularly local area networks (the Ethernet). Nevertheless, implementing a system to take advantage of the possibilities of hypertext and the Internet had not occurred in the first decade and a half after the emergence of the personal computer. Based on the work of some key individuals, as well as corporations and other organizations, this would change in the early- to mid-1990s.

In 1980, Tim Berners-Lee began work as a software consultant at CERN, the famed international particle physics laboratory in Geneva, Switzerland. In his spare time, he wrote a program, Enquire, which helped link data relevant to his work (to keep track of relationships between projects, people, machines, etc.). The only way to add information on Enquire was to link it to other data already on the system. The program/database ran on an individual computer, not a network, and when Berners-Lee departed after six months to work on another consulting assignment, he left Enquire behind.

Berners-Lee had enjoyed his time at CERN, and in the mid-1980s he applied for a fellowship to return to the center. He began to think about his old program and started to recreate it. He became increasingly focused on the possibility of developing a networked hypertext system that could link computers within CERN, and more broadly, computers around the world through the networking infrastructure of the Internet.[16] Between October and December of 1990, on a NeXT computer (NeXT was a firm founded in the mid-1980s by Steven Jobs), Berners-Lee programmed protocols for such a system: Hypertext Transfer Protocol (HTTP), a language for computers to communicate to each other; Uniform Resource Identifiers (URIs, later renamed Uniform Resource Locators, or URLs); Hypertext Markup Language (HTML), which describes how to format pages with hypertext links; and, finally, a browser tool to navigate through documents. By Christmas 1990, he had set up a server for his HTML documents at info.cern.ch. He named his system the World Wide Web.[17] Prior to the World Wide Web, transferring or accessing data was typically achieved through the more arduous process of File Transfer Protocol (FTP) servers and clients—a system that worked in small groups, but led to the fragmentation of data rather than widespread access.

Berners-Lee's site on the World Wide Web received a hundred hits a day in the summer of 1991, one thousand a day the following year, and 10,000 a day by the summer of 1993.[18] He created pages explaining the protocols and promoted the system through visits to leading centers such as MIT's Laboratory for Computer Science (LCS) and Xerox PARC. More and more people were setting up servers and Web sites during 1992 and 1993, and the need grew for efficient and effective software tools to locate particular sites and navigate through them.

A number of early attempts were made to produce navigational software tools called browsers. Some systems to share documents, such as Gopher at the University of Minnesota, had menus rather than hypertext links. The most sophisticated and polished of the browsers in the early- to mid-1990s was developed at the University of Illinois National Center for Supercomputing Applications (NCSA). A student, Marc Andreeson, programmed most of the code for this browser, which was named Mosaic. The NCSA made Mosaic publicly available in November 1993. More than 40,000 copies were downloaded the first month, and the technology clearly had commercial possibilities.[19] Andreeson left NCSA to join Enterprise Integration Technology and soon met businessman Jim Clark. Andreeson and Clark founded Mosaic Communications Corporation to commercialize the browser software. They hired others from NCSA who had contributed to Mosaic, relocated to Mountain View,

California, renamed their firm Netscape, and soon came out with a revised, more efficient, and more secure version of the system called Navigator.

Around this time, other companies emerged to create software tools to help people find information on the World Wide Web. These typically started as projects to index sites, but as the number of sites and indexes grew, software spiders, or programs that search the Web and collect information, were often developed and used to automate the process. Early movers in this area included Excite and Yahoo (unofficially standing for Yet Another Hierarchical Officious Oracle). Yahoo was a firm initiated by Stanford University graduate students David Filo and Jerry Yang in 1994.[20] Other companies in this field also started in the mid-1990s, including Infoseek, Alta Vista, and Lycos. The latter took an early lead, but many found Yahoo more user-friendly, and coupled with effective branding, Filo and Yang's firm soon moved to the forefront. Like its competitors, Yahoo had yet to achieve net earnings at the time of its initial public offering (IPO) in 1996, but following a rapid rise in its stock, Yahoo reached more than $9 billion in capitalization during 1998.[21] That same year, a new powerhouse in search engines, Google, was launched: a private company that used software that ranked pages based on inbound links. Google rapidly moved into the number one position in search engine technology, and the America Online (AOL) and Yahoo portals soon began to use Google's search mechanism.[22] Google remained private for more than half a decade before having a well-publicized Dutch-auction initial public offering in August 2004.[23]

With browsers, search engines, and Berners-Lee's protocols and programs underlying the World Wide Web, the ARPANET/Internet had been transformed from a mere research tool and system commonly used for e-mail by a relatively small number of individuals within government, universities, and other organizations, to an increasingly broad-based communication device. For the World Wide Web to achieve ubiquity however, other infrastructure, both equipment and software, was necessary.

JOHN CHAMBERS AND CISCO SYSTEMS: MANAGING ACQUISITIONS AND BUILDING THE COMPUTER NETWORKING EQUIPMENT INDUSTRY

Only a relatively small number of individuals had access to the ARPANET during the 1970s. By the early- to mid-1980s, local area networks (LANs) gave a larger number of people exposure to computer networking technology. LAN users, however, were often frustrated by the inability of different LANs, especially nearby local networks, to facilitate data sharing and inter-LAN communication. A married couple at Stanford University, Sandra Lerner of the business school and Leonard Bosak of the computer science department, along with several other colleagues, designed routers to meet this challenge. Bosak, and an engineer at Stanford University Medical School, Bill Yeager, led the effort to create a router (based on a DEC minicomputer) to connect the Medical School local area network with the university's computer science department LAN.[24] A router is a computer that allows individual LANs to remain distinct, but enables the forwarding of data packets between them using the most expedient route based on traffic load, line costs, speed, and other factors. Software routines are programmed to facilitate the interoperability of different LANs. The unauthorized project of Bosak, Yeager, and others, once successful, was adopted by Stanford University to connect LANs throughout the campus in the early 1980s. All of a sudden people on campus could communicate and share data—the school no longer had twenty incompatible e-mail systems.[25]

In 1984, Lerner and Bosack founded cisco Systems (a couple of years later it was renamed Cisco Systems) to commercialize this technology.[26] They had little capital and used credit cards to get the firm started. Cisco Systems' first product was a multiprotocol router, a device that supported a number of protocols such as IP (Internet Protocol) and DECnet. A widely accessible international communication internetwork, or the World Wide Web, would not have been possible without the past networking technologies (packet-switching and standard protocols) of the ARPANET/Internet, as well as certain devices, including routers and switches, to facilitate communication between individual computers, LANs, and WANs.

In the first couple of years Cisco Systems charged between $7,000 and $50,000 for its routers. Its early customers were universities, corporations, and other large organizations. By early 1986, the firm was generating a profit of several hundred thousand dollars a month. Cisco routers had an open architecture that allowed customers to adjust and add source code to meet their specific needs. Many of these large organizations had a vast array of computer hardware and software to internetwork, and routers enabled their mainframes, minicomputers, and personal computers to share data.

By 1987, other networking companies were emerging to meet the growing demand for routers, and Bosack and Lerner reasoned that Cisco Systems had to grow quickly or lose its place. The couple sought out venture capital (VC), but initially had a difficult time, as more than seventy VC firms turned them down. Finally, Don Valentine, founder and general partner of Sequoia Capital, took on the venture. He provided $2.5 million for a 32 percent stake in the firm.[27]

Sequoia, a company initiated in 1972, had demonstrated vision in providing early investment capital for Atari, Oracle, Apple Computer, and 3Com. Valentine recognized the great opportunity that existed in networking equipment and software. He understood computing technology better than most Silicon Valley venture capitalists, and provided much-needed leadership, becoming the Cisco chair of the board from the time of Sequoia's investment in 1987 until his retirement from the position in 1995.

With venture capital from Sequoia in place, Sandy Lerner and Len Bosack agreed to take the positions of president of customer service and chief technology officer, respectively. Lerner was extremely customer-driven, establishing a culture that would long remain central to Cisco Systems. Valentine recruited a CEO for the firm, John Morgridge, the former president of a struggling portable computer firm, Grid Systems. Morgridge, who had come from a sales background (with Honeywell), had difficulty with Lerner from the start. Lerner sought to exert a disproportionate amount of control relative to her position, and seven of the firm's vice presidents threatened to leave if Morgridge and Valentine did not fire her. In August 1990 Valentine acquiesced and fired Lerner; cofounder Len Bosack left shortly thereafter. Earlier that year the firm had gone public, and given the company's higher profile and the recent awkwardness in dismissing the founders, Valentine recognized the importance of a smooth succession of leadership in the future—he believed it would be essential to maintaining and extending the Cisco Systems' brand as a symbol of quality and reliability. Morgridge, who came to Cisco Systems at age fifty-seven, and Valentine, soon sought an executive to groom to be the new chief executive. They selected John Chambers for this role, and he was brought on as senior vice president of world operations.

John Chambers, born in Charleston, West Virginia, in 1949, completed his M.B.A. at the age of twenty-six, and spent the next fourteen years in sales and management positions at IBM and Wang Laboratories. At Wang, Chambers managed the firm's Asia Pacific business before the firm's founder and chief executive, An Wang, brought him back to the United States to be vice president of operations. Wang Laboratories was a minicomputer manufacturer that, like Digital Equipment Corporation, missed the opportunity as the industry shifted to much less expensive personal computers. As the market for Wang products declined, the organization was left with a tremendous overcapacity, and Chambers was left with the responsibility of laying off more than 5,000 employees.[28] This was a difficult experience for Chambers, and when he became the leader of Cisco Systems, he was committed to not letting technology pass his firm by, and thereby avoiding lay offs.

Cisco Systems had developed a culture of customer commitment and frugality that had transcended the changes in executive personnel—even top executives flew coach class on business trips. At the same time, by the early- to mid-1990s the computer-networking environment was going through a major transformation. The World Wide Web brought many new opportunities for networking firms, but it also created a great deal of attention and an increasing amount of competition. In 1993 Morgridge, Chambers, and the firm's chief technology officer, Ed Kozel, engaged in formal strategic planning for Cisco Systems' future. They came up with the four strategic goals that guided the firm's activities in the coming years: (1) providing end-to-end networking solutions for customers, (2) making acquisitions a key structural process to maintain the firm's position at the forefront of new technology, (3) defining the networking industry's protocols, and (4), forming appropriate strategic alliances when important firms did not meet Cisco's tough acquisition criteria.[29]

In early 1995, Chambers became the new Cisco Systems CEO. While some members of the management team questioned Chambers' lack of technical background, his interpersonal skills and customer focus fit the needs of the corporation. Chambers was focused on growth and rapidly dismantled the centralized managerial structure that had existed under Morgridge. By this time, the firm's annual revenue had exceeded $2 billion and it had more than four thousand employees. The centralized structure that had worked for Cisco previously, would likely be debilitating in the future, Chambers believed, especially given the company's 1993 strategic goals.

In its early days, Cisco had developed a reputation as a technological leader through internal development. With competition intensifying in the early- to mid-1990s from dedicated networking equipment providers such as 3Com and Bay Networks, as well as from computer industry giants Digital Equipment Corporation, Hewlett-Packard, and IBM, Cisco shifted to a strategy of being a leader in making and managing acquisitions and becoming a broad end-to-end network equipment and software provider. Influenced by the business philosophy of General Electric's long-time CEO Jack Welch, Chambers was committed to being either the first or the second leading company in all of its businesses.[30]

Growing through acquisition is a challenging endeavor for firms in any industry, but is especially difficult in high technology. Chief among the hurdles is the integration of a new business in a timely manner. Examples of successful, long-term, major acquisition strategies in the high technology fields are few and far between in U.S. history. At the end of the nineteenth century and beginning of the twentieth century, American Telephone & Telegraph (AT&T) was successful at acquiring and integrating dozens of independent telephone companies into its network. Led by Theodore Vail, AT&T demonstrated insight and aversion to risk in its aggressive acquisition strategy at a time of rapid technological change and political and legal uncertainty. This included great indeterminacy regarding potential antitrust litigation, coupled with concomitant and seemingly contradictory political movements to municipalize or nationalize industries that appeared to be "natural monopolies."[31]

Similarly, another giant in the history of American industry, General Motors (GM), engaged in a rapid acquisitions strategy during the first two decades of the twentieth century. GM acquired dozens of other automobile firms and component suppliers to transform itself from a mere automobile assembler into an integrated automobile manufacturer. GM's strategy, led by two different tenures of GM founder William Durant, resulted in the near collapse of the firm on a couple of occasions due to its overaggressive acquisitions just prior to major market downturns. In both cases, Durant lost control of his firm to financiers. The company did not successfully integrate its operations until a subsequent GM president, Alfred P. Sloan, instituted a now-famous centralized managerial structure based on independent but centrally coordinated divisions in the early 1920s.[32]

Cisco Systems would have been at tremendous risk if it had suffered a similar number of integration struggles as had GM in the early twentieth century. Cisco's history more nearly matches the comparatively smooth acquisition and integration activity of Vail at AT&T. Cisco Systems' experience, however, did differ in part from both AT&T and GM in that it was taking over firms to gain their technological products, patents, and expertise, and manufacturing operations and existing physical infrastructure were not fundamental considerations with regard to most of the firms it acquired.

The only IT firm of the second half of the twentieth century that can possibly lay claim to being as successful with acquisitions as was Cisco Systems in the 1990s would be the software firm Computer Associates (CA) during the 1970s and 1980s. CA was the first software company to reach $1 billion in annual revenue (in 1989), and remains one of the top software firms to this day, with more than $3 billion in revenue in 2004. Behind the leadership of founder and long-time CEO Charles Wang (and recently, Sanjay Kumar—Wang's successor in 2002—and current Interim CEO Kenneth D. Cron), CA has shown foresight in entering and navigating high-growth areas such as security software and enterprise software.

Another factor that has helped CA retain currency is that its business model focuses on offering flexible licensing arrangements, including shorter-term licensing than many of its competitors (a month as opposed to three months, a year, or more). From its origins in the mid-1970s, CA has also concentrated on business software and corporate markets—and has long been responsive to meeting its customers changing needs and building strong long-term relationships (despite, and perhaps in part as a result of, its willingness to accept short-term contracts). This has been possible, in part, because CA provides many corporations with critical behind-the-scenes systems for internal functions that have major switching costs.[33]

As CA has taken over many of the first generation of the leading software product companies, including Informatics, Applied Data Research, and Cullinet, CA has provided a bridge to the past. In many respects, CA has defied the odds in selling a broad and arguably somewhat disparate set of business software tools. It has, however, been very successful at determining products with future growth potential, cross-selling, and serving corporate and organizational customers many business software needs.

Computer Associates has also combined its extensive acquisitions with an increasing emphasis on internal research and development to create and refine software products, and to build capabilities to provide more extensive and deeper support services. In fiscal year 2004, more than 20 percent of CA's annual revenue was invested in research and development. While Charles Wang and Sanjay Kumar both left CA early in this new century as the firm faced a number of accusations regarding its accounting practices, for many years they led the way in getting bargain prices for quality companies (with quality products) during periods of relative decline. These leaders did not concern themselves with the particular culture of an acquisition target and were dedicated to cost control, which was often achieved through firing the personnel of the acquired firm.[34]

Not unlike Wang and Kumar, John Chambers instituted practices that helped Cisco Systems to mitigate some of the risk of rapid acquisitions. Some aspects of Cisco's strategy demonstrated modest similarities to CA's, while other elements could not be more different. Chambers and his team carefully analyzed the direction of networking equipment technology and what the firm needed to meet its goal of providing a full range of networking equipment supplies and services. It avoided targeting firms that did not fit in well with Cisco's technological goals. In implementing this strategy, Cisco Systems, like CA, listened carefully to its customers. Second, it consciously avoided firms that had corporate cultures that differed significantly from that of Cisco's—a fundamental difference from CA.

Cisco Systems acquired primarily smaller firms in the mid-1990s, and successful integration was highly dependent on retaining the engineers and scientists of the acquired firm.[35] In the words of Chambers, "When we acquire a company, we aren't simply acquiring its current products, we're acquiring the next generation of products through its people."[36] By empowering the managers and engineers of acquired firms and offering attractive stock options, Cisco did a far better job than most at retention of personnel. Cisco Systems' strategy of employee retention could not stand in starker contrast to that of CA, a firm that focused more on the acquisition of products than on people.

With the advent and proliferation of the World Wide Web at mid-decade, coupled with Cisco's rapid and consistent growth in revenue and profits, the firm's stock began a meteoric rise. The ever-expanding capitalization of the company allowed it to go shopping for the most promising of the smaller networking equipment firms, and in time, to buy established, larger companies as well. While Cisco purchased many small and young firms, most were able to rapidly add to Cisco's bottom line, further fueling a cycle of profit growth, rising market capitalization, and future acquisitions. When firms met Cisco's acquisition criteria, it would pay seemingly high prices in inflated Cisco stock. When firms did not meet Cisco's acquisition criteria, it succeeded at forming strategic alliances. This typically included Cisco taking a significant minority ownership stake in the partnering firm, as well as joint work in research and development, marketing, and sales.

Cisco remained committed to not focusing too heavily on a single type of networking technology. Instead, the firm hedged its bets, provided a range of networking solutions, and prepared itself for different contingencies as the networking industry evolved. Though the company started as a supplier of routers and became the leading firm in this area, it also acquired capabilities in LAN switches. LAN switches, a technology and industry sector that began to take off in the early 1990s, offered a far less expensive alternative to routers. The other relatively inexpensive technology that had been competing with routers, intelligent hubs, did not increase bandwidth, a critical deficiency in an era of rapidly expanding computer-networking demand.

Prior to Cisco's waves of acquisitions, it had demonstrated its ability to use such a strategy to remain at the technological forefront of the networking-equipment industry. In 1993, it paid $95 million for a fifty-two-person firm that was just starting to make the new technology of LAN switches: Crescendo Communications. Though it took criticism in the financial press for overpaying for this company, which was expected to only have $10 million in revenue the following year, it got Cisco in the switches business, which represented 40 percent of the firm's products by decade's end. Based on its overall capitalization in 2000, its switches business had an approximate value of $200 billion.[37]

Likewise, Cisco used acquisitions to get into the Fast Ethernet and Asynchronous Traffic Mode (ATM) markets. Cisco had listened to its customers and quickly recognized new Fast Ethernet technology could speed up LANs to operate ten times quicker than past Ethernet technology. It took over leading Fast Ethernet firm Grand Junction for about $400 million in stock in the second half of 1995.[38] Cisco's primary networking competitors, 3Com and Bay Networks, were also interested in the company, but Chamber's ability to move quickly and offer a generous price, landed Cisco the deal.

Fast Ethernet had five times the industry revenue of Asynchronous Traffic Mode (ATM) technology, but this strictly hardware-based networking technology (unlike routers, which used a combination of hardware and software) facilitated digital emulation of traditional phone networks. Chambers and Cisco have the long-term goal of being at the forefront of digital communications, which includes not only data, but also voice and video. There were two major players in ATM technology in the mid-1990s, Cascade and StataCom. Chambers decided to target the latter, in part, because of its nearby location, often a fundamental factor in Cisco's acquisitions due to both the greater likelihood of common corporate cultures as well as easier direct managerial contact. In 1996, through exchanging stock, Cisco paid $4.5 billion for StrataCom, by far its largest acquisition until 1999.[39]

With these key acquisitions, as well as others, Cisco Systems had achieved a full range of networking technologies. By the end of 1997, Cisco had completed nineteen acquisitions totaling more than $7 billion dollars in Cisco stock.[40] Besides outright acquisitions of established firms like StrataCom, Cisco also employed another strategy: "spinning-in" new firms. With promising start-up companies that had not produced important products yet, Cisco considered making an investment, helping the firm along, and later acquiring it *if* it succeeded. It did this with San Jose–based Ardent Communications Corporation in the mid-1990s to gain technology and expertise to further its efforts to combine data, video, and voice networking across ATM networks. Cisco set a purchase price ($156 million) and determined ten goals for Ardent. Cisco had the ongoing option of acquiring the firm at the specified purchase price, while Ardent Communications, if it came through on the technological goals Cisco established, could require Cisco to acquire it at that same price. In June 1997, shortly before Ardent Communications completed the final of the ten goals that Cisco had set, Cisco acquired all remaining shares (it had previously owned about one-third of the firm).[41]

During the second half the 1990s, Cisco Systems continued to acquire firms to stay at the forefront of computer networking technology. While it suffered from a small number of deals that in retrospect were mistakes, the vast majority of Cisco's acquisitions added to the firm's technological and business leadership, as well as its revenue and profits. This helped it thrive in an increasingly competitive environment in which Canadian firm Nortel (Northern Telecom until its acquisition of Cisco-rival Bay Networks for $7 billion in 1998) has consistently proven itself a formidable adversary.[42]

The 1990s were a decade in which Cisco developed a formal growth and leadership through acquisition strategy that it carefully adhered to and executed. It benefited from the tremendous rise in demand for networking technology with the Internet, and from highly optimistic individual and institutional investors. Ever-inflating Cisco Systems stock allowed the firm to acquire companies that fit its strategy, regardless of the price. By early 2000, Cisco Systems briefly became the largest capitalized firm in the United States, surpassing much older industrial giants such as General Electric and General Motors, as well as software leader, Microsoft.

In the second half of the 1990s and in the year 2000, Chambers increasingly became the leading IT industry spokesperson for the future benefits of the Internet. He presented the Internet to the U.S. Congress, the media, and the public as an unprecedented tool that would improve peoples' lives.[43] While he likely believed much of what he said in his Internet evangelizing, the continued growth of the Internet was absolutely fundamental to building the Cisco Systems' brand, keeping investors optimistic, and helping his firm to grow at its frenetic pace. Eventually, Cisco's good fortunes would reverse as computing and networking technology suffered a major downturn in 2000 and 2001. Though Cisco and Chambers survived, unlike many firms and the tenures of their CEOs, things would not be the same as in the 1990s, a decade, in retrospect, of irrational expectations of endless growth in computing, software, and especially, networking. Chambers laid off thousands of Cisco employees during 2001, and the firm's stock slipped from more than $80 per share at its high in 2000, to the lower teens in 2001. Cisco's acquisition engine came to a grinding halt. Though Cisco fared better than many IT firms, has now returned to profitability, and is beginning to hire again, it is not likely that it will acquire firms at the same pace as in the 1990s anytime in the near future.

E-COMMERCE AND THE DOT.COM SHAKEOUT

John Chambers and other industry leaders' proselytizing for the business and societal benefits of the Internet, the growing number of connected users, the expanding success of networking and software firms, and the media attention on the IT revolution, all helped to fuel an environment of business optimism and perceptions of unlimited future growth. With its long leadership in semiconductors, personal computers, software, and equally important, venture capital enterprises, Silicon Valley was the epicenter of both the activity and excitement in IT that accelerated throughout the 1990s. The rapid rise of leading firms such as Cisco Systems led to skyrocketing stock prices on the technology-laden NASDAQ market—a market that since February 1971 had depended on computer networking (initially, two UNIVAC 1108 computers, 20,000 miles of circuitry, and hundreds of networked Bunker Ramo 2217 terminals) rather than a trading floor like the New York Stock Exchange.[44] The share prices of established industry leaders such as Cisco Systems, Intel, and Microsoft rose substantially, but so too did a number of much smaller start-up companies during the second half of the 1990s. These firms often had no proven track record and sometimes lacked experienced leaders, completed products, profits, or even revenue. An idea and rudimentary business plan were often enough to attract substantial venture capital.

Many of these start-ups either sought to sell goods or services on the Internet, or to generate enough traffic so they could sell advertising space on their Web pages. Some companies, like the online book retailer Amazon.com, quickly shot forward, gained widespread attention, and achieved leadership in a particular niche. While profits proved elusive until recently for Amazon, it was rapidly adding to its customer base, which was the fundamental long-term plan of the firm's leader Jeff Bezos. Amazon moved into many areas beyond books to continue to increase its millions of regular customers. For most Internet retailers, however, profitability was not the only elusive metric. Many failed to come through on projections to generate substantial revenue and grow a large customer base. Revenue from online advertising, perceived by many to be a significant new business, failed to even approach the optimistic expectations that were common within the industry and in the media during the mid- to late-1990s.

Concerns about the Y2K problem, coupled with anecdotal evidence and skyrocketing NASDAQ stocks, led many corporations to invest in information technology infrastructure as never before in the last years of the twentieth century. The Y2K problem extended from widespread international concern that systems and data from the mainframe era that used only two rather than four digits to designate year-dates in software code would cause computers to crash or not function properly at the turn of the millennium (the shortened dates were to save memory back when memory was far more expensive). The combination of Y2K passing as a nonevent, depleted corporate capital funds for IT, the failure of many e-retailers to attract customers, and a struggling economy, led to the rapid decline and failure of electronic commerce and other IT firms in 2000 and 2001.[45] More than anything, too many firms were built on the unrealistic idea that consumers would rapidly shift from making their purchases from bricks-and-mortar retailers to Internet retailers. The impact of large-scale deregulation, deceptive accounting, conflicts of interests between investment banks and their stock market analysts, and widespread greed among investors, also played a significant role.[46]

Though more substantial than many dot.coms, Webvan Group, Inc., characterized the unrealistic expectations for rapid Internet retailing growth, expectations that in retrospect seem quite naive. In 2000, this online grocery store delivery service had a peak capitalization of more than $1 billion and served Chicago, Los Angeles, San Francisco, Seattle, Portland, and San Diego, with plans to operate in nineteen additional markets. In the middle of 2001 the firm collapsed. Webvan Group, or Webvan.com, had been backed by such IT venture capital heavyweights as Benchmark Capital and Sequoia Capital, and was the most heavily funded online retailer next to Amazon. Nevertheless, it had a business model that could not sustain it. Its stock went from a November 1999 initial public offering high of more than $30 per share to $.06 per share just prior to its bankruptcy. While some online grocers that are concentrating on one or a small number of markets are showing improvement and may survive, such as Minneapolis' Simon Delivers, the model of large numbers of people rapidly switching to buy groceries online was clearly overly optimistic.[47]

The technology-heavy NASDAQ stock market index reached a peak of more than 5,100 during March 2000 only to hit an interday low of just over 1,100 in October 2002—an unprecedented 78.4 percent decline. The "irrational exuberance" of the overvalued stock market (especially the NASDAQ) that Federal Reserve Chairman Alan Greenspan had warned of back in 1996 when the New York Stock Exchange and NASDAQ markets were much lower, became an often-quoted phrase to describe what later came to pass early in the new century. This decline led to increasing speculation, and some skepticism, about the contributions of IT to the larger economy.

RENEWED DEBATE ON THE QUESTION OF PRODUCTIVITY

Economists and others have long debated the relative costs and returns of IT investments. Given that many government and non-government figures on computer research and development expenditures are only estimates, and the fact that the attribution of productivity gains to a single class of technology is often difficult, the so-called productivity question, whether the overall investment in IT has paid off in heightened productivity, will not likely be answered in a clear and definitive way anytime soon. A number of prominent economists and computer scientists, including the late Michael Dertouzos, longtime head of computer science at MIT, Stephen Roach, senior economist at Morgan Stanley, and Paul Strassmann, former chief of computing at Xerox, have concluded that computers have not had much of a positive impact on productivity.[48]

Anecdotal evidence supports that expenditures on computing

technology have aided some individuals, firms, and organizations on certain tasks in recent decades, but other cases, in other areas, have shown different results. In the aggregate, ascertaining costs is challenging, and some current projects in implementing computer technology rest upon early developments funded by the government to advance the nation's defense, and thus, are difficult to factor into economic analysis. In many cases, new investments in IT represented a risky and difficult decision for firms and other organizations given the uncertainties of the near-term and longer-term payoffs. For other companies, meeting new industry standards have forced major IT investments—such as OEMs or higher-tier suppliers requiring electronic data interchange (EDI) technology to implement just-in-time manufacturing and delivery throughout a supply chain.

Opinions differed on the profitability of IT investments before the bursting of the dot.com bubble, yet during the 1990s, most industry leaders and business journalists seemed to buy into the notion of the new wonders of IT for efficiency and its role in the growth of the new economy—an economy that operated on "Internet time" and was not necessarily subject to the economic rules and cycles of the so-called old economy. At the same time, expenditures for Y2K compliance were estimated to be $100 billion in the United States and $500 billion internationally—numbers that should, at least temporarily, put questions to rest about whether overall gains in IT have equaled or exceeded expenditures. Furthermore, average labor productivity figures have actually declined, from a post–World War II average of 3.4 percent growth per year, to 1.2 percent between 1979 and 1994—leading to talk of a "productivity paradox." On the other hand, there was a 2.5 percent gain in productivity during the first half of the 1990s (versus the 1979 to 1990 period) in computer-using sectors of manufacturing.[49] Furthermore, average Gross Domestic Product (GDP) and the estimated IT contribution to GDP grew significantly in the last half-decade of the century, suggesting the World Wide Web was a positive force for productivity.[50]

While of justifiable interest to many economists, business historians, and policy makers, the productivity paradox or productivity question may not be pertinent for individual firms or organizations. These entities have to ignore the sunk costs of their organization, or the broader aggregate, to answer the question of whether specific types of *new* investment in information technology will aid future productivity sufficiently to add to their bottom line. At the same time, corporations must be cognizant of whether

IT investment is necessary to ensure their ability to compete in a particular business area. History may or may not be a proper guide. More broadly, the notion that a critical mass has been reached where future investment in IT will yield new productivity gains is more plausible than it was two decades ago, but highly optimistic interpretations such as this have to be viewed with a degree of caution, much like those at the other end of the spectrum that immediately dismiss the possibility of any new economic realities extending from IT.[51]

SOCIAL AND ETHICAL ISSUES IN COMPUTING AND THE COMPUTER INDUSTRY: THE DIGITAL DIVIDE AND COMPUTER SECURITY

Of far greater importance to many people than the productivity question or productivity paradox is the broader societal impact of computing technology. Personal computers and the World Wide Web have altered the way large numbers of people live their lives and the way businesses are run. Some individuals spend great amounts of time on online chat rooms, playing interactive games, or surfing the Web. Each year more and more information is on the Web, and it can now be a fundamental tool to figure out a tax question, identify an educational opportunity, apply for a job, design products, or manage a supply chain. The U.S. Department of Commerce began to study the impact of networking technology on society shortly after the advent of the World Wide Web.

Previous technologies, including electricity, transportation infrastructure, and telecommunications, paved the way for an early recognition that new technologies could have differential impacts on certain segments of American society. In 1995, the U.S. Commerce Department began to produce a series of major reports entitled *Falling Through the Net*. The subtitle of the first such report, *A Survey of the "Have Nots,"* indicates the likely legacy of the aforementioned past technologies for framing the issue in terms of technological *access*. Three subsequent U.S. Department of Commerce reports have been distributed, all with a focus on the "Digital Divide" or the differential *access* to computer networking technology.

So-called cyber-optimists have argued for the World Wide Web as the great equalizer. Numerous advocates have presented this technology as a great force for democracy and grassroots organization in an era when lobbyists and corporate donations have made many skeptical of the political process. At the same time, critics have focused on the World Wide Web as a tool that further stratifies society and exacerbates existing inequalities by creating an information-rich and an information-poor. The 2000 *Falling Through the Net* report indicates that differential access to computers and the Internet based on race, education, and income still exists, but progress is being made. For instance, 23.5 percent of blacks had home Internet access in mid-2000 versus 11.2 percent twenty months earlier. While this trend is positive and has likely continued over the past four years given the declining costs of personal computers and dial-up Internet connections, the 2000 figure is still far from the national average of 41.5 percent and is only partially accounted for by differences in income level.[52] Also, high speed Internet access is becoming more and more critical to navigating some sites and costs significantly more than dial-up service.

Access remains an important first step toward technological equality, but defining the Digital Divide, as most have, in terms of access alone is problematic. The benefits the Web can provide depend not only upon access, but also on the choices made by Web users, as well as the education and skills of these individuals to utilize the Internet effectively. The amount of information and misinformation in cyberspace grows rapidly each year, and strategies for conducting searches and sifting out, avoiding, or disregarding poor information, become increasingly important. In this sense, most metrics for examining the Digital Divide appear limiting.

Strictly focusing attention on access made more sense with some past technologies, such as electricity and telecommunications. An analogy that goes beyond access appears more appropriate for the World Wide Web. Returning to Vannevar Bush's conception of Memex, an all-inclusive hyperlinked microfiche-type machine, and thinking of the Web as a vast store of information, like a library, might be more useful. Questions such as whether an individual goes to a library, which library they use, what they choose to look for, how they use the mechanisms to find information, and how they interpret what they find, are fundamental concerns that deal far more with education than mere access.[53] In the case of the Web, no vetting has occurred (unlike the vetting done by publishers of print volumes and acquisition decisions made by trained librarians), making education all the more critical.

Another fundamental social issue related to computing is computer security. Computer security is often spoken of in tandem with computer privacy, and though the issues are often interrelated, they are conceptually distinct. Computer privacy has both cultural and legal components, and the latter extend from a long history of the notion of a right to privacy that grew out of the use and abuse of handheld cameras in the late nineteenth century.[54] The right to privacy was first formally articulated in 1890, in a famous *Harvard Law Review* article by Samuel D. Warren and future Supreme Court Justice Louis D. Brandeis.[55] Despite this early legal focus, only a scattering of state privacy laws followed in the coming decades. Certain landmark Supreme Court decisions, however, were based on the right to privacy in the 1960s and 1970s (*Griswald v. Connecticut*, 1965, on the right to use birth control; and *Roe v. Wade*, 1973, on abortion rights).

In 1974, privacy was the focus, rather than merely the underpinning, of a new federal law, the Privacy Act. The Privacy Act of 1974 was in direct response to growing concern about government computer databases on individuals. In 1967, President Lyndon B. Johnson's proposed National Data Center (which would have combined the databases of twenty federal agencies) was abandoned as the result of mass opposition. Popular books, such as Arthur Miller's *The Assault on Privacy: Computers, Data Banks, and Dossiers* (1971), continued to fuel public concerns. Such concerns, and the rising use of Social Security numbers as universal identifiers, led Secretary of Health, Education, and Welfare Elliot Richardson to establish the Advisory Committee on Automated Personal Data Systems (APDS), a committee led by RAND Corporation computer scientist Willis Ware. Ware had previously chaired the Defense Science Board Task Force on Computer Security. While greater information privacy was the goal, computer security, an area in which Ware had unique expertise, was perceived as a primary means to that end. The Privacy Act of 1974 followed the recommendations presented by Ware's APDS.[56]

The Privacy Act gave some protections to individuals (such as a right to inspect records on oneself) and imposed some modest restrictions on government. This helped address potential abuses at the federal level, what was believed to be the greatest threat to privacy during the 1970s. Increasingly, during the 1980s, and particularly over the past decade given the widespread use of the World Wide Web, the real abusers of personal data are now generally believed to be corporations and computer criminals. Sharing and selling financial, medical, and other types of information has resulted in businesses that flood peoples' postal and electronic mailboxes. Pre-existing medical conditions are widely known and insurance companies can refuse to take on the most needy. Meanwhile, computer crime has grown immensely.

In the 1970s, the term "hacker" referred to a talented amateur programmer and had positive connotations. Over the past two decades the term has come to refer to individuals who maliciously and illegally infiltrate computer networks of the government, companies, other organizations, and individuals. Identity theft, which is often perpetrated through gaining information from computer databanks, has become an epidemic that has plagued millions of Americans in recent years. This problem has cost many billions of dollars, and the numbers continue to grow rapidly. Longtime information security and computer-crime expert Donn Parker, who spent many years researching the topic while at SRI, has written on how computer crime, like other forms of crime, historically has been the result of people who have or develop personal problems and end up misusing their access or betraying the trust of their organization. More recently, he has warned of the future likelihood of automated computer-crime programs—programs that might infiltrate a bank or brokerage account, transfer money out to a foreign account, exit the system, and erase any traces of the transaction. Such crimes could potentially be placed on disks and bought and sold on the black market—the ones that work best will be in the greatest demand until law enforcement catches on and criminals switch to focus upon other automated computer-crime programs.[57]

As the Digital Divide diminishes, combating social stratification appears increasingly dependent on reducing economic and educational disadvantage in broad terms. Computer crime and computer surveillance (by employers, criminals, and increasingly in the wake of terrorism concerns, government), on the other hand, demand both new and more traditional remedies, but offer no easy solutions. Parker indicates that looking forward, varying daily routines, both in terms of how individuals interact with computers (such as frequently changing passwords), as well as software that disrupts and randomly changes the operations of certain computer functions, represent the best opportunity to combat computer criminals. Computer surveillance by employers or government, on the other hand, is an ethical and legal decision that will involve balancing the value of threats to productivity and safety with protections for personal privacy. Security exists simultaneously as a means to achieve greater information privacy and protection (through antivirus software, firewalls, etc.) as well as a justification (typically by government or large organizations) to protect people through surveillance (often reducing privacy). Only time will tell how these competing interests will play out in the future.

NOTES

1. Robert Metcalfe served in various top positions at 3Com, including chief executive officer and chair of the board of directors, before retiring in 1990. Ethernet became the most common LAN protocol. Other LAN protocols however also gained significant use, such as AppleTalk for Macintosh systems.

2. The differential access to computing technology had been an issue prior to widespread computer networking, but gained new urgency with the advent and growing ubiquity of the World Wide Web during the 1990s.

3. Building on top of MS-DOS took considerable memory and inhibited performance, particularly on the first iteration of Windows. Macintosh users, who tend to be fiercely loyal to Apple, often claim that the latest versions of Windows have never reached the performance and reliability of the latest version of Macintosh operating systems. Apple has had some successful products and financial peaks and troughs over the past decade and a half, but has continued to be particularly resilient in some educational markets and among design professionals.

4. Recently Intel and AMD have leapfrogged each other in having the highest performance microprocessors—but Intel has generally held this distinction.

5. While Intel has a dominant market share of microprocessors in personal computers, it only holds a modest position, and has a number of competitors in the imbedded microprocessors market (for many electronic consumer goods, vehicles, etc.).

6. Youngme Moon and Christina Darwall, *Inside Intel Inside*, Case 0-502-083 (Cambridge, MA: Harvard Business School, June 5, 2002). In addition to outlining the history of "Intel Inside," this case presents the context of the firm's contemplation of extending the "Intel Inside" campaign beyond personal computers.

7. Personal computer firms differed in the degree to which they outsourced components, but most outsourced key components, including microprocessors and operating systems.

8. Michael Dell with Catherine Fredman, *Direct from Dell: Strategies that Revolutionized an Industry* (New York: HarperBusiness, 1999), 8–9.

9. Ibid., 18–19.

10. Brands, choice of components, quality of assembly, design, and other factors have continued to be areas of differentiation with personal computers, but this differentiation is often lessened by the fact that the so-called box makers frequently (but not always) use the same Intel processors and Microsoft software.

11. Dell with Fredman, *Direct*, 38–39.

12. Mass customization is the most challenging process strategy a firm can undertake. Dell has not only been at the forefront of mass cus-

tomization in the computer industry, but is one of the most frequently cited examples of successful mass customization in any industry.

13. Compaq continued to have higher international sales and held the lead in worldwide personal computer market share.

14. Dell Corporation, *Annual Reports: 1994 and 2001.*

15. Haim Mendelson, *Dell Direct,* Case EC-17 (Stanford, CA: Graduate School of Business Stanford University, November 2000).

16. Tim Berners-Lee with Mark Fischetti, *Weaving the Web: The Original Design and Ultimate Destiny of the World Wide Web by Its Inventor* (San Francisco: HarperSanFrancisco, 1999), 9.

17. Ibid., 12, 28–30.

18. Ibid., 75.

19. Bruce R. Schatz and Joseph B. Hardin, "NCSA Mosaic and the World Wide Web: Global Hypermedia Protocols for the Internet," *Science* 265 (1994): 897.

20. Karen Angel, *Inside Yahoo! Reinvention and the Road Ahead* (New York: John Wiley & Sons, 2002), 123–124. Yahoo differed from the others in that it was a directory of human-classified Web sites, rather than a true search engine using spiders to search the Web for keywords.

21. Ibid., 105. Yahoo achieved its first net earnings during 1998, something that many IT firms with high flying stocks, like Amazon.com, did not achieve for more than half a decade.

22. Ibid., 248–249. The term "portal," which came into widespread use in 1998, refers to a site that gives an entry point to the Web and can send you down a proper road on the "information superhighway" or let you conduct a search. The goal with portals was to get people to the site and make money off advertising. While Yahoo uses Google's search engine, the first listings of a search are often sponsored ones that provide revenue for Yahoo.

23. Dutch-auction share distribution gives individual investors a greater opportunity to participate by allowing bids to be entered, and the lowest accepted offer price (based on a predetermined share volume and working from highest offers down) becoming the price everyone pays at the offering.

24. David Bunnell, *Making the Cisco Connection: The Story Behind the Real Internet Superpower* (New York: John Wiley & Sons, 2000), 4–5.

25. Ibid., 4, 6–7.

26. Cisco Systems (with an uppercase C) is used throughout this chapter regardless of the time period under discussion.

27. Bunnell, *Making,* 11–12.

28. Robert Slater, *The Eye of the Storm: How John Chambers Steered Cisco Through the Technology Collapse* (New York: HarperBusiness, 2003), 99–101.

29. Bunnell, *Making,* 32–35.

30. While true of most of Cisco's businesses, with some areas such as the fiber optics or the pipes of networks, Cisco has become a player, but is not among the top two. Nortel Networks has a lead in these areas.

31. Gerald W. Brock, *The Telecommunications Industry: The Dynamics*

of Market Structure (Cambridge, MA: Harvard University Press, 1981); Susan E. McMaster, *The Telecommunications Industry* (Westport, CT: Greenwood Press, 2002).

32. Jeffrey R. Yost, "Components of the Past and Vehicles of Change: A History of the American Automobile Supply Industry, 1895–1930," (diss., Case Western Reserve University, 1998).

33. Charles Forelle and Joann S. Lublin, "Kumar Gives Up Leadership Posts Under Pressure: Computer Associates Board Worried Embattled CEO Faces Indictment in Probe," *Wall Street Journal* (April 22, 2004): A1.

34. Computer Associates, *Annual Report: 2004*; Ken Belson, "A Host of Challenges at Computer Associates," *New York Times* (April 22, 2004): C1.

35. James McJunkin and Todd Reynders, *Cisco Systems: A Novel Approach to Structuring Entrepreneurial Ventures*, Case EC-15 (Stanford, CA: Graduate School of Business Stanford University, 2000); Bunnell, *Making*, 64–68.

36. McJunkin and Reynders, *Cisco*, 5.

37. Slater, *Eye*, 202–203. This figure is based on the heavily inflated market valuation prior to the firm losing roughly three-quarters of its value as its stock declined markedly in 2001. Nevertheless, its switching business remained worth tens of billions.

38. Bunnell, *Making*, 69–72.

39. Ibid., 79–82.

40. McJunkin and Reynders, *Cisco*, 5.

41. Ibid., 16.

42. Larry MacDonald, *Nortel Networks: How Innovation and Vision Created a Network Giant* (New York: John Wiley & Sons, 2000). Competitors such as Lucent, Juniper Networks, and others make the growing field of networking increasingly competitive.

43. John K. Waters, *John Chambers and the Cisco Way: Navigating Through Volatility* (New York: John Wiley & Sons, 2002), 105–124.

44. Jeffrey R. Yost, "NASDAQ," in *Encyclopedia of Computers and Computer History*, ed. Raul Rojas (Chicago: Fitzroy Dearborn Publishers, 2001), 563–564.

45. Opinions differ on whether the large expenditures on Y2K compliance prevented widespread problems, or if concerns were overblown. Many countries that spent and did far less, did not suffer any major setbacks. The truth probably lies somewhere in between—that some problems were prevented through investment in preparedness, but that premillennium worries were inflated.

46. Paul Krugman, *The Great Unraveling: Losing Our Way in the New Century* (New York: W. W. Norton, 2003); Roger Lowenstein, *Origins of the Crash: The Great Bubble and Its Undoing* (New York: Penguin Press, 2004).

47. "Webvan Group, Inc.," *Wall Street Journal*, eastern ed. 239:9 (January 14, 2002); Stewart Alsop, "The Tragedy of Webvan," *Fortune* 144, no. 3 (August 13, 2001): 52.

48. Thomas K. Landauer, *The Trouble with Computers: Usefulness, Usability, and Productivity* (Cambridge, MA: MIT Press, 1995), 13.

49. Matt Siegel, "Do Computers Slow Us Down?" *Fortune* 137, no. 6 (March 30, 1998).

50. James W. Cortada, *The Digital Hand: How Computers Changed the Work of American Manufacturing, Transportation, and Retail Industries* (New York: Oxford University Press, 2003).

51. Roger Alcaly, *The New Economy: What It Is, How It Happened, and Why It Is Likely to Last* (New York: Farrar, Straus, and Giroux, 2003). Alcaly's broad-based popular account provides an optimistic picture of IT-based productivity gains and offers some compelling analysis, but contains some incorrect information on the history of computing.

52. U.S. Department of Commerce, *Falling Through the Net: Toward Digital Inclusion, A Report on Americans' Access to Technology Tools* (Washington, DC: GPO, October 2000), xv–xvii.

53. The question of access alone is more significant in looking at wealthy versus poor countries. For an international examination of the Digital Divide, see Pippa Norris, *Digital Divide: Civic Engagement, Information Poverty, and the Internet Worldwide* (Cambridge: Cambridge University Press, 2001).

54. Robert E. Mensel, "'Kodakers Lying in Wait': Amateur Photography and the Right to Privacy in New York, 1885–1915," *American Quarterly* 43 (March 1991): 24–45.

55. Samuel Warren and Louis D. Brandeis, "The Right to Privacy," *Harvard Law Review* IV, no. 5 (December 15, 1890): 193–200.

56. Jeffrey R. Yost, "Reprogramming the Hippocratic Oath: An Historical Examination of Early Medical Informatics and Privacy," in *The History and Heritage of Scientific and Technological Information Systems*, eds. Boyd Rayward and Mary Ellen Bowden (Medford, NJ: Information Today, Inc., 2004), 46–55.

57. Donn Parker, interview by Jeffrey R. Yost, May 14, 2003, Los Altos, CA (Charles Babbage Institute, University of Minnesota).

Conclusion:
Looking Backwards and
Looking Ahead

Despite the social and policy challenges, and the open question concerning the contribution of computer technology to productivity (at least with some types of applications and within certain contexts), the future of the computer industry looks much brighter than it did several years ago. While undoubtedly there will be future IT bubbles and shakeouts, these events, while economically painful to some individuals and firms in the short term, often lead to both innovation and more reasoned resource allocation in the longer term.

With the advent and widespread use of the World Wide Web, computers are a part of peoples' lives at work, at home, and on the go as never before. The importance of computer technology will almost certainly grow in the future, but in what directions remains uncertain. J.C.R. Licklider, Robert Taylor, Douglas Engelbart, and others created a new paradigm for computing, one focused on human-computer interaction. They provided a challenge to the existing model that dominated the mainframe computer era, one where computing was largely limited to a so-called priesthood of computer engineers and software programmers who primarily operated computers for large corporations and government entities. Much of the work toward greater human-computer interaction and more user-friendly interfaces resulted from IPTO funding in the 1960s, while additional and often complementary research was carried out by many of the same scientists and engineers at Xerox PARC in the 1970s. The work funded by these organizations helped to produce both the Internet and the graphical user interface (GUI) of the Apple Macintosh operating system and Microsoft Windows. The extent to which subsequent developments have followed through on this rich past has been subject to debate in recent years.

Donald A. Norman, who has served in executive posts at Hewlett-Packard and Apple Computer, and as a professor of cognitive science at the University of California at San Diego, has argued that the personal computer has failed to continue to evolve to best meet peoples' needs following the achievement of GUI-based operating systems. He believes that the personal computer is designed to be all things to all people. This has led to a high level of complexity and a less-than-optimal tool for a number of different tasks for which people now use computers. He believes GUI-based systems, with windows and icons, worked well when computers had twenty things to display, but as the number has escalated, it has only added confusion. Meanwhile, IT companies continually build new features for their hardware and software to entice individuals and organizations to frequently upgrade. Norman cites that Microsoft Word had evolved to have 311 distinct commands by 1992, far more than most people use. By 1997, however, Microsoft Word grew to include 1,030 commands. Norman claims that for many tasks that people regularly engage in, such as writing a business memo, they have to use a number of different applications—they might need a word processor, calendar, and budget tables (all best accomplished by individual programs).[1]

While Norman's emphasis on the problematic nature of today's personal computers and software might be overstated, the idea of personal computers being more customer-oriented and specialized to best meet individual consumers is an emerging trend that appears to be accelerating. Last year the revenue for laptop computers exceeded that of desktop computers for the first time. While both are general-purpose machines, the portability of laptops is something many people value. The increasing ease of obtaining wireless Internet connections has added to this phenomenon.

Designing software that takes complexity away for most users is something that people crave. Donn Parker has emphasized that, given the current computer security threats of viruses, worms, and other malicious programs and users, consumers want to know that their computer is as secure and protected as possible. At the same time, he emphasizes, that people do not want to see the security, they do not want to think about the possible risks that underlie the need for security software, and they do not want to contemplate that the security system they are using is taking away memory and processing power. In many respects, Parker is highlighting a theme common to Norman, that people want computers to be easier, smoother, and less complex.[2]

In addition to the added complexity resulting from features many people do not use, monopolies are often cited as inhibitors to innovation. The Department of Justice spotlight, long centered on IBM within the IT field, shifted to Microsoft during the mid- to late-1990s. Microsoft was slow to recognize the importance of the Internet and the advent of the World Wide Web, but once Netscape Navigator took off (when Netscape started to give away this program for free downloads in 1994 in order to create a product lock-in), Gates and his firm moved quickly. Microsoft acquired a license to use and build upon the browser technology of a firm named Spyglass, another descendant of the University of Illinois' Mosaic. In mid-1995 Microsoft bundled its browser, Explorer, with its Windows operating system. That same year the firm entered into a consent decree, an agreement with the U.S. Department of Justice that it would not use its operating system monopoly as a vehicle to force sales of other types of software. Despite this agreement, subsequent versions of both Windows and Explorer were closely integrated.[3] The so-called browser war between Microsoft and Netscape had begun, and by 1997, with Explorer 4.0 tightly integrated with Windows, Netscape and the U.S. Department of Justice focused on Microsoft's alleged anticompetitive tie-in practice and its failure to operate under the consent decree. The Department of Justice was also concerned with the software firm's legal, but controlling, practice of billing personal computer manufacturers by the total number of computers installed (sold or leased) rather than by the number of machines that actually contained a version of Windows (customers could choose to have a different operating system, but if they did, they would indirectly have to pay for Windows as well).

The Department of Justice initiated a complaint against Microsoft in October 1997 and was joined by a number of states. The case focused on whether Microsoft had broken its recent consent decree and whether customers could remove the Explorer icon that came with all versions of Windows on the computer desktop. Judge Thomas Penfield Jackson ruled against Microsoft on June 7, 2000, and ordered that Microsoft split the company in two (an operating system firm and an applications firm). Microsoft lawyers, however, argued that Jackson was biased against the firm. In the end, Jackson's decision was not recognized, and he was dismissed from the case. In late 2001 Microsoft settled, agreeing to pay a substantial financial penalty and pledging to operate with greater restrictions. A minority of states chose not to settle, and some foreign governments also have pending cases against Microsoft. The primary settlement was a relatively benign penalty for Microsoft considering the potential outcome of dividing the company in two.

The Microsoft case was about customer choice: Did consumers have a viable option to use an alternative technology, such as Netscape, instead of Internet Explorer? While customers may have been denied a true choice between Explorer and Navigator in the mid- to late-1990s, another development did offer a choice and has provided a small-scale, but accelerating challenge to Microsoft's dominance in operating systems: Linux.

At the end of the 1960s, Linus Torvalds developed a PC-based version of UNIX, called Linux, while he was a student at the University of Helsinki in Finland in 1991. UNIX was a software system designed by Dennis Ritchie and Ken Thompson at Bell Labs at the end of the 1960s. AT&T, as a restricted monopoly, let the technology for this C language–based program disseminate outside of the firm, and it found a happy home in many universities. It was a simple but elegant program with minimal structure. Users could program the elements they wanted, and thus UNIX evolved, based on many contributions from a large community of users. Along with Linux, a number of other "free" (to the consumer—developed by programmers often on release time or their spare time), open-source UNIX-based products have been developed, including the most commonly used Web server software, Apache, and the most widespread mail-router program, Sendmail.

Many Linux users like the flexibility of the program versus Windows. Linux and other UNIX-based software represent the drive to develop programs that are more responsive to particular users' needs, and more reliable. The ongoing peer-review of prominent open-architecture (or open-source) programs like Linux by the user community tends to result in fewer bugs—Linux usually runs longer before crashing than versions of the leading closed-architecture operating system, Microsoft Windows. The open-source movement, and users of open-source programs such as Linux, is still small, but is growing rapidly. Some estimates place the number of contributors of code to Linux at over 100,000. The voluntary contributions made by the open-source community are remarkable and defy the theory of public good's prediction of few participants and many freeloaders.[4] While the future of Linux and open source look promising, the continuance of volunteerism and cooperation of the user community, the long-term impact, and the extent of the threat posed to Microsoft are all difficult to predict.[5]

Despite the ongoing business challenges that Microsoft may face from Linux, Microsoft and the other IT industry leaders appear in good shape. Microsoft, Intel, Cisco Systems, Hewlett-Packard, and Dell all emerged from the dot.com collapse in a relatively strong position—as smaller competitors suffered more of a blow, and some never recovered.[6]

Hewlett-Packard, led by Chief Executive Officer Carleton (Carly) Fiorina, a history and philosophy double-major from Stanford University and former Lucent Technologies executive, successfully engineered a controversial takeover of Compaq (for $19 billion). In the process, she created the leading personal computer firm—battling with board member and son of the founder, Walter Hewlett, on this acquisition every step of the way.[7] In leaving Lucent in 1999, after successfully spinning off this division of AT&T to great fanfare, Fiorina became the first female CEO of a leading IT firm or a Dow Jones Industrial (Dow 30) company. The firm Bill Hewlett and David Packard founded six decades earlier had long focused on teamwork, or "the HP Way."[8] This strategy and corporate culture had produced great success, but also built a bureaucratic structure that challenged the rapid innovation necessary at the turn of the millennium. Fiorina, in attempting to hold on to aspects that made the firm successful, but also push it to be more flexible and innovative in the future, pursues a task that is easier said than done. Even with the Compaq acquisition, the most lucrative part of Hewlett-Packard's (HP) current business remains printers and printer cartridges, and HP faces a tough road ahead with Dell and IBM as its primary competitors.[9]

During the economic downturn in 2000 and 2001, Hewlett-Packard could count on reliable cash flow from its peripherals business, while Compaq faced increasing challenges from Dell and the large number of box makers. Back in 1997, Compaq had taken over the struggling Digital Equipment Corporation, a firm that had rode a crest behind VAX (Virtual Address eXtession). VAX was an innovative, large cabinet-sized computer developed first in 1977 (VAX-11 /780). This multi-user system could process one million operations per second, a speed offering compelling performance as a minicomputer that challenged much more expensive mainframes. In later incarnations, VAX models offered additional capabilities, including vector processing and multiple processors. By the early 1990s, VAX systems peaked with more than a half-million installations worldwide. VAX was a successful technology and lucrative line that was in many respects the last hurrah prior to the growing competitive forces brought from personal computers. DEC, which made its name offering powerful computers at a price that attracted many new businesses and scientific laboratories into the world of computing, was bypassed by personal computing technology that further extended the affordability of computers. At the time of Compaq's acquisition of DEC, the once-mighty minicomputer manufacturer was clearly on the decline.[10]

Meanwhile, the other firm that started in 1957 and initiated a new sector of the computer industry, Control Data Corporation (supercomputing), also faced major challenges in the early 1990s. During the 1980s, Control Data had continued to become more diversified in its range of businesses in the information technology field, and maintaining focus was increasingly difficult. In 1989, CDC dismantled its hemorrhaging supercomputing division, but had many other struggling disparate business areas that remained. After suffering declining revenue and net losses between 1990 and 1991, the firm decided to engage in major restructuring the following year. The payroll and business services unit—the primary part of the business by this time—was spun off as Ceridian Corporation, while the remaining high-end computer engineering business was renamed Control Data Systems, Inc. Neither would approach the fundamental role CDC played in the computer industry from the early 1960s through the 1970s. Ceridian was in an increasingly competitive service field, while VAX, other minicomputers, and even personal computers, were beginning to erode the business areas of Control Data Systems.[11] DEC and CDC stand as two fundamental examples of the difficulty technology firms face in transitioning into fundamental new areas. DEC more nearly matched the experience of earlier computer firms in clinging to profitable technologies and areas of the past as powerful new industry sectors emerged (not unlike Sperry Rand, Burroughs, and NCR), while CDC sought to jump into many new areas, but lacked a clear and focused strategic plan and many of the capabilities to achieve success.

Unlike the technological transformations that reshaped the playing field in the computer industry, the market collapse at the beginning of the new century was extremely broad. Dell and online auction firm eBay were two of the few large IT firms to see relatively modest declines in share price as the vast majority of technology companies lost anywhere from half to all of their value in 2000 and 2001. Both firms had carved out niches that limited competition.

In 1995 eBay was founded in San Jose, California. Like Amazon.com in online book retailing, it benefited from its first-mover advantage. In contrast to more traditional electronic retailers, eBay was the first major online consumer-to-consumer (C2C) company.

The auction firm continues to generate substantial revenue and profits, and benefits from the fact that it is a business that requires relatively little overhead—its customers do both the selling and the buying, it is largely just engaging in marketing and technological infrastructure.

Like these electronic commerce firms, Dell also seems well-positioned for the future; however, its ongoing success will rest on its ability to continue to be an innovator in supply-chain management and the leader in customer service. The latter came under challenge recently as it outsourced some customer service phone operations to India, but later reversed this move in the face of customer dissatisfaction. More broadly, the issue of outsourcing IT services to other nations will undoubtedly remain a trend and continue to generate uncertainty, anxiety, individual hardship, and controversy, as well as potentially new opportunities as our economy transitions.

IBM suffered heavily after its failure to remain a leader in the personal computer field. Big Blue, a firm that many had long thought invincible, and a company that had enjoyed decades of uninterrupted annual net earnings (usually growing significantly from year to year), faced several consecutive years of annual net losses in the early 1990s. IBM rebounded strongly during the second half of the decade behind the leadership of CEO Louis Gerstner. Key among the strategic changes was the push into some areas where substantial market opportunities existed that the firm had not focused on previously, at least not as businesses: services and software.[12] IBM's Global Services Division produced 48 percent of the firm's revenue in fiscal year 2003 and is the only division that has grown substantially over the past three years. The Software Division's revenue has risen modestly, while hardware declined slightly between 2001 and 2003.[13]

Emphasizing IBM's transition, the firm sold its PC business to the Chinese firm Leveno in late 2004 (retaining a 19 percent stake). IBM has long had strong organizational capabilities in services and software, but in previous decades, these were perceived and used primarily as tools to sell and lease more hardware. Both fields have now become substantial business divisions and revenue and profit generators. While IBM remains the leading mainframe computer firm and still produces a number of innovative hardware products, it has built upon its past strength in software and services, as well as its grand scope, to offer more complete end-to-end IT solutions for its corporate and institutional customers and clients. This has continued during the last few years under its new leader Samuel Palmisano. This expertise allows firms like IBM-client Charles Schwab to focus on investment management as IBM provides a team of consultants to maintain Schwab's complex information technology needs.[14]

More than ever, IBM is concentrating on promoting Linux, a move that will likely hurt Microsoft, may cut into IBM's future software sales in some areas (as open-source programs are developed to replicate some of IBM's software products), but will probably provide another big boost to IBM's Global Services unit. It also can simplify things for IBM by having a single system that runs on all IBM computers. Anticipation of this business has led IBM to create twenty Linux training centers in developing nations, have 12,000 IBM employees devote at least part of their time to Linux (including 3,000 Global Services employees who were trained to help customers migrate to Linux), purchase shares of Linux distributors Red Hat and SuSe, and spend billions of dollars to make Linux the world's leading operating system.

In 2000, IBM's vice president for Technology and Strategy Irving Wladawsky-Berger stated that open source "throws technical innovation into perpetual fast forward; and it guarantees the world that Linux will always remain beyond the control of a single vendor."[15] IBM continues to have many successful businesses, but does not retain the dominant market share in fundamental areas the way it did historically. Microsoft has had a larger capitalization than IBM in recent years and as a result of an early contract with IBM (and many subsequent events), still holds the greatest monopolies (operating systems and basic applications) in the information technology field. Ironically, IBM may play a fundamental role in gradually destroying the ability for a fundamental IT monopoly (Microsoft Windows) by supporting Linux.[16]

Meanwhile a number of software companies have embraced Linux and open source. Computer Associates (CA) was one of the founding members of Open Source Development Laboratories, an organization created to advance open-source software that is headed by Linus Torvalds. Moreover, CA has long evangelized the virtues of open source to its customers, despite the fact that it does business with Microsoft. Recently, CA has been questioned within some open-source circles for its signing a licensing agreement with SCO Group, Inc., of Lindon, Utah, to use Linux software, a firm claiming proprietary rights to Linux. Computer Associates, however, maintains that it continues its long-standing position of support for open source and keeping Linux free. While the firm signed the license with SCO, it did not provide any funds to this firm.[17]

What transpires in the computer industry in coming decades remains to be seen and history rarely provides an unobstructed view of what the future holds. What computer technology will look like and its particular functionality and applications have always been difficult to predict years and decades out. Information technology, at least in many areas, continues to change more rapidly today than in the past, making projections even less reliable. At the same time, the history of the computer industry offers some basic themes that may replay in the future. The rise of fundamental new areas of IT, such as the advent of the software and networking (after the World Wide Web) businesses, led to excesses in outlook and investment capital, followed by a subsequent shakeout. Important new areas of IT will almost certainly emerge and similar types of reactions will probably occur. The rise of the personal computer, personal computer software, and networking sectors led many to focus on the entrepreneurial spirit and venture capital upon which these new areas seemingly rested. Also fundamental however, were many years of government investment (particularly by the Department of Defense) in developing key underlying technologies that made this possible. Government-funded technologists and managers also provided critical insight and ongoing infrastructure for change (sometimes within the private sector, such as former IPTO-funded scientists and engineers at Xerox PARC). The belief that the industry has reached a critical mass, where government investment is no longer advantageous, is naive given that most fundamental developments in the history of computing technology have strong connections to government funding. Finally, existing IT companies will likely have a difficult time transitioning into new IT areas, but the path will be far less challenging if underlying organizational capabilities, such as IBM's in software and services, have long been present.

NOTES

1. Donald A. Norman, *The Invisible Computer: Why Good Products Can Fail, the Personal Computer Is So Complex, and Information Appliances Are the Solution* (Cambridge, MA: MIT Press, 1998), 80–81.
2. Donn Parker, interview May 14, 2003.
3. Paul Ceruzzi, "A War on Two Fronts: The U.S. Justice Department, Open Source, and Microsoft, 1995–2002," *Iterations: An Interdisciplinary Journal of Software History* 1 (September 13, 2002): 6.
4. Steven Weber, *The Success of Open Source* (Cambridge, MA: Harvard University Press, 2004).
5. Peter Wayner, *Free for All: How Linux and the Free Software Movement Undercut the High-Tech Titans* (New York: HarperBusiness, 2000); Dan Orzech, "Open Source," in *Encyclopedia of Computers and Computer History*, ed. Raul Rojas (Chicago: Fitzroy Dearborn Publishers, 2001),

592–594. Computer scientist Richard Stallman started the Free Software Foundation to promote open-architecture software. The "Free" in this organization's name refers to freedom, not necessarily free of cost to create or distribute. A firm, Red Hat, is a leading distributor of Linux. Both individuals and firms (such as IBM on code for Apache) have contributed substantially to open-source programs.

6. The possible exception is Intel, which is once again facing strong pressure from Advanced Micro Devices (AMD). Personal Computer industry leader Hewlett-Packard has a long-standing relationship with AMD.

7. George Anders, *Perfect Enough: Carly Fiorina and the Reinvention of Hewlett-Packard* (New York: Portfolio, 2003).

8. David Packard, *The HP Way: How Bill Hewlett and I Built Our Company* (New York: HarperBusiness, 1996).

9. Majorie Scardino, "Carly Fiorina: Inventing a New Hewlett-Packard," *Time,* April 26, 2004, 72.

10. John Deane, "VAX," in *Encyclopedia of Computers and Computer History,* ed. Raul Rojas (Chicago: Fitzroy Dearborn Publishers, 2001), 794–795.

11. Michael Allen, "Control Data Plans Spinoff of Its Computer Operations," *Wall Street Journal* (May 28, 1992): B4.

12. Louis V. Gerstner, Jr., *Who Says Elephants Can't Dance: Inside IBM's Historic Turnaround* (New York: HarperBusiness, 2002), 128–145.

13. International Business Machines, *Annual Report: 2003,* 51.

14. David Kirkpatrick and Christopher Tkaczyk, "IBM Case Study: Schwab," *Fortune* 149, no. 12 (June 14, 2004): 94–95.

15. International Business Machines, *Annual Report: 2000.*

16. Michael Maiello and Susan Kitchens, "Kill Bill," *Forbes* 173, no. 12 (June 7, 2004): 86–91.

17. Charles Forelle, "Free Use of Linux Is Dealt a Setback; Computer Associates Signed SCO Licenses, in a Surprise to Open-Source Coalition," *Wall Street Journal* (March 8, 2004): B7.

Appendix: Company Profiles

Many companies contributed to the growth of the computer industry, but the following firms were particularly important for their early achievements in new sectors and/or their ability to produce significant results over long periods of time. They are divided into three categories: hardware, software/programming services, and networking/e-commerce. These companies are categorized by their original primary business (a few companies, such as IBM, have successfully transitioned into new businesses—IT consulting services). Categorization is based on the businesses, not the activities of firms. For instance, software/programming is in many cases the most fundamental activity of networking companies (such as Cisco Systems). In the 1950s and 1960s, several of the firms were generating substantial revenue/profits outside the computing field (particularly Sperry Rand as a conglomerate involved in many areas and IBM in the tabulating machine and punched-card field). Financial information is generally at five-year intervals, but additional years were added (or omitted) based on their relevance to discussions within the book, understanding important trajectories, and the availability of reliable data. With existing companies, the last five years are always included to indicate potential trends. All market capitalization data is from the end of September 2004, while employment numbers are from the end of 2003 or early 2004. Most of the financial information was taken from annual reports (generally from the year the numbers were originally reported) and archival records held at the Charles Babbage Institute in CBI's corporate records or product literature collections. Some data was obtained from contacting the companies. Please be aware that companies sometimes restate financial results and these numbers may differ from previously reported figures. When data comes from material other than company documents or company representatives, these sources are cited in the notes.

HARDWARE

Apple Computer, Inc.

Founded in 1976 (on April Fool's Day) by Steven P. Jobs and Stephen Wozniak

Chief Products/Services Historically: Apple II (1977), Macintosh (1984), Powerbook 100 (1991), Power Macintosh series (1993), iMac (1998), iPod (2003)

Date Firm Went Public: December 1980

Key Acquisitions: Orion Network Systems, Inc. (1988); Coral Software Corp. (1989); NeXT (1997)

Historic and Current Financials (in millions of dollars)—FY-close at end of September

Fiscal Year	Revenue	Profit/(Loss)
1985	$1,918	$61
1990	$5,558	$475
1995	$11,062	$424
2000	$7,983	$786
2001	$5,363	($25)
2002	$5,742	$65
2003	$6,207	$69

Current Chief Executive: Steven P. Jobs

Current Primary Businesses: Personal computers, laptop computers, portable music players

Current Number of Employees: 10,912

Current Market Capitalization: $14.5 billion

Burroughs Corporation

Founded in 1886 by William Seward Burroughs as the American Arithmometer Company

Name Changes: Burroughs Adding Machine Company (1905), Burroughs Corporation (1953)

Chief Products/Services Historically: Burroughs E-101 (1954), Burroughs (ElectroData) 205 (1954–1956), Burroughs 220 (1958), Burroughs B5000 (1961), B5500 (1964), B6500 (1967)

Key Acquisitions: ElectroData Corporation (1956), Memorex (1980), System Development Corporation (1981)

Historic Financials (in millions of dollars)—FY-close at end of December

Fiscal Year	Revenue	Profit/(Loss)
1950	$87.4	$8.02
1952	$151	$9
1954	$169	$7.80
1956	$273	$14.2
1958	$294	$6.41
1960	$389	$9.24
1962	$423	$9.49
1964	$392	$10.2
1966	$494	$31
1968	$651	$43.3
1970	$893	$66.5
1972	$1,053	$87.5
1974	$963	$143
1976	$1,070	$186
1978	$1,384	$253
1980	$1,614	$82
1982	$2,486	$118
1984	$3,241	$245
1985	$5,038	$248

Merged with Sperry Corporation to form Unisys in 1986

Control Data Corporation

Founded in July 1957 by William Norris

Chief Products/Services Historically: CDC 1604 (1960), CDC 6600 (1964), CDC 7600 (1969), CDC STAR-100 (1974)

Key Acquisitions: Cedar Engineering, Inc. (1957); Bendix Corporation Computer Division (1963); Computers Laboratories, Inc. (1964); TRG, Inc. (1964); C-E-I-R, Inc. (1967); Computer Peripherals, Inc. (formed as joint venture with NCR-1973)

Historic Financials (in millions of dollars)—FY-close at end of June (pre-1968) and December (1968 forward)

Fiscal Year	Revenue	Profit/(Loss)
1958	$0.63	($0.12)
1960	$9.67	$0.55
1962	$41	$1.54
1964	$121	$6.07
1966	$168	($1.91)
1968	$438	$45.5
1970	$354	($3.21)
1972	$664	$62.4
1974	$535	$3.73
1976	$664	$48.6
1978	$921	$89.5
1980	$1,473	$151
1982	$3,301	$155
1984	$3,755	$31.6
1986	$3,347	($265)
1988	$3,628	($1.7)
1990	$1,691	$2.7

Spun off into two separate firms: Ceridian and Control Data Systems, Inc. (1992)

Dell Computer Corporation

Founded in 1984 by Michael Dell

Name Changes: Dell Computer Corporation (1987), Dell, Inc. (2003)

Chief Products/Services Historically: Various models of built-to-order desktop computers, laptop computers, and servers; Internet sales infrastructure (1994)

Date Firm Went Public: June 1988

Key Acquisitions: ConvergeNet (1999), Plural, Inc. (2002)

Historic and Current Financials (in millions of dollars)—FY-close at end of January

Fiscal Year	Revenue	Profit/(Loss)
1995	$3,475	$213
2000	$25,265	$1,860
2001	$31,888	$2,310
2002	$31,168	$1,780
2003	$35,404	$2,122
2004	$41,444	$2,645

Current Chief Executive: Kevin B. Rollins

Current Primary Businesses: Personal computers; laptop computers; servers, printers, storage; services; software

Current Number of Employees: 50,000

Current Market Capitalization: $87.5 billion

Digital Equipment Corporation

Founded in 1957 by Kenneth Olsen and Harlan Anderson

Chief Products/Services Historically: DEC PDP-1 (1960), DEC PDP-8 (1965), VAX 11/780 (1977)

Date Firm Went Public: August 1966

Historic Financials (in millions of dollars)—FY-close at end of June

Fiscal Year	Revenue	Profit/(Loss)
1972	$188	$15.3
1974	$422	$44.4
1976	$736	$73.4
1978	$1,437	$142
1980	$2,368	$250
1982	$3,881	$417
1984	$5,584	$329
1986	$7,590	$617
1988	$11,475	$1,306
1990	$12,943	$74
1992	$13,931	($2,796)

Acquired by Compaq (1998)

Hewlett-Packard Company

Founded in January 1939 by David Packard and William Hewlett in Palo Alto, California

Chief Products/Services Historically: HP 215-A (1967), HP 35 scientific calculator (1970), HP 3000 computer (1972), HP LaserJet printer (1984), RISC microprocessor (first major computer firm to incorporate, 1986), HP DeskJet 500C color printer (1991), HP OfficeJet printer/fax/copier (1994), HP Services (2001)

Date Firm Went Public: November 1957

Key Acquisitions: F. L. Mosely Company (1958), F&M Scientific (1965), Apollo Computer (1989), Compaq (2002)

Historic and Current Financials (in millions of dollars)[1]—FY-close at end of October

Fiscal Year	Revenue	Profit/(Loss)
1960	$60.7	$4.23
1965	$165	$14
1970	$352	$23.1
1975	$981	$83.6
1980	$3,090	$269
1985	$6,505	$489
1990	$13,233	$739
1995	$31,519	$2,433
2000	$41,653	$3,697
2001	$37,498	$408
2002	$72,346	($928)
2003	$73,061	$2,539

Current Chief Executive: Carleton Fiorina

Current Primary Businesses: Laser printers, servers, handhelds, PCs, services

Current Number of Employees: 140,000

Current Market Capitalization: $56.1 billion

Intel Corporation

Founded in 1968 by Robert Noyce and Gordon Moore

Chief Products/Services Historically: Various DRAM chips (focus before mid-1970s), microprocessors (focus after mid-1970s)

Date Firm Went Public: 1971

Key Acquisitions: Dialogic (1999); Basis Communications (2000); Ambient Technologies (2000); Ziatech (2000); Picazo Communications (2000); Xircom, Inc. (2001); West Bay Semiconductor, Inc. (2003); Mobilian (2003); Envara (2004)

Historic and Current Financials (in millions of dollars)—FY-close at end of December

Fiscal Year	Revenue	Profit/(Loss)
1972	$23.4	$3.1
1974	$135	$19.8
1976	$226	$25.2
1978	$399	$44.4
1980	$855	$96.8
1982	$900	$38
1984	$1,629	$198
1986	$1,265	($203)
1988	$2,839	$453
1990	$3,921	$650
1992	$5,844	$1,067
1994	$11,521	$2,288
1996	$20,847	$5,157
1998	$26,273	$6,068
2000	$33,726	$7,314
2001	$26,539	$1,291
2002	$26,764	$3,117
2003	$30,141	$5,641

Current Chief Executive: Craig R. Barrett

Current Primary Businesses: Microprocessors; computing, networking and Communications products

Current Number of Employees (December 2003): 78,000

Current Market Capitalization: $129.1 billion

International Business Machines Corporation

Founded in 1896 as Tabulating Machine Company by Herman Hollerith

Name Changes: Tabulating Machine Company merges with Computing Scale Company of America and International Time Recording Com-

pany to become Computer-Tabulating-Recording Company or C-T-R
(1911); C-T-R changes name to International Business Machines or
IBM (1924)

Chief Products/Services Historically: Various tabulation machines and
punched cards, IBM 701 (1953), IBM 650 (1964), IBM 1401 (1960),
IBM System 360/40 (1965), IBM 4300 (1979), IBM PC (1981), IBM
Thinkpad (1992)

Date Firm Went Public: 1911

Key Acquisitions: Lotus 1-2-3 (1995), PricewaterhouseCoopers' Consulting Division (2002), Rational Software (2003), Venetica (2004)

**Historic and Current Financials (in millions of dollars)—FY-close
at end of December**

Fiscal Year	Revenue	Profit/(Loss)
1950	$266	$37
1955	$696	$73
1960	$1,817	$205
1965	$3,573	$477
1970	$7,504	$1,018
1975	$14,437	$1,990
1980	$26,213	$3,397
1985	$50,718	$6,555
1990	$68,931	$5,967
1991	$64,766	($2,861)
1992	$64,523	($4,965)
1993	$62,716	($8,101)
1994	$64,052	$2,937
1995	$71,940	$4,178
2000	$88,396	$8,093
2001	$83,067	$7,713
2002	$81,186	$3,579
2003	$89,131	$7,583

Current Chief Executive: Samuel J. Palmisano

Current Primary Businesses: Mainframe computers, personal computers,
servers, storage devices, business software, networking systems, IT
consulting services

Current Number of Employees (December 2003): 319,273

Current Market Capitalization: $141.4 billion

Remington Rand, Inc./Sperry Rand Corporation

Founded in January 1927 by James Henry Rand with the merger of Rand Kardex and Rand Kardex Bureau, Inc., along with the acquisition of Dalton Adding Machine Company and Powers Accounting Machine Company

Name Changes: Sperry Rand (1955) after merger with Sperry Corporation (Sperry incorporated as Sperry Gyroscope in 1929), Sperry Corporation (dropping "Rand" from name, 1979)

Chief Products/Services Historically: Various accounting machines and typewriters (1920s–1950s), UNIVAC (1951), UNIVAC 1103 (1953), UNIVAC II (1957), UNIVAC 1105 (1958), UNIVAC LARC (1960), UNIVAC III (1962), UNIVAC 1107 (1962), UNIVAC 1050 (1963), UNIVAC 1004 (1964), UNIVAC 9700 (1971)

Key Acquisitions: Powers Accounting Machine Company by Remington Rand (1927), Dalton Adding Machine Company by Remington Rand (1927), Merger with Sperry Corporation (1955), RCA's Computer Division (1971)

Historic and Current Financials (in millions of dollars)—FY-close at end of March (years prior to 1955 represent the combined revenue and earnings of the two separate firms)

Fiscal Year	Revenue	Profit/(Loss)
1948	$237	$20.8
1950	$250	$13.4
1952	$468	$26
1954	$690	$28
1955	$699	$44.6
1956	$711	$46.3
1958	$864	$44.4
1960	$1,173	$37.2
1962	$1,183	$24.4
1964	$1,279	$26
1966	$1,280	$31.9
1968	$1,563	$64
1970	$1,755	$81
1972	$1,824	$60.8
1974	$1,944	$112
1976	$2,455	$145

1978	$2,824	$177
1980	$3,717	$277
1982	$4,195	$222

Merged with Burroughs Corporation to form Unisys in 1986

Unisys Corporation

Founded in 1986 through the merger of Burroughs Corporation and Sperry Rand Corporation

Chief Products/Services Historically: Micro A (1989), IT Services unit (1992), Cellular Multi-Processing (1998), ES7000 servers (2000), 3D Visible (2004)

Date Firm Went Public: 1986

Key Acquisitions: Timeplex (1988); Convergent Technologies (1988); Pioneer Systems, Inc. (1997); TechHackers, Inc. (1999); Publishing Partners International (1999)

Historic and Current Financials (in millions of dollars)—FY-close at end of December

Fiscal Year	Revenue	Profit/(Loss)
1991	$5,715	($1,393)
1992	$5,400	$361
1993	$4,705	$564
1994	$4,078	$101
1995	$6,342	($625)
1996	$6,371	$50
1997	$6,636	($854)
1998	$7,244	$376
1999	$7,544	$511
2000	$6,885	$225
2001	$6,018	($67)
2002	$5,607	$223
2003	$5,911	$259

Current Chief Executive: Lawrence Weinbach

Current Primary Businesses: High-end servers, systems integration, IT consulting

Current Number of Employees: 37,000

Current Market Capitalization: $3.36 billion

SOFTWARE/PROGRAMMING SERVICES

Applied Data Research

Founded in 1959 by Martin Goetz, Ellwood Kauffman, Steve Wright, Dave McFadden, Bob Wickenden, Bernie Riskin, and Sherman Bluementhal

Chief Products/Services Historically: Programming/computing Services (1959 forward), Autoflow (1964), ROSCOE and Librarian (1967–1968)

Date Firm Went Public: 1965

Key Acquisitions: Datacom (1978)

Historic Financials (in millions of dollars)—FY-close at end of December

Fiscal Year	Revenue	Profit/(Loss)
1968	$4.78	$0.35
1969	$6.15	$0.15
1971	$6.44	($0.35)
1972	$8.88	$0.07
1975	$9.61	$0.43
1976	$12.91	$1.44
1977	$16.93	$1.64
1978	$22.63	$1.98
1979	$28.69	$0.52
1982	$65.35	$4.74
1983	$85.48	$6.98
1984	$124.23	$9.66

Acquired by Computer Associates in 1988

C-E-I-R, Inc.

Founded in 1952 as Council for Economic and Industrial Research, a nonprofit firm; became for profit corporation called C-E-I-R, Inc., under the leadership of Herbert Robinson in 1954

Chief Products/Services Historically: Programming services, computer time-sharing, proprietary control programs

Key Acquisitions: General Analysis Corporation and Data-Tech (late 1950s)

Historic Financials (in millions of dollars)—FY-close at end of September

Fiscal Year	Revenue	Profit/(Loss)
1954	$0.121	($.002)
1956	$0.683	$0.02
1958	$1.374	$.042
1960	$9.549	($0.25)^2
1962	$16.99	($1.91)
1964	$16.36	$1.57
1966	$22.36	$1.45

Acquired by Control Data Corporation in 1967

Computer Associates International, Inc.

Founded in 1976 by Charles Wang

Chief Products/Services Historically: CA-Sort (1976), CA-Sentinel (1983), CA-Universe (1984), CA-DB (1990), ACCPAC (1991), Unicenter TNG (1995), Brightstar (2001), CleverPath Portal (2002)

Date Firm Went Public: 1980

Key Acquisitions: Capex Corporation (1982); UCCEL (1987); Applied Data Research (1988); ASK Group, Inc. (1994); Cheyenne Software, Inc. (1996); PLATINUM Technology, International, Inc. (1999); Sterling Software, Inc. (2000)

Historic and Current Financials (in millions of dollars)—FY-close at end of March

Fiscal Year	Revenue	Profit/(Loss)
1993	$1,841	$246
1994	$2,148	$401
1995	$2,623	$432
1996	$3,505	$752
1997	$4,040	$3,505
1998	$4,206	$1,169
1999	$4,666	$626
2000	$6,103	$696
2001	$4,198	($591)
2002	$3,116	($267)

2003	$2,964	($1,102)
2004	$3,276	($36)

Current Chief Executive: Kenneth Cron (interim)

Current Primary Business: Management software

Current Number of Employees: 15,000 (approximate)

Current Market Capitalization: $15.8 billion

Computer Sciences Corporation

Founded in April 1959 by Fletcher Jones and Roy Nutt

Chief Products/Services Historically: Fully Automatic Compiling Technique or FACT (1960), various computer and programming services, systems integration services

Date Firm Went Public: 1963

Key Acquisitions: Communications Systems, Inc. (1965); Intelcom (1965); CIG-Intersys Group (1989); ARC Professional Services Group (1994); Ploenzke AG–SAP Consultancy (1994); Datacentralen A/S (1996); Continuum (1996); CSA Holding, Ltd. (1999); Nichols Research (1999); GE Capital Information Technology Solutions (1999); Mynd Corporation (2000); DynCorp (2003)

Historic Financials (in millions of dollars)—FY-close at end of March

Fiscal Year	Revenue	Profit/(Loss)
1964	$3.93	$0.248
1968	$53.4	$3.30
1972	$128	($35.7)
1982	$630	$17.8
1986	$839	$23.9
1990	$1,500	$65.5
1994	$2,896	$72.3
1998	$6,601	$260
2000	$9,346	$403
2001	$10,493	$232
2002	$11,379	$344
2003	$11,347	$440
2004	$14,768	$519

Current Chief Executive: Van B. Honeycutt

Current Primary Business: IT services

Current Number of Employees: 90,000

Current Market Capitalization: $8.9 billion

Electronic Data Systems Corporation

Founded in June 1962 by H. Ross Perot; in 1984 the firm was sold to and became a division of General Motors Corporation, but in 1996 GM divested in EDS and it went back to being an independent company

Chief Products/Services Historically: Information technology services

Date Firm Went Public: 1968

Key Acquisitions: A. T. Kearney (1995), MCI's Systemhouse Division (1999), Advanced Computing (1999)

Historic and Current Financials (in millions of dollars)—FY-close at end of December

Fiscal Year	Revenue	Profit/(Loss)
1968	$10	$2
1970	$64	$8.9
1975	$123	$15
1980	$417	$33
1985	$3,407	$190
1990	$6,022	$497
1995	$12,422	$822
2000	$18,856	$1,143
2001	$21,033	$1,363
2002	$21,359	$1,116
2003	$21,476	($1,698)

Current Chief Executive: Michael Jordan

Current Primary Businesses: Professional services; e-commerce; mainframe, data center, application maintenance and development, and business processes outsourcing; product lifecycle management software, and various other IT-related services

Current Number of Employees: 120,000

Current Market Capitalization: $9.8 billion

Informatics General Corporation

Founded in 1962 by Walter F. Bauer, Werner L. Frank, Richard H. Hill, and Francis V. Wagner (along with Erwin Tomash, who became the first Chair of the Board—Informatics was a wholly owned subsidiary of Tomash's DataProducts until it became independent in 1969)

Name Changes: Informatics General Corporation (1982)

Chief Products/Services Historically: Mark IV (1967), data services, custom services

Key Acquisitions: Ruckers Data Centers (1969), Computer Technology (1969), Equimatics (1974)

Historic Financials (in millions of dollars)[3]—FY-close at end of March

Fiscal Year	Revenue	Profit/(Loss)
1963	$0.2	($0.06)
1965	$2.2	$0.09
1970	$14.7	$0.46
1975	$39	($4.37)
1980	$126	$4.06
1982	$170.1	$5.46

Acquired by Sterling Software (1985)

Microsoft

Founded in 1975 by Paul Allen and William Gates

Chief Products/Services Historically: Basic Interpreter (1975), MS DOS (1981), MS Word (1983), MS Excel (1984), MS Windows (1985), Windows 3.0 (1990), Windows 95 (1995), MS Explorer 4.0 (1997), Microsoft Office 2000 (1999), MS Windows 2000 (2000)

Date Firm Went Public: March 1986

Key Acquisitions: Web TV Networks (1997), Hotmail (1998)

Key Joint Ventures: Joint venture with NBC (50 percent stake) to form MSN, a cable channel and Internet news service (1995); joint venture with Comcast (10 percent stake, 1997)[4]

Historic and Current Financials (in millions of dollars)—FY-close at end of June

Fiscal Year	Revenue	Profit/(Loss)
1985	$140	$24
1990	$1,186	$279

1995	$6,075	$1,453
2000	$22,956	$9,421
2001	$25,296	$7,346
2002	$28,365	$5,355
2003	$32,187	$7,531
2004	$36,835	$8,168

Current Chief Executive: Steve Ballmer

Current Primary Businesses: Operating systems, office software applications, Internet navigation software, server software, game consoles

Current Number of Employees: 57,086

Current Market Capitalization: $296.7 billion

Oracle Corporation

Founded in 1977 by Larry Ellison as System Development Laboratories

Name Changes: Oracle Corporation (1982)

Chief Products/Services Historically: Oracle VI (1978), SQL RDMS (1979), Oracle V2 (1980), Oracle V3 (1982), VAX-mode Database (1983), Oracle V4 (1984), Oracle V5 (1986), PL/SQL (1988), CDE (1993), CRM Suite (1998)

Date Firm Went Public: March 1986

Key Acquisitions: Thinking Machines Corporation Data Mining Division (1999), Indicast (2002)

Historic and Current Financials (in millions of dollars)—FY-close at end of May

Fiscal Year	Revenue	Profit/(Loss)
1982	$2.5	$0.3
1985	$23.1	$1.6
1990	$971	$117
1995	$2,967	$442
2000	$10,231	$6,297[5]
2001	$10,961	$2,561
2002	$9,673	$2,224
2003	$9,475	$2,307
2004	$10,156	$2,681

Current Chief Executive: Lawrence Ellison

Current Primary Businesses: Database software, business applications software

Current Number of Employees: 42,000

Current Market Capitalization: $56.1 billion

System Development Corporation

Founded in 1956 as a spin-off of the RAND Corporation. Like RAND, it was a nonprofit corporation. In 1968 System Development Corporation became a for-profit corporation

Chief Products/Services Historically: Programmed the software and did system integration for the Semi-Automatic Ground Environment (1955 as System Development Division of RAND into the late 1950s in first iterations). In the 1960s and 1970s the firm diversified into a range of computing and software services and equipment (often done on a contract basis)

Key Acquisitions: Mechanics Research, Inc. (1972); Investment Data Corporation (1972); Condura Corporation Data Systems Division (1974); Applied Information Development (1974); Aquila BST (1974)

Historic Financials (in millions of dollars)—FY-close at end of June

Fiscal Year	Revenue	Profit/(Loss)
1958	$25.55	$1.07
1960	$42.43	$1.45
1962	$47.80	$0.43
1964	$56.82	$0.34
1966	$51.30	($0.61)
1968	$53.38	$0.69
1970	$55.58	($0.55)
1972	$49.35	$1.21
1974	$90.16	$0.77
1976	$109.94	$1.91
1978	$145.04	$1.55
1980	$168.27	$7.03

Acquired by Burroughs Corporation in 1981

NETWORKING/E-COMMERCE

Amazon

Founded in 1994 by Jeffrey Bezos

Chief Products/Services Historically: Internet-based book retail sales (1994 forward)

Date Firm Went Public: May 1997

Key Acquisitions: Jungalee Corp. (1998), PlanetAll.com (1998), Pets.com (1999), Joyo.com (2004)

Historic and Current Financials (in millions of dollars)—FY-close at end of December

Fiscal Year	Revenue	Profit/(Loss)
1995	$511	($303)
2000	$2,762	($1,411)
2001	$3,122	($567)
2002	$3,933	($149)
2003	$5,264	$35

Current Chief Executive: Jeffrey P. Bezos

Current Primary Businesses: Internet-based book retail sales, broad-based Internet retail sales

Current Number of Employees (December 2003): 7,800

Current Market Capitalization: $16.7 billion

Cisco Systems, Inc.

Founded in December 1994 by Len Bosack and Sandy Lerner

Chief Products/Services Historically: Routers and networking solutions (1985 forward), LAN switches (1990 forward), Asynchronous Traffic Mode (ATM) switches (1995 forward)

Date Firm Went Public: February 1990

Key Acquisitions: Crescendo Communications (1993), Grand Junction Networks (1995), StrataCom (1996), Ardent Communications (1997), GeoTel Communications Corporation (1999), ArrowPoint (2000)

Historic and Current Financials (in millions of dollars)—FY-close at end of July

Fiscal Year	Revenue	Profit/(Loss)
1995	$2,233	$456
1996	$4,101	$915

1997	$6,452	$1,047
1998	$8,489	$1,331
1999	$12,173	$2,023
2000	$18,928	$2,668
2001	$22,293	($1,014)
2002	$18,915	$1,893
2003	$18,878	$3,578

Current Chief Executive: John T. Chambers

Current Primary Businesses: Networking equipment, telecommunications equipment

Current Number of Employees: 33,371

Current Market Capitalization: $122.4 billion

eBay, Inc.

Founded in September 1995 by Pierre Omidyar and Jeff Skoll

Chief Products/Services Historically: Internet auction Web site

Date Firm Went Public: September 1998

Key Acquisitions: Billpoint, Inc. (1999); Kruse International (1999); Butterfield & Butterfield (1999); Paypal, Inc. (2002); Internet Auction Co. (2004)

Historic and Current Financials (in millions of dollars)—FY-close at end of December

Fiscal Year	Revenue	Profit/(Loss)
1996	$32	$3.4
1997	$41	$7.1
1998	$86	$7.3
1999	$225	$9.6
2000	$431	$48.3
2001	$749	$90.4
2002	$1,214	$249.9
2003	$2,165	$441.7

Current Chief Executive: Margaret Whitman

Current Primary Businesses: Internet auctions, Internet retailing

Current Number of Employees: 5,700

Current Market Capitalization: $59.0 billion

Yahoo, Inc.

Founded in March 1994 by David Filo and Jerry Yang

Chief Products/Services Historically: Internet portal

Date Firm Went Public: April 1996

Key Acquisitions: Broadcast.com (1999); Inktomi (2003); Overture (2003); Software Company, Ltd. (2004); Outpost (2004)

Historic and Current Financials (in millions of dollars)—FY-close at end of December

Fiscal Year	Revenue	Profit/(Loss)
1995	$1.4	($0.8)
1996	$19.7	($4.3)
1997	$67.4	($22.9)
1998	$245	($13.6)
1999	$592	$47.8
2000	$1,110	$70.8
2001	$717	($92.8)
2002	$953	$42.8
2003	$1,625	$237.9

Current Chief Executive: Terry Semel

Current Primary Businesses: Internet portal, Web-based products and services, e-commerce, Internet advertising (Yahoo Search, Hot Jobs, Yahoo Autos, etc.)

Current Number of Employees: 5,500

Current Market Capitalization: $44.3 billion

NOTES

1. 1960–2000 revenue numbers from company Web site (where figures are rounded).

2. Figures for 1960 and 1961 include subsidiaries of C-E-I-R, Inc. acquired during 1960 and 1961.

3. Richard L. Forman, *Fulfilling the Computer's Promise: The History of Informatics, 1962–1982* (Informatics, 1985).

4. With the exception of the QDOS product purchased from Seattle Computer Products, acquisitions have been less important, and most expansion has occurred internally. Microsoft has formed a number of joint ventures with ownership stakes, and thus, a few key partnerships are listed here.

5. Includes $4 million gain from sale of Oracle Japan.

Suggestions for
Further Reading and Research

GENERAL WORKS

Over the past decade several high-quality works of synthesis have been published on the history of computers. These include historians Martin Campbell-Kelly and William Aspray's *Computer: A History of the Information Machine* (New York: Basic Books, 1996) and Paul Ceruzzi's *History of Modern Computing* (Cambridge, MA: MIT Press, 1998). While the former provides a broader overall introduction to the history of computers, the latter also contains much information and insight. Both concentrate on the technology of computing, but include substantial discussion and analysis of the computer industry. Though somewhat dated, economist Kenneth Flamm published two books during the late 1980s that provide a meaningful macroeconomic picture of the industry, as well as an early attempt to characterize the role of the government in funding the development of computer technology: *Targeting the Computer* and *Creating the Computer* (Washington, DC: Brookings Institution, 1987 and 1988, respectively). More recently, leading business historian Alfred D. Chandler, in *Inventing the Electronic Century: The Epic Story of the Consumer Electronics and Computer Industries* (New York: Free Press, 2001), provided a meaningful and informative economic examination of a range of communications and information technology sectors in the United States and Japan. Few quality works have been completed that focus on the history of individual firms. Emerson Pugh's *Building IBM: Shaping an Industry and Its Technology* (Cambridge, MA: MIT Press, 1995) is an exception. This provides a strong overview of the development of this longtime leading computer company, from its origins with the tabulation machine technology of Herman Hollerith in the 1890s into the early PC era of the 1980s. In doing so, it deftly examines both technical and business issues. For a quality work that puts the history of computing within the broader context of the history of information in the United States, see Alfred D. Chandler and James W. Cortada, eds., *A Nation Transformed by Information: How Information Has Shaped the United States from Colonial Times to the Present* (Oxford: Oxford University Press, 2000).

CHAPTER 1

There is one exceptional book on the prehistory of computing and the computer industry: James W. Cortada's *Before the Computer* (Princeton, NJ: Princeton University Press, 1993). This work provides a wealth of data and quality analysis on early leaders of the U.S. information machine industry that transitioned into the computer trade. Another significant work on the prehistory of computing is Paul Ceruzzi's *Reckoners: The Prehistory of the Digital Computer from Relays to the Stored Program Concept, 1935–1945* (Westport, CT: Greenwood Press, 1983). This takes a more concentrated approach to examine specific technological antecedents of digital computing. The best examination of the origins of tabulating machines and the contributions of Herman Hollerith is Geoffrey D. Austrian's biography *Herman Hollerith: Forgotten Giant of Information Processing* (New York: Columbia University Press,1982). Other than Pugh's *Building IBM* (1995), there are no histories that stand out on an individual mainframe computer firm's entire history, nevertheless several participants in this trade provide useful information in their memoirs. Noteworthy among these are Stanley C. Allyn's *My Half Century with NCR* (New York: McGraw Hill, 1967) and Thomas J. Watson, Jr.'s, *Father, Son & Co.: My Life at IBM and Beyond* (New York: Bantam Books, 1990). The best account of the adoption and use of office machines in the United States is management scholar JoAnne Yate's *Control Through Communication: The Rise of System in American Management* (Baltimore, MD: Johns Hopkins University Press, 1989). With regard to primary resources, The Charles Babbage Institute holds the records of the Burroughs Corporation and the Hagley Museum and Library holds the records of Sperry Rand Corporation.

CHAPTER 2

The best account of the first decade of the computer industry is the forthcoming monograph by historian Arthur L. Norberg, *Computers and Commerce: A Study of Technology and Management at Eckert-Mauchly Computer Company, Engineering Research Associates, and Remington Rand, 1946–1957* (Cambridge, MA: MIT Press, 2005). This book does a particularly strong job of addressing and integrating the technological and organizational histories of the pioneering firms of the mainframe industry. Prior to this book, the standout work was Nancy B. Stern's *From ENIAC to UNIVAC: An Appraisal of the Eckert-Mauchly Computers* (Bedford, MA: Digital Press, 1981). This book gives very little sense of organizational and business development, but provides some good information on early mainframe technology. The fullest account of Semi-Automatic Ground Environment (SAGE) computing is Kent C. Redmond and Thomas M. Smith's *From Whirlwind to MITRE: The R&D Story of the SAGE Air Defense Computer* (Bedford, MA: MITRE Corporation, 1986). A fascinating, insightful, and elegantly written cultural and political history of early computing in the context of the Cold War is provided in information scholar Paul N. Edwards' *The Closed World: Computers and the Politics of Discourse in Cold War America* (Cambridge, MA: MIT Press, 1996). There are a small number of articles on computing developments at early mainframe firms, but only two achieve an outstanding level of depth and rigor: management scholar Richard S. Rosenbloom's "Leadership, Capabilities, and Technological Change: The Transformation of NCR in the Electronic Era," *Strategic Management Journal* 21, no. 3 (March 2000): 1083–1103; and historian Steven Usselman, "IBM and Its Imitators: Organizational Capabilities and the Emergence of the International Computer Industry," *Business and Economic History* 22, no. 2 (Winter 1993): 1–35.

CHAPTER 3

Mainframe computing was transformed by new developments in semiconductors (transistors followed by integrated circuits, and later, microprocessors) that initiated a continuing path toward ever-greater processing power and miniaturization. The most readable and insightful of the books on the history of the transistor and the emergence of integrated circuits is Michael Riordan and Lillian Hoddeson's *Crystal Fire: The Invention of the Transistor and the Birth of the Information Age* (New York: W. W. Norton,

1998). A monograph that provides a fuller account and analysis of the industry context of integrated circuits is Ernest Braun and Stuart MacDonald's *Revolution in Miniature: The History and Impact of Semiconductor Electronics* (Cambridge, London: Cambridge University Press, 1978). For a detailed look at the IBM System 360 and 370 series of computers, see Emerson W. Pugh, Lyle R. Johnson, and John H. Palmer's *IBM's 360 and Early 370 Systems* (Cambridge, MA: MIT Press, 1991). For an analysis of the introduction of computers into the world of business, see James W. Cortada's *The Digital Hand: How Computers Changed the Work of American Manufacturing, Transportation, and Retail Industries* (New York: Oxford University Press, 2003). In addition to this important work, Cortada is currently producing additional volumes (for Oxford University Press) on the introduction and impact on computing in other industries. For a reference source to some of the more significant literature and primary sources on computer applications in the biological, physical, medical, and cognitive sciences, see Jeffrey R. Yost's *A Bibliographic Guide to Resources in Scientific Computing, 1945–1975* (Westport, CT: Greenwood Press, 2002).

CHAPTER 4

The historical literature on the supercomputing and minicomputer sectors of the computer industry, and the development of the leading firms in these two sectors, Control Data Corporation (CDC) and Digital Equipment Corporation (DEC), is sorely lacking. For this reason, a number of primary sources, oral histories, and other resources at CBI were used for this chapter (CBI holds the corporate records of Control Data Corporation). James W. Worthy's biography, *William C. Norris: Portrait of a Maverick* (Cambridge, MA: Ballenger Publishing Company, 1987) offers some extensive information on developments at Control Data, but is far from a complete history of this important firm. Glenn Rifkin and George Harrar's biography on DEC's longtime leader, *The Ultimate Entrepreneur: The Story of Ken Olsen and Digital Equipment Corporation* (Chicago: Contemporary Books, 1988) is far more limited, as is the company-published, James Parker Pearson, ed., *Digital at Work: Snapshots from the First Thirty-Five Years* (Burlington, MA: Digital Press, 1992). On the other hand, Tracy Kidder's account of minicomputer product development work at DEC-competitor Data General, in *Soul of a New Machine* (New York: Avon Books, 1981), is a masterful narrative that stands with the very best accounts of business and technological development in the twentieth century.

CHAPTER 5

The history of software, and particularly the software industry, is a field that has been neglected until the past decade, but is starting to gain momentum. Martin Campbell-Kelly's excellent book on the software industry, *From Airline Reservation to Sonic the Hedgehog: A History of the Software Industry* (Cambridge, MA: MIT Press, 2003) is the most important work in this field. It provides meaningful analysis and hitherto unavailable economic data on this trade. While it concentrates more on the macroeconomics of the services, software product, and system integration sectors, it also gives some useful insights on what is happening within individual firms. It takes the literature beyond David C. Mowery's edited volume, *The International Software Industry: A Comparative Study of Industry Evolution and Structure.* (New York: Oxford University Press, 1996), a strong work of scholarship admirable for its breadth of coverage, but one that lacks the depth achieved by Campbell-Kelly's more focused study. Additional important sources include articles on the labor history and software user groups: Nathan Ensmenger and William Aspray's "Software as Labor Process," in *History of Computing: Software Issues*, eds. Ulf Hashagen, Reinhard Keil-Slawik, and Arthur L. Norberg, (Berlin: Springer-Verlag, 2002); and Atsushi Akera, "Volunteerism and the Fruits of Collaboration: The IBM User Group, SHARE," *Technology and Culture* 42, no. 4 (2001): 710–736. Other chapters in the Hashagen, Keil-Slawik, and Norberg volume explore a broad range of significant scientific, technical, and historiographical issues involved with studying software's past. Two company-produced books provide some useful information, but lack rigorous analysis: Claude Baum, *The System Builders: The Story of SDC* (Santa Monica, CA: System Development Corporation, 1981); and Richard L. Forman, *Fulfilling the Computer's Promise: The History of Informatics, 1962–1982* (Informatics General Corporation, 1985). The Charles Babbage Institute recently (in February 2004) completed a four-year $488,000 National Science Foundation project, "Building a Future for Software History" to expand resources, literature, and understanding on the history of software. This project consisted of producing a software-history dictionary and software-history bibliography (with over 2,500 sources); as well as conducting, transcribing, and making available thirty-five oral histories with software pioneers from industry and academe, and editing and publishing the ongoing peer-reviewed scholarly journal *Iterations: An Interdisciplinary Journal of Software History.* All of these resources are at the CBI Web site: http://www.cbi.umn.edu. Additionally, the records of Applied Data Research's Software Products Division and the papers of its founder, Martin Goetz, as well as the papers of C-E-I-R, Inc., the System Development Corporation, and many other primary resources on software technology and the software industry are available at CBI.

CHAPTER 6

There are several standout works on the role of government, and particularly the U.S. Department of Defense (DoD), in funding research and development in computing. Chief among these is Arthur L. Norberg and Judy O'Neill's *Transforming Computer Technology: Information Processing for the Pentagon, 1962–1986* (Baltimore, MD: Johns Hopkins University Press, 1996). This book provides the first historical account of the development of the Arpanet/Internet, and more broadly, an institutional history of ARPA's Information Processing Techniques Office. Also significant is the National Research Council's *Funding a Revolution: Government Support for Computing Research* (Washington, DC: National Academies Press, 1999). Science writer Michael Hiltzik has produced the most thorough, engaging, and balanced study of developments at Xerox PARC in his book, *Dealers in Lightning: Xerox PARC and the Dawn of the Computer Age* (New York: HarperBusiness, 1999). Another science writer, M. Mitchell Waldrop, provides a well-crafted biography, *The Dream Machine: J.C.R. Licklider and the Revolution that Made Computing Personal* (New York: Viking, 2001), which speculates meaningfully on the long-term implications of Licklider's early insights. An exceptional monograph on the history the Internet is Janet Abbate's *Inventing the Internet* (Cambridge, MA: MIT Press, 1999). This book stands out for its insightful analysis on the importance of users in the development of computer networking and associated software technology.

CHAPTER 7

The historical literature on the personal computer is at the stage the literature and resources on the early history of the software trade were at a decade ago. Aside from participant and journalist accounts, the literature is nearly nonexistent. Several of these journalistic accounts, however, offer insights and are quite informative. Most significant among these is Robert X. Cringely's *Accidental Empires: How the Boys of Silicon Valley Make Their Millions, Battle Foreign Competition, and Still Can't Get a Date* (Reading, MA: Addison-Wesley, 1992). This book is often quick to judge particular historical actors, but is nevertheless an informative and insightful account of the history of personal computers and personal computer software. Paul Freiberger and Michael Swaine's *Fire in the Valley: The Making of the Personal Computer*, 2nd ed. (New York: McGraw-Hill Trade, 1999) is less analytical, but gives an even broader overview of the history of the personal computer and the PC trade. Journalists' books on the development of individual machines, most notably, Steven Levy's *Insanely Great: The Life and Times of Macintosh, the Computer that Changed Everything* (New York: Viking, 1994), are also informative. The highest quality work of scholarship addressing this period is a study of the primary component of personal computers, microprocessors: Ross Bassett's *To the Digital Age: Research Labs, Start-Up Companies, and the Rise of MOS Technology* (Cambridge, MA: MIT Press, 1990).

CHAPTER 8

The literature on the computer networking industry is largely limited to journalistic books on companies, many of which were done without gaining access to either key individuals in the firms or the existing corporate records held by these companies. Two books on Cisco Systems are of higher quality than most journalistic studies in the literature: Robert Slater, *The Eye of the Storm: How John Chambers Steered Cisco Through the Technological Collapse* (New York: HarperBusiness, 2003); and David Bunnell, *Making the Cisco Connection: The Story Behind the Real Internet Superpower* (New York: John Wiley & Sons, 2000). Management scholars' articles and case studies produced for graduate-student instruction are also good sources of information. Stanford University Business School has a particularly strong set of case studies on IT firms in the 1990s and the first half-decade of the twenty-first century—see http://gobi.stanford.edu/cases/. Tim Berners-Lee provides an engaging participant account of his development of the World Wide Web in *Weaving the Web: The Original Design and Ultimate Destiny of the World Wide Web by Its Inventor* (San Francisco: HarperSanFrancisco, 1999). For an insightful analysis of the impact of computer networking on society see Manuel Castell's trilogy, *The Rise of the Network Society*, *The Power of Identity*, and *End of the Millenium* (Oxford: Blackwell Publishers, 1997, 1998, 1998, respectively); as well as Mark Poster's *What's the Matter with the Internet* (Minneapolis, MN: University of Minnesota Press, 2001). For an intriguing personal account of the life of a programmer in the 1990s, see Ellen Ullman's *Close to the Machine: Technophilia and Its Discontents* (San Francisco: City Lights, 1997). A cottage industry has emerged to produce books on Microsoft, and particularly, Bill Gates. Of the Microsoft studies, there is one scholarly work that stands out for both its access to the firm and its quality analysis: Michael A. Cusumano's *Microsoft Secrets: How the World's Most Powerful Software Company Creates Technology, Shapes Markets, and Manages People* (New York: Free Press, 1998). Of the increasing number of books on the Digital Divide, one internationally focused examination distinguishes itself above others: Pippa Norris, *Digital Divide: Civic Engagement, Information Poverty, and the Internet Worldwide* (Cambridge: Cambridge University Press, 2001). Another insightful book is Mark Warschauer's *Technology and Social Inclusion: Rethinking the Digital Divide* (Cambridge, MA: MIT Press, 2003). For extensive data on access to networking technology among demographic groups, see the U.S. Department of Commerce's *Falling Through the Net* at http://www.ntia.doc.gov/ntiahome/digitaldivide. Regarding Linux and the movement toward open source, the best source is Steven Weber, *The Success of Open Source* (Cambridge, MA: Harvard University Press, 2004).

Index

About the Author

JEFFREY R. YOST is Associate Director of Charles Babbage Institute for the History of Information Technology at the University of Minnesota. He has published and edited scholarship in a number of areas on the business, social, cultural, scientific, and intellectual history of computing, software, and networking.